EVALUATING CLASSROOM INSTRUCTION

JAMES S. CANGELOSI *Utah State University*

Longman
New York & London

Evaluating Classroom Instruction

Copyright ©1991 by Longman Publishing Group

Longman, 95 Church Street, White Plains, N.Y. 10601

Associated companies:
Longman Group Ltd., London
Longman Cheshire Pty., Melbourne
Longman Paul Pty., Auckland
Copp Clark Pitman, Toronto

To Chris

Executive editor: Raymond T. O'Connell
Development editor: Virginia L. Blanford
Production editor: Camilla T. K. Palmer
Cover design: Anne M. Pompeo
Text art: Fine Line Studio
Production supervisor: Joanne Jay

Library of Congress Cataloging-in-Publication Data
Cangelosi, James S.
    Evaluating classroom instruction / James S. Cangelosi.
      p.   cm.
    Includes bibliographical references.
    ISBN 0-8013-0391-5
    1. Teaching—Evaluation.   2. Teachers—United States—Rating of.
I. Title.
LB1027.C254   1990
371.1'44—dc20   90-31115
                                               CIP

ABCDEFGHIJ-AL-99 98 97 96 95 94 93 92 91 90

Contents

Appendixes   213

Preface

There was a time when preservice teachers were expected to collect the tools of teaching (e.g., understanding of subject content, educational psychology, learning theory, classroom management, curriculum planning, instructional methods, and assessment methods) from college and university teacher preparation programs. Obtaining a teaching position, and thus becoming an in-service teacher, required poise during interviews and, in some cases, passing scores on "teaching competency" tests. Once in the classroom, in-service teachers were generally on their own to learn how to use the tools of teaching acquired at their alma maters. As long as they kept their students from disrupting other classes, didn't accumulate too many complaints about their work, cooperated with colleagues and administrators, and avoided social indiscretions, the principal's high "evaluation" ratings virtually ensured job security.

During those times, both exemplary teaching performances by many and gross instructional malpractice by many others could escape detection by supervisors and school administrators. Occasionally, outstanding instruction would be recognized, and sometimes even rewarded. When gross malpractice in the classroom was detected, it was difficult to prove. Consequently, teaching incompetence or malpractice was rarely given as a reason for dismissing or reassigning a teacher to noninstructional responsibilities. Most dismissal cases were based on charges of teacher insubordination, social misconduct, or failure to "get along."

Evaluations of instruction were in the hands of school administrators who had virtually no preparation in the science of measurement and the art of evaluation.

Since that time, enlightened scholarship has demonstrated the following truths:

1. Preservice teacher preparation programs provide beginning teachers with necesssary, but insufficient, competencies to be successful \in-service teachers. Effective instruction depends on teachers further developing

those competencies from in-service experiences (Duke, Cangelosi, & Knight, 1988).

2. To be consistently effective, especially in the first few years of their careers, in-service teachers gravely need support, guidance, and feedback as they develop curricula, conduct lessons, manage students, and assess achievement (Evans, 1989).

3. Providing teachers with properly directed, efficient help requires access to accurate information about their teaching performances (McGreal, 1988).

In response to these needs, the field of instructional supervision has emerged as the hope for leading classroom practice into an era in which students will benefit from productive learning experiences systematically designed and conducted by thoughtful, expert teachers. Research-based models whereby instructional leaders work with, not over, teachers have proven successful (Harris, 1989, pp. 1–28). However, all such models (e.g., the clinical models, peer tutoring, self-assessment, and mentor teacher models) depend on nonthreatening programs of feedback on teaching performances. In other words, instructional supervision cannot succeed without accurate formative evaluations of instructional behaviors.

The accuracy of such evaluations depends on the linking of sound principles and practices from the field of measurement and evaluation with those from the field of instructional supervision. In the past, that linkage has been almost nonexistent. Professional organizations for instructional supervisors (e.g., the Association for Supervision and Curriculum Development [ASCD] and those for measurement and evaluation specialists (e.g., the National Council on Measurement in Education [NCME]) never had to worry about members complaining that the meetings of one conflicted with the meetings of the other. There was almost no overlap of membership.

The success of instructional supervision programs, as well as programs for controlling the quality of instruction in schools, depends on our understanding of what constitutes effective instruction. How should teachers go about developing curricula, conducting learning activities, managing classrooms, eliciting students' cooperation, and assessing achievement? This is a question addressed by research studies on teaching. Researchers conducting such studies, like administrative supervisors and instructional leaders, need to base judgments of teaching performance on tenable measurement and evaluation methods.

This book is directed at the following groups:

1. *Instructional supervisors* who need nonthreatening methods of evaluating instruction to guide how they help teachers and provide teachers with feedback on their instructional activities.

2. *Teachers* who need to assess their own teaching performances and those of colleagues with whom they work in cooperative partnerships.

3. *Administrative supervisors* who are responsible for school quality control programs (e.g., those pertaining to hiring, retention, and promotion of teachers).

4. *Researchers* examining variables involving teaching competence, performance, or outcomes.

Evaluating Classroom Instruction illustrates how research-based principles from the field of measurement and evaluation can be realistically integrated into programs for evaluating instruction for purposes of improving instruction, quality control, and research studies. It is designed as a textbook for graduate students in education who are conversant with fundamental teaching/learning principles and are aware of the realities of today's schools.

The book is presented in four parts:

Part I, Fundamental Principles, contains four chapters:

- Chapter 1 illustrates the various functions of evaluations of instruction and introduces some fundamental principles to be considered in designing programs for carrying out those functions.
- Chapter 2 introduces fundamental principles relevant to the selection and development of measurements for evaluating instruction and proper interpretation of the results of those measurements.
- Chapter 3 suggests how to utilize cost-effective classroom observations as data sources for evaluating instruction.
- Chapter 4 examines the advantages and disadvantages of different types of measurements and suggests how to complement classroom observations with additional data sources.

Part II, Formative Methods, contains two chapters:

- Chapter 5 illustrates how summative evaluations that affect the security and status of teaching positions (e.g., in retention, promotion, or salary decisions) can be prevented from interfering with programs for providing teachers with formative feedback leading to improvement of instructional performance. This chapter also presents a model for subdividing teaching responsibilities into manageable components so that feedback helps rather than overwhelms teachers.
- Chapter 6 presents a model by which teachers in cooperation with instructional supervisors receive formative feedback at key points as they plan, design, prepare, implement, and assess outcomes of teaching units and lessons.

Part III, Summative Methods, contains four chapters:

- Chapter 7 suggests ways of resolving issues and problems related to summative evaluations for beginning teachers. The design of a model program is illustrated.
- Chapter 8 presents ideas for designing summative evaluations of instruction for use within an advancement program for expert teachers.
- Chapter 9 suggests ways of resolving issues and problems related to summative evaluations used in decisions regarding whether or not marginal teachers should be retained, dismissed, or reassigned. The design of a model program is illustrated.
- Chapter 10 points out critical differences between evaluations of instruction

that affect individual teachers' futures and summative evaluations for purposes of research studies. Advantages and disadvantages of two evaluation approaches for researchers are illustrated.

Part IV, Looking Ahead, contains the final chapter:

• Chapter 11 reflects on the dismal history of evaluations of instruction in schools but points out that the recent advancements in both instructional supervision and measurement and evaluation suggest a much brighter future.

The appendices contain some of the artifacts (primarily measuring instruments) of the many examples used to illustrate principles, techniques, and programs for evaluating instruction. Comprehension of the text's contents depends on the reader's referring to appendices as indicated in the chapters.

I am indebted to the many students and professional educators with whom I have worked over the past 20 years; their experiences are the sources for the 125 realistic examples used in this book. Although these examples reflect aspects of actual events, they are presented here with fictitious names, locations, and institutions. Circumstances, actions, and situations are likely to appear familiar to any reader acquainted with the realities of schools, but any similarities to names, locations, and institutions alluded to in these examples are strictly coincidental.

Special thanks to Izar Martinez, whose administrative genius creates opportunities for scholarship at Utah State University and Barb Rice, who expertly served as advisor and copyreader. Working with the professionals at Longman—especially Ray O'Connell, Richard Bretan, and Camilla Palmer—has proven to be both satisfying and enjoyable.

PART I
Fundamental Principles

CHAPTER 1

Who Evaluates Instruction and for What Purposes?

Goal of Chapter 1

Chapter 1 identifies the people responsible for evaluating instruction and illustrates their purposes for doing it. Specifically, this chapter is designed to help you:

1. Define evaluation.
2. Distinguish between evaluations of instruction and evaluations of teachers and explain why it is important for teachers, supervisors, and researchers to make that distinction.
3. Describe how the teachers', supervisors', and researchers' decisions are dependent on evaluations of instruction.
4. Classify evaluations of instruction according to whether they focus on teaching competence, teaching performance, or student outcomes.
5. Distinguish between examples of formative and summative evaluations of instruction and explain why the two should be clearly separated.
6. Explain the role of formative evaluations of instruction both for guiding one's own instructional practices and for instructional supervision.
7. Explain the role of summative evaluations of instruction for quality control and for research on teaching.

EVALUATE INSTRUCTION, NOT THE TEACHER

Evaluation

An *evaluation* is a judgment about the quality, value, effectiveness, or impact of something (e.g., a product, process, person, organization, or collection). Tables 1.1 and 1.2 list examples of evaluations made by instructional supervisors, teachers, or researchers. How do the two lists differ regarding *what* was evaluated?

Evaluations Focusing on Instruction

Table 1.1's evaluations focus on: the relationship between the effectiveness of Ms. Green's lesson and the rate of disruptive student behavior; Mr. Manion's accomplishments with his life-science students; the impact of Dan's problem-solving outline; the ratio of application-level to knowledge-level items that Ms. Matsumoto should use on her next test; and the degree to which teachers display an assertive communication style.

These five evaluations relate to aspects of teachers' instruction or the impact of that instruction, not on the teachers themselves.

Evaluations Focusing on Teachers

On the other hand, the questions addressed by the evaluations listed in Table 1.2 were directed at the value of the teachers themselves rather than the quality, value,

---

TABLE 1.1. EXAMPLES OF EVALUATIONS OF INSTRUCTION

A district reading supervisor: "Ms. Green's lesson was ineffective because of a high rate of disruptive student behavior."

A middle school principal: "Mr. Manion accomplished more with his life-science students this year than I had thought was possible."

A department head: "Dan, that 'problem-solving outline' you gave them really focused their attention during the questioning session!"

Ms. Matsumoto: "On my next test, I'm going to use more application-level items, and fewer knowledge-level ones."

A researcher: "The teachers who attended the workshop are now more likely to display an assertive communication style than those in the control group."

TABLE 1.2. EXAMPLES OF EVALUATIONS OF TEACHERS

A district reading supervisor: "Mr. Calhoun is a poor disciplinarian."

A middle school principal: "Ms. Marino is as fine a life-science teacher as I ever hoped to have on my faculty."

A department head: "Sue, you are one fantastic teacher!"

Mr. Galbreth: "I'm a rotten test designer."

A researcher: "Most of the teachers who attended the workshop are now better than those in the control group."

effectiveness, or impact of their instructional activities. Each of Table 1.2's evaluations resulted in the labeling of a teacher as either a "poor disciplinarian," "fine life-science teacher," "fantastic," "rotten test designer," or "better." Labeling teachers does not provide them with the information they need to determine how to better practice their art. Administrators can hardly defend personnel decisions based on the strengths of such labels.

A Critical Difference

Competently conducted evaluations of *instruction* have the potential of providing information that can be examined, analyzed, and utilized without threatening teachers' self-esteem and stimulating defensive responses. Methods suggested in Chapters 5–10 of this text are designed to do just that. However, virtually any evaluations of *teachers themselves* lead to destructive outcomes (Cangelosi, 1988a, pp. 83–85; Ginott, 1972; Medley, Coker, & Soar, 1984, pp. 3–31; Oliva, 1989, pp. 52–54). For example:

Following her initial observation in the fourth grade classroom of John Gonzales, a first-year teacher, Principal Margaret Roth engages John in the following conversation:

MARGARET: I really enjoyed your class this morning; you're quite a teacher! With a little more experience, you'll be a superstar!

JOHN: Why thank you. [As John thinks to himself, "Hooray, she likes *me*! Good thing she caught me today, not when I made a fool of myself handling Scott's misbehavior."]

MARGARET: I'll bet you're even better when I'm not in the room. Some new teachers freak out the first time they're observed.

JOHN: Oh! Did I seem nervous? [Thinking to himself, "Oh-oh! She thinks I'm too nervous."]

MARGARET: No, you were just fine. But it's natural to be a little jittery until you get your feet on the ground.

JOHN: When will you visit the class again? Please come by anytime. [Thinking to himself, "She thinks I'm jittery! I'll be ready for her next time. I'll be so calm she'll think I'm a cool customer."]

Margaret set the unfortunate tone of the exchange by labeling John as "quite a teacher" and a "potential superstar." This communicated to John that *he*, not his instruction, is the object of Margaret's evaluations. He became quite defensive, attempting to protect his image as "quite a teacher on the threshold of superstardom." Of course, "superstars" don't "freak out" or appear nervous. Because Margaret made John the issue, rather than how he teaches, John now views her visits as times to hide weaknesses and display strengths rather than as opportunities for constructive feedback.

People are far more likely to accept and make constructive use of feedback about what they *do*, than on who they *are*. Your responsibilities as a supervisor, teacher, or researcher require you to evaluate instruction, not teachers.

RESPONSIBILITY FOR EVALUATING INSTRUCTION

Evaluating One's Own Instruction

Some teachers expertly and systematically evaluate their own instruction; others use more haphazard approaches. But no teacher can avoid making judgments about her or his instruction. Teachers' evaluations, accurate or not, influence their goals, how classrooms are organized, methods for managing student behavior, lesson designs, how lessons are conducted, and how student achievement is assessed. The two teachers in the following examples recognize the need to evaluate their own instruction:

> Nettie McCullah is trying to determine which of two grouping patterns is more effective for her first graders' reading lessons. One pattern uses interest groups; the other groups according to comprehension levels. She decides to try each for a week and then continue with the more successful one.

> Reading an article in a journal for mathematics teachers leads Sam Ortega to wonder if he overemphasizes computational skills with his pre-algebra students and neglects their application-level learning. Thus, he decides to monitor and analyze the lessons in his next teaching unit to assess whether he has an appropriate balance between skill-level and application-level activities.

Instructional Supervision

Among their other roles, school principals, assistant principals, mentor teachers, department heads, cooperating teachers working with student teachers, school district area specialists (e.g., for social studies, vocational education, special education, and science), and state office area specialists serve as instructional supervisors. Instructional supervision is helping teachers to be more effective with their students (Cooper, 1984a, pp. 1–2). However, an instructional supervisor cannot know how to help teachers in the absence of evaluations of their instruction. For example:

> Maude Nelson considers providing help and support to teachers to be her most important responsibility as principal of Malaker Middle School. She embarks on a program for evaluating instruction to identify specific needs of individual teachers for which she can provide assistance.

> Al Quintana, an experienced teacher, has been appointed as the mentor teacher who helps Anna Gray during her first year of teaching. Anna expresses concern over

maintaining student engagement during lessons and handling off-task behaviors. Thus, they develop a plan by which Al advises her on classroom management strategies based on periodic evaluations.

Quality Control

Instructional supervision is concerned solely with improving the instructional practices of individual teachers. There is, however, another supervisory responsibility for which administrators and other professional educators are responsible. To maintain standards of quality in the teaching profession, incentives should be provided for expert teaching, and ineffective teachers who are unresponsive to instructional supervision should be replaced. Evaluations of instruction yield the bases for the difficult decisions made in this arena. For example:

In the Carolton School District, teachers are assigned probationary status during their first three years in the district, then they are either awarded tenure or released. According to school board policy, Len Young-Jun, one of Carolton's principals, must semiannually provide the district office with a recommendation for each of his probationary teachers. Each recommendation is to include a judgment regarding progress toward tenure, of either "satisfactory," "questionable," or "unsatisfactory" for two areas: "level of professionalism" and "instructional effectiveness." Judgments in the area of instructional effectiveness require Len to implement a tenable process for evaluating instruction.

As her district's assistant superintendent for health and physical education, Roberta Ayers is responsible for selecting the physical education teachers to be nominated for a merit pay raise for "outstanding teaching." The way she evaluates instruction will be subject to careful scrutiny.

It is Jon Garon's first month as assistant principal for instruction at Bayview High School. He has just observed Ms. White conduct a history class and is appalled by what he saw and heard. He bursts into Principal May Watkins' office, where the following confidential conversation ensues:

MAY: Better sit down Jon, you look a little out of joint.

JON: I've just observed one of Ms. White's classes.

MAY: That explains your chagrin.

JON: For 55 minutes, I watched the subversion of everything we're trying to build with these kids!

MAY: Do you really think she can do that by herself?

JON: She created conflict, labeled students, vacillated between passivity and hostility—never was assertive! It took her a record 13 minutes to extinguish Josh Boyer's on-task behavior! Even I was in danger of being permanently turned off to history! Now, I need deprogramming!

MAY: (laughing) You probably got out of there just in time!

JON: You're laughing about this?

MAY: I'm laughing at you. I've already cried over the way she teaches, but I don't know what to do. She's a nine-year veteran with tenure. Three years ago when I took this job, I discovered the bad news. But she has nothing but positive evaluations from her previous supervisors and administrators.

JON: Did I just catch her on a bad day?

MAY: Probably not any worse than most days. Nothing you said surprises me. Actually, I've tried to neutralize her teaching by keeping her loads down and being selective about who gets in her classes. You know, she's such a remarkably pleasant person. She loves the kids and really tries. But she just doesn't have the ability or personality to teach.

JON: Don't get me wrong. I like her personally. I'm just shocked at how she teaches.

MAY: Part of the problem is that she's so likable that no one wants to confront her about what goes on in her classroom. She'd be very hurt.

JON: But the students are the ones being hurt and they're our responsibility!

MAY: I can't argue with that. It's gone along long enough. We start solving this problem right now. This situation falls under the district's provision for *marginal teachers.*

JON: What's that?

MAY: It's a tricky-to-use policy by which tenured teachers with records of negative teaching evaluations are assigned "marginal" status.

JON: But you said Ms. White's evaluations have been positive to this point.

MAY: That's true. In fact, one of the reasons I recommended you for this position is because I needed someone with evaluation skills who could work with me in making the difficult decisions like this one. Before now, I didn't have anyone who could provide me with evaluation results that can stand up in the face of a legal appeal.

JON: I won't be your "hit" man.

MAY: I don't want you to be. I want you to design effective evaluations of instruction that tell us how to do better.

JON: I will be happy to do that. But finish telling me about this marginal teacher policy.

MAY: A principal can recommend marginal status for tenured teachers with a history of negative teaching evaluations. If the assistant superintendent for instruction accepts the recommendation and appeals are unsuccessful, a year-long program of instructional supervision is cooperatively planned with the marginal teacher. If the evaluations of instruction in the year following the program are markedly improved, then the teacher is returned to tenured status. If not, either the teacher is released or some compromise is reached. Compromises usually lead to early retirement.

JON: So what about Ms. White?

MAY: I would like to give her every opportunity to prove my perception of her teaching to be inaccurate. And I don't want to be doing anything behind her back. We need to develop an evaluation plan, but she should be involved in its design.

JON: Give me until tomorrow afternoon to pull together some ideas. Then we'll meet and decide how to approach Ms. White.

MAY: Four-fifteen right here. Thanks.

Research on Teaching

What we know about how to teach and how to help teachers be more effective in the classroom is dependent on the findings of research studies that address questions such as: What is the relationship between teachers' scores from the NTE Core Battery Tests (Mitchell, 1985, pp. 1063–70) and cognitive levels of the lessons they conduct? Do teachers who consistently use assertive communication styles deal with student off-task behavior any more or less efficiently than teachers who consistently use hostile communication styles (Canter & Canter, 1976, pp. 156–60; Render, Padilla, & Krank, 1989)? Are mathematics teachers who completed preservice teaching programs in mathematics more successful teaching middle school mathematics than crossover teachers whose preservice preparations were in other subject areas, such as English or elementary education (Jesunathadas, 1990)?

For studies to address questions such as these, they must include evaluations of instruction. But, unlike evaluations used for guiding one's own teaching practices, for instructional supervision, or for quality control, these evaluations are not intended to influence the teachers whose instruction is analyzed. Here are two examples:

For his Master's thesis, Damien Yoder examines the degree to which teachers who demonstrated improved teaching methods upon completion of an in-service program maintain that level of improvement over time. To conduct the study, Damien will have to evaluate his subjects' teaching methods. The evaluations are to be used to learn more about the effects of the in-service program, not to learn about the practices of the subjects themselves.

Rolfe Robicheaux, the in-service director for Silver Isle School District, is assessing the cost-effectiveness of a mentoring program for beginning teachers. He designs a study to compare the instructional effectiveness of second-year teachers who participated in the program the previous year to those who did not. Rolfe's evaluations of instruction will influence judgments about the future of the mentoring program, not the future of the teachers who serve as study subjects.

THREE VARIABLES

A *variable* is a quality, characteristic, or quantity that differs according to subjects, circumstances, or other factors. For example, *success of a lesson* is a variable because one lesson can be highly successful, another might be a miserable failure, and others may fall anywhere between the two extremes. A typical evaluation of instruction focuses on one of the following variables: *teaching competence, teaching performance*, or *student outcomes*.

Teaching Competence

In one of the previous examples, Jon Garon evaluated Ms. White's teaching performance in a particular history class to be appallingly poor. This observation motivated his discussion with May Watkins. Recall that midway through the conversation Jon and May shifted the topic from Ms. White's teaching performance for that one history class period to questions about Ms. White's ability to teach. Apparently, the accumulation of evaluations of Ms. White's *teaching performance* led May to question her *teaching competence*.

Evaluations of teaching competence are concerned with the degree to which teachers demonstrate characteristics, abilities, skills, and attitudes that are considered essential for effective instruction. Such evaluations address questions such as: How familiar is the teacher with subject matter content and with accepted pedagogical principles and techniques? Does the teacher display personality characteristics such as warmth, decisiveness, and self-assurance, typically associated with effective instruction?

The certification of teachers (e.g., through college preservice programs) is dependent on evaluations of teaching competence. And, although the practice is criticized in the professional literature, teaching competence seems to be the variable of concern of most evaluations of instruction occurring in schools (Cangelosi, 1986). Focusing the evaluation on teaching competence has been criticized for many reasons.

First, some say that research findings do not clearly support notions about relationships between teacher characteristics and student learning (Coker, Medley, & Soar, 1980; Guthrie, 1970; Lewis, 1982). It is also claimed that measurement instruments and procedures (e.g., observer rating scales, personality tests, student rating forms, and teacher competency tests) typically used as data sources for evaluations of teaching competence fail to meet conventional standards of measurement validity (Cangelosi, 1984; Peterson, 1983; Quirk, Witten, Weinberg, 1973; Soar, Medley, & Coker, 1983). Also, the teaching styles and personality characteristics appear to vary as much among teachers judged as highly competent by students, supervisors, and peers as they vary for teachers in general (Allen, Davidson, Hering, & Jesunathadas, 1984).

Ideas for overcoming these weaknesses in some of the limited circumstances in which evaluations should focus on teaching competence are included in Chapters 2–4.

Teaching Performance

Evaluations of *teaching performance* are more likely than evaluations of teaching competence to provide the accurate information needed in most situations for guiding one's own instructional practices, instructional supervision, quality control, and research on teaching. Instead of focusing on what teachers are capable of doing, evaluations of teaching performance are concerned with the relevance and quality of the lessons they plan and conduct. Questions such as the following are addressed (Cangelosi, 1986):

1. Are the teacher's goals appropriate? In other words: (a) Are the learning objectives consistent with the school's curriculum guidelines? (b) Do the objectives address students' needs? (c) Are the objectives sufficiently, but not overly, ambitious?
2. Considering the aptitudes and prior achievements of the students and the amount of time and resources available to the teacher, what pedagogical principles apply and what procedures should be followed to help students achieve the learning objectives? In other words, how should the lessons be designed and conducted?
3. How well do the teacher's lessons adhere to the principles and procedures identified in the answer to question 2?
4. Are the lessons conducted in an efficient and expert manner that not only should help students achieve the learning objectives, but also should be an overall positive experience for them?

Designing and implementing procedures for evaluating teaching performance are challenging tasks requiring an expertise that most teachers, supervisors, and researchers have yet to acquire. The remainder of this text is designed to help you gain that expertise.

Student Outcomes

Schools are established to serve students. The success of a school depends on what its students learn. Student achievement is the goal of instruction. Thus, doesn't logic dictate that evaluations of instruction should depend on how well students achieve learning goals? One school of thought that is especially popular among politicians who control funds for schools answers that question in the affirmative. Advocates of this view insist that teachers should be held accountable for student achievement and, thus, evaluations of instruction should focus on *student outcome* variables (Popham, 1982). Their evaluations would address questions such as: To what degree did students achieve the learning goals specified by school curricula? What other influences did the instruction have on the students?

The rationale for this type of evaluation includes the assumption that the quality of a product reflects the quality of the process that produced the product. However, the complexities of the teaching/learning process (Arends, 1988) and the realities of today's schools (McLaren, 1989) may render that assumption inapplicable to evaluations of instruction. For one thing, a student's prior achievements, aptitudes, attitudes, motivation for learning, history, family's influence, emotional maturity, work ethic, and temperament are among the complex factors that influence what that student achieves under the tutelage of a teacher; however, the teacher cannot control these factors (Lamb & Thomas, 1981). Second, assessments of student achievement are typically dependent on standardized tests with questionable validities for the learning goals of the vast majority of teachers (Cangelosi, 1982, pp. 343–51). Third, some commonly used statistical manipulations (e.g., computing post- pretest gain scores) of test results for purposes of assessing student achievement are untenable for reasons (e.g., regression effects) that are not widely understood by school personnel (Shavelson & Russo, 1977; Soar, Medley, & Coker, 1983; Veldman & Brophy, 1974). Finally, the influence of students' test scores on judgments of teaching performance encourages teachers to limit their curricula to what the tests measure (Shine & Goldman, 1980).

Focusing on teaching performance variables rather than student outcome variables is preferable for most evaluations of instruction.

FORMATIVE VERSUS SUMMATIVE EVALUATIONS

Formative Evaluations of Instruction

An evaluation of instruction is *formative* if its sole purpose is to provide information that is useful for decisions about how to teach. Teachers make formative evaluations whenever they evaluate their own instruction for guidance in organizing, designing, or planning lessons. For example:

Prent Jeiko videotapes one of the questioning strategy sessions he conducts with his fifth graders. Later, he views the tape to help him decide if he is inadvertently discouraging some students from participating. He decides that next time he will have all students write down answers to each question before calling on some to reply orally.

An evaluation of instruction is always formative if it is made by an individual serving in the capacity of an instructional supervisor. For example:

Anna Gray is concerned that a significant number of her students frequently fail to follow her directions. She suspects they stare at her without really attending to what she is saying. Al Quintana, her mentor teacher, suggests that the students have become accustomed to her repeating directions and consequently don't bother to listen when she first begins to speak. They agree that if subsequent observations support Al's contention, they will devise a cue to remind Anna not to repeat directions.

Chapters 5 and 6 explain and illustrate specific suggestions for developing and conducting formative evaluations of instruction.

Summative Evaluations of Instruction

An evaluation of instruction is *summative* if it is a judgment of instructional effectiveness that is used for purposes other than helping the teacher decide how to teach. Unlike formative evaluations, summative evaluations may influence administrative decisions about that teacher (e.g., regarding retention, salary, or promotion). For example:

Jon Garon, Bayview High assistant principal, cooperatively designs a summative evaluation plan with Ms. White and his principal that will be used to decide if Ms. White's tenure status should be changed to "marginal."

When an evaluation is made as part of a research study, the evaluation is summative, since the sole purpose is not to influence the way the teachers who serve as study subjects teach. For example:

In-service Director Rolfe Robicheaux evaluated the instructional effectiveness of two groups of second-year teachers: (1) those who participated in the district's mentoring program the previous year and (2) those who did not. The results of his study influenced his recommendation to the superintendent that the program be continued and required for all beginning teachers the following year. Rolfe revealed only aggregate evaluation results obtained from each *group* of teachers. Results for any individual were kept confidential.

The Need for Maintaining Separation

Instructional supervisors are responsible for helping teachers be more effective with their students. They can hardly meet this responsibility without making accurate formative evaluations of the teachers' instructional practice. However, if teachers suspect that the instructional supervisors' formative evaluations may influence administrative decisions regarding their retention, salaries, or promotions, the trusting, collegial relationship necessary for effective instructional supervision is threatened (Sergiovanni & Starratt, 1983). Consequently, formative evaluations of instruction can hardly serve their purpose unless they are completely divorced from summative evaluations of instruction (Scriven, 1988). Popham (1988, pp. 281–82) states:

The initial shortcomings in current teacher appraisal practices, a problem encountered in almost all public school districts, is that the officials of those districts have thoughtlessly merged two different missions of teacher evaluation. The two evaluative functions are splendid if separate, but counterproductive when combined. The first of these two missions, *formative* teacher evaluation, is to help teachers become more effective. A second, and equally important, function of teacher evaluation is to isolate those weak teachers who, if they cannot be improved, should be removed from their teaching positions. The latter mission, of course, is *summative* teacher evaluation.

Summative teacher evaluation, in addition to being used for the dismissal of teachers, can also be employed to help assign teachers to levels of a career ladder (merit pay) and to grant or deny tenure to beginning teachers. Summative teacher evaluation has as its primary function, however, the determination of teacher competence—not the augmentation of that competence. Summative evaluation makes no pretense about helping a teacher get better. Improving the teacher's performance is the job of formative teacher evaluation.

Almost all American teacher evaluation systems attempt to combine these two teacher evaluation functions so that both can be carried out simultaneously. Yet, the combination constitutes a classic instance wherein the coalescing of inherently contradictory functions renders both dysfunctional.

Typical of the language encountered in most public school teacher appraisal procedures is that found in the teacher appraisal law recently enacted by one state legislature. According to that law, "the results of the appraisal of teachers shall be used for career ladder purposes, and may be used for contract renewal and staff development considerations." In the same law, however, legislators require that the evaluation instrument for teachers "be used to assess specific skills primarily for the purpose of remediation and improvement." Not surprisingly, a dual-purpose statewide teacher appraisal system was developed consonant with legislative intent.

Chapter 5 illustrates how to maintain a separation between formative and summative evaluations of instruction.

SELF-ASSESSMENT EXERCISES FOR CHAPTER 1

The self-assessment sections at the end of each chapter provide exercises to help you (1) evaluate your achievement of the chapter's objectives so that you can identify your areas of proficiency and the topics you need to review, and (2) reinforce and extend what you have learned from the chapter.

Here are the exercises for Chapter 1:

I. Define *evaluation* in your own words. Like the definition on page 4, yours should include an emphasis on qualitative judgment or decision making.
II. Write "instruction" by each of the following examples in which instruction is the target of the evaluation. Write "teacher" by those in which a teacher is the target.
   A. Mr. Bradley is most worthy of being named "Teacher of the Year."
   B. Helena is a poor communicator in the classroom.
   C. Eva tends to use descriptive rather than judgmental language with her students.
   D. Estasvus efficiently handled that discipline problem.
   E. Her tests are well-constructed.

    F. She is an excellent test designer.

Now compare your answers to the following and resolve any difference by discussing them with someone else who engaged in these self-assessment exercises: "Instruction" for C, D, and E; "Teacher" for A, B, and F.

III. Do you agree or disagree with the following statement: "People are far more likely to accept and make constructive use of feedback about what they *do* than on who they *are*." In a paragraph explain the rationale for your answer. Then share your paragraph with someone and discuss the implications for evaluating instruction.

IV. For each of the following, recall an example and describe it in several sentences:

    A. In a particular situation, you modified how you teach because of an evaluation you made about your own instruction.

    B. A supervisor misadvised a teacher about how to teach because the supervisor had not accurately evaluated the teacher's performance.

    C. An evaluation of instruction affected a teacher's position on a school faculty.

    D. A research project was conducted that examined the quality of instruction.

Without revealing names or violating professional confidences, share your examples with another professional educator and discuss the role of evaluations of instruction.

V. Five examples of evaluations of instruction are described below. Classify each according to:

    1. Whether the *evaluation variable* of focus is *teaching competence* (TC), *teaching performance* (TP), or *student outcomes* (SO).

    2. Whether it is *formative* (F) or *summative* (S).

    3. Whether it appears to be used primarily for purposes of *guiding one's own instruction* (GO), *instructional supervision* (IS), *quality control* (QC), or *research on teaching* (RT).

Here are the examples:

    A. On the basis of the results of a diagnostic achievement test she administered to her students, a teacher decides to emphasize application-level objectives in subsequent lessons.

    B. A teacher education professor decides that one preservice teacher is not yet ready to begin student teaching.

    C. A principal forms the opinion that graduates from five-year teacher preparation programs tend to be more capable of becoming effective teachers than those from four-year programs.

    D. Based on the consistent indications that she applies accepted pedagogical principles, an elementary teacher is awarded tenure.

    E. A mentor teacher decides that the beginning teacher assigned to her needs to streamline his use of classroom transition time.

Compare your responses with the following key and resolve any discrepancies with someone else who also engaged in this exercise:

A: SO, F, GO.
B: TC, S, QC.
C: TC, S, RT.
D: TP, S, QC.
E: TP, F, IS.

CHAPTER 2

Measurement and Evaluation Principles

Goal of Chapter 2

Chapter 2 acquaints you with fundamental principles relevant to the selection and development of measurements for evaluating instruction and properly interpreting the results of those measurements. Specifically, this chapter is designed to help you:

1. Define measurement.
2. Explain how evaluations of instruction are dependent on measurements and measurement results.
3. Distinguish between examples of actual and pseudo measuring instruments used in processes for evaluating instruction.
4. Distinguish between evaluations of instruction that are norm-referenced and those that are criterion-referenced.
5. Explain why a measurement's relevance depends on the degree to which it focuses on the specific variable to be evaluated.
6. Explain why a measurement's reliability depends on the adequacy of its test–retest, internal, and observer consistencies.
7. Explain why a measurement's validity depends on its relevance and reliability.
8. Explain why the cost-effectiveness of a measurement depends on its validity and usability.
9. Explain the role of data analysis in interpreting measurement results for the purposes of evaluating instruction.
10. Describe in nontechnical terms general principles for assessing the validities of measurements used in evaluating instruction.

17

11. Explain why it is necessary to specify the purpose of an evaluation and define the evaluation variable prior to selecting or developing measurements.

12. Given a vaguely defined task to evaluate instruction within a situation that is familiar to you, define the evaluation variables specifically enough to allow valid measurements to be selected or developed.

MEASUREMENTS AND EVALUATIONS

Measurement

Think about one of the many evaluations of instruction you have made in your work as a teacher, supervisor, or researcher. Write out the specific evaluation that you have in mind.

Now list the empirical observations (i.e., things you heard, saw [including read], felt, tasted, or smelled) that influenced you to make the evaluation of instruction that you just recalled and articulated in writing.

Three of the evaluations of instruction from examples in Chapter 1 are repeated in Table 2.1 (pages 20–21), each juxtaposed with two lists: (1) the empirical observations that influenced the evaluation and (2) the results of those observations.

Your evaluations are value judgments that are influenced by *information* acquired through your empirical observations. If that information is accurate and relevant to the evaluation variable, then you are in a position to make an informed, rather than a naive value judgment. The process of making an empirical observation and recording the resulting information (i.e., facts or data) is a *measurement*. Thus, evaluations depend on measurements.

Each of the three evaluations listed in the second column of Table 2.1 were made in light of the corresponding measurement results of column 4. The results were obtained by the measurements described in column 3.

By definition, a measurement is an objective process. For example, it is a fact that the middle school principal (from Table 2.1) overheard June say, "How do you think Manion's experiment will turn out today?" and Norman reply, "I don't know; I spent hours thinking about it last night!" As long as that principal was only observing and recording, only measurements were being made. An evaluation was made when the principal decided to interpret that measurement result as an indication of Mr. Manion's accomplishments with his students. It is a fact that the students said what the principal heard, but it is a matter of opinion as to what, if anything, their conversation indicates about Mr. Manion's instructional practice. Evaluations involve subjective judgments, whereas measurements involve only acquiring and recording information. Table 2.2 (page 22) reflects the roles of measurements and measurement results in the process of evaluating instruction.

The primary purpose of this and the next two chapters is to help you, whenever you need to evaluate instruction, (1) to select or develop practical measurements that will provide accurate results that are relevant to your particular evaluation variable, and (2) to interpret properly the measurement results (i.e., facts or data).

Measurement Results

Facts. Since a measurement is an objective process whereby observations are made and recorded, its results are facts. Sometimes measurement results may be misleading or irrelevant, but they are still facts. Consider these two examples:

As part of a communications lessons for her fifth graders, Mabel Molitor role-plays assertive, passive, and hostile responses to a situation in which someone asks her to do something she doesn't want to do. Just as she begins demonstrating the hostile response, her principal, Carl DeVarona, steps into her room and observes the following exchange:

DEBBIE:　　　Miss Molitor, don't give us any homework tonight! We really worked hard today.

MS. MOLITOR:　You're just trying to get out of doing work, and don't tell me you worked hard today! You don't know what hard work is!

Carl DeVarona thinks to himself, "That was an inappropriate way for Mabel to speak to that child. I'd better monitor her classes more closely and find ways to help her change that attitude."

As Lakeland School District's social studies specialist, Pam Soldweldel completes a school board mandated "evaluation rating form" each time she observes a teacher's class. The form yields an overall score for "Teaching Performance" that is the sum of three subscores: "Knowledge of Content," "Methodology," and "Professional Conduct."

As she observes Pruitt Austin-Brown's civics class, she thinks, "I'll have to rate him at the bottom for 'professional conduct' because no teacher should wear jeans with an old wrinkled shirt like that." Consequently, the overall "Teaching Performance" score is low compared to those Pam awards for the teaching of others she observes.

Carl DeVarona's measurement left him with the *fact* that Ms. Molitor's response to a student was, "You're just trying to get out of work, . . . what hard work is!" But because he was unaware of why she gave that hostile reply, the measurement result misled Carl's evaluation.

Pam Soldweldel's observation provided the *fact* that Mr. Austin-Brown wore jeans and a wrinkled shirt to class. But how relevant is it to an evaluation of his teaching performance?

Scores. The facts or information yielded by some measurements are in the form of *scores* (i.e., numbers). Such formal measurements typically utilize structured instruments or recording devices. Appendix A illustrates an example.

Instrumentation and Recording Devices

Appendix A's instrument, when properly used by a trained observer, produces measurement results relevant for evaluations about the communication style a teacher uses in the classroom (Struyk, 1990). The instrument's directions explain

TABLE 2.1. EXAMPLES OF EVALUATIONS, MEASUREMENTS AND MEASUREMENT RESULTS

Evaluator	Evaluation	Empirical Observations or Measurements	Measurement Results
A middle school principal	"Mr. Manion accomplished more with his life-science students this year than I had thought was possible." (student outcome variable)	The middle school principal:	
		1. Overheard two students, June and Norman, talking in the hallway before school. (Both had high absentee rates last year and for the first month of this year.)	1. June: "How do you think Manion's experiment will turn out today?" Norman: "I don't know; I spent hours thinking about it last night!"
		2. Checked the absentee rates of Mr. Manion's students this year and compared it to rates for last year.	2. Absentee rates for those students since September of this year are well below last year's.
		3. Read the science department head's report of two in-class observations of Mr. Manion's lessons.	3. The report indicated that at least 90% of the students were on-task at all times and that most of the lessons involved students in higher-cognitive thinking processes.
		4. Examined a sample of 20 of Mr. Manion's students midterm examinations.	4. 12 students correctly answered more than 75% of the application-level items and 18 had more than 75% of the knowledge-level items correct.
Jon Garon (assistant principal, Bayview H.S.)	"[Ms. White] created conflict, labeled students, vacillated between passivity and hostility … extinguished[ed] Josh Boyer's on-task behavior! …"	Jon:	
		1. Visited one of Ms. White's history class sessions for 45 minutes, informally (i.e., without recording de-	1. Approximately 15 minutes expired before the lesson began. In that time, students engaged in conversations (none relating to history were detected) as Ms. White sat at her desk ac-

(teaching performance variable)

vices), watching and listening to the activities.

Anna Gray's repetition of directions conditions some students to ignore her when she first speaks. She should devise other means for communicating directions. (teaching performance variable)

knowledging students who came in late with comments such as the one she made to Georgina Floyd: "Thought you'd skip the first part of today's class? Too bad, we waited for you because you just love history!" For the next 30 minutes students took turns reading aloud from the textbook. Student engagement appeared low as (1) three appeared to sleep and (2) only two of the eight students who read (in the order in which they were seated) started reading without first being told where the previous reader stopped. Twice Josh Boyer silently raised his hand but was not acknowledged until he spoke out saying, "Mrs. White, I've got a question." She replied, "I wish you people wouldn't speak out." At the bell Ms. White assigned the rest of the chapter to read and the chapter questions to answer.

Al Quintana (mentor teacher for Anna Gray, beginning teacher)

Al Quintana:

1. Discussed Anna's concerns with her in the hallway before school.

2. Made three one-hour observations in Anna's class using a recording instrument for measuring efficiency of classroom transitions.

1. Anna said too many students don't follow her directions, just stare instead of listening.

2. Seven transition periods occurred in which directions were given. Six of the seven transitions were extended while 10 or more students waited for directions to be repeated before engaging in the learning activities.

TABLE 2.2 THREE OF THE STAGES OF AN EVALUATION OF INSTRUCTION

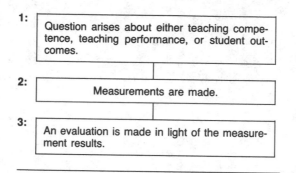

1: Question arises about either teaching competence, teaching performance, or student outcomes.

2: Measurements are made.

3: An evaluation is made in light of the measurement results.

the observation, recording, and computation procedures for obtaining a (1) descriptive to judgmental ratio for teacher talk, (2) supportive to nonsupportive ratio for teacher replies to students' comments, (3) ratio for teacher to student talk, (4) ratio for teacher-asked to student-asked questions, (5) ratio of high-level to low-level teacher-asked questions, and (6) ratio of high-level to low-level student-asked questions. This instrument, designed for use in formative evaluations of teaching performance, produces a score for each of six different variables. Thus it is an example of a measuring device that yields *multiple scores*.

Besides classroom observational instruments, a variety of other types of measurement devices (e.g., student achievement tests, teacher competency tests, and document examination forms) produce scores used in evaluating instruction. The middle school principal alluded to in Table 2.1 based an evaluation about Mr. Manion's instruction partially on 20 students' scores from a midterm examination.

Too often, both single- and multiple-score devices are misused for evaluations of instruction. Chapters 3 and 4 provide hints for avoiding the misuses and for constructively using well-designed instruments.

Pseudo Measuring Instruments

Appendix B contains an example of an evaluator's rating form that is often mistaken for a measuring instrument. This particular form is supposed to yield opinions that are relevant for summative evaluations of overall teaching performance. One must *evaluate*, not simply gather and record information to determine the degree to which the "observed" teacher (1) displayed knowledge of subject matter, (2) was well prepared for the lesson, (3) had the classroom well organized, (4) used effective and appropriate communications, (5) maintained students on-task and engaged in the lesson, (6) displayed a professional manner and attitude, and (7) projected enthusiasm for learning. To make this pseudo measuring instrument into a true measuring instrument, each of the eight statements to be evaluated should be replaced by a number of observable indicators relevant to that item. Appendix A includes observable indicators relevant to "effectiveness and appropriateness of communications;" Appendix C shows a measuring instrument for "how well a lesson is prepared."

Completing forms like the one in Appendix B should not be confused with making measurements. However, there are times when the opinions recorded on such forms serve as measurement results for subsequent evaluations. For example:

Brian Tufts serves as "lead" fifth-grade teacher in one of Drake School District's larger elementary schools. Using the district's "Supervisor's Classroom Observational Rating Form" (see Appendix B), he observed Anyla Hardman's fifth-grade class on three occasions. A district social studies specialist, Elaine Gillingham, also used the pseudo measuring instrument for one of Ms. Hardman's civics lessons.

The school's principal, Ms. Nelson, examines the four completed rating forms as she thinks: "Brian's ratings are consistently positive for items 1, 7, and 8, but each of the other five items are negative for at least two of the three observations. The total 'scores' didn't go up over time either. Negative two, negative one, and the last one's negative four! I see Gillingham's total is plus eight with plus ones for every item, but she does that for everybody. I trust Brian's evaluations. It looks like I should get some help for Anyla in the areas of methods, organization, and classroom management. I'll speak with her tomorrow to plan a program of instructional supervision."

Note that Mr. Tufts *evaluated* when completing Appendix B's rating form. However, Ms. Nelson *measured* by reading Mr. Tuft's evaluations. Her evaluation that Ms. Hardman needed help with methods, organization, and classroom management was influenced by the *fact* that Mr. Tuft's evaluations of her performance in those areas were relatively low.

NORM-REFERENCED EVALUATIONS

Interpretations of measurement results depend on the standards to which they are compared. The choice of standards determines whether the evaluation is norm-referenced or criterion-referenced. Here is an example in which a norm-referenced evaluation of instruction is made:

Two teachers, Aaron Wilkes and Betsy Yen, are discussing the results Betsy obtained when she used the instrument from Appendix A for one of Aaron's class periods:

AARON: What does this supportive to nonsupportive ratio score of 1.7 mean?

BETSY: Let's see—ahh, 12 of your 19 opportunities for supportive replies were, in fact, supportive. So, the ratio is twelve to seven or 1.7.

AARON: That's not what I asked; that's how the ratio is calculated. I want to know if that's a high or low score.

BETSY: Well, the average for the 40 teachers with whom the instrument has been used runs about .03. Without special training in active listening, most teachers hardly ever make a supportive reply.

AARON: So, my replies tended to be very supportive.

BETSY: Yes, 1.7 is high even compared to the scores of the 12 teachers who were in the active listening workshop. The average for that group was only 1.2.

An evaluation of a teacher's instruction is *norm-referenced* if it is based on a comparison of the results of measurements with standards established through measurements of the instruction of a group of teachers. Labels such as "above average," "normal," "not as effective as most," "better than I've seen anyone else do that before," and "lower quartile" suggest norm-referenced evaluations.

CRITERION-REFERENCED EVALUATIONS

Here is an example in which a criterion-referenced evaluation of instruction is made:

Two teachers, Zina Neville and Art Thompson, are discussing the results Zina obtained when she used the instrument from Appendix A for one of Art's class periods:

ART: What does this supportive to nonsupportive ratio score of 1.7 mean?

ZINA: Well, being in that active listening workshop convinced me that supportive replies relieve student frustration, defuse conflicts, and teach students to listen to us. The guy that ran the workshop said those benefits come with ratios above 2.

ART: So, I should try to get mine up.

An evaluation of a teacher's instruction is *criterion-referenced* if it is based on a comparison of the results of measurements with standards established independently of measurements of the instruction of others. Labels such as "adequate performance," "lack of with-it-ness," "sufficiently organized," "excessive use of praise," and "competent to use computers effectively" suggest criterion-referenced evaluations.

MEASUREMENT VALIDITY

The veracity of both norm-referenced and criterion-referenced evaluations are dependent on the *validity* (i.e., accuracy) of the measurements that influence those evaluations. For example:

Maxine Spencer, personnel director for Mount Hope School District, and Principal Tom Leckner are discussing the applications for a fifth-grade teaching position at Tom's school:

MAXINE: Now that we've gone through all the files, who do you want to interview?

TOM: There are at least four I'd like to talk to. This fellow Mike Brown really has high NTE scores, but his letters of recommendation aren't as impressive as some of the others.

MAXINE: Brown is the only one with every subtest score above the 75th percentile. That's a pretty good indication of competence.

TOM: I don't trust those scores that much. How can competence to teach be measured with a bunch of multiple-choice items?

MAXINE: The NTE is not all multiple choice; there are essay sections too.

TOM: Yeah, that's right. But measurement error still influences those scores.

MAXINE: I agree that the test items relate to only a minute portion of the competencies it takes to be effective in the classroom, but that's better than nothing.

TOM: Maybe, but then there's the problem of the dependability of those kinds of tests. Brown may have been having a "good" day when he was tested and some of the others a "bad" day!

MAXINE: So to varying degrees these scores reflect *both teaching competence* and *measurement error*.

TOM: The greater the measurement error, the less valid the test and the *less* stock we should put in the scores.

MAXINE: And the less measurement error, the more valid the test and the *more* stock we should place in these scores.

Maxine and Tom were concerned about the *measurement validities* of teaching competency tests. They recognized the following relationship:

A teaching competency test score depends on the actual level of the teacher's competence to teach and measurement error.

To varying degrees measurement error contaminates all measurement results used in the evaluation of instruction. Maxine and Tom's discussion focused on the validities of written-response teacher competency tests, but measurement error is also a cause for concern for all types of measurements (e.g., classroom observations, interviews, and document examinations) used in evaluating instruction.

In general: *Measurement results used in evaluating instruction depend on two other variables:* the true answer to the question about instruction that the evaluation addresses, and measurement error. Furthermore, *the less measurement error influences measurement results, the more valid the measurement that produced those results*.

Maxine demonstrated her awareness of the fact that a lack of *relevance* contributes to measurement error when she commented, "I agree that the test items relate to only a minute portion of the competencies it takes to be effective in the classroom, but that's better than nothing." Tom showed his concern for another source of measurement error, inadequate *reliability*, when he said, "Maybe, but then there's the problem of the dependability of those kinds of tests. Brown may have been having a 'good' day when he was tested and some of the others a 'bad' day!"

A measurement is *valid* to the same degree that it is both *relevant* and *reliable*.

MEASUREMENT RELEVANCE

The relevance of a measurement used in an evaluation of instruction depends on how well its results pertain to the question addressed by that evaluation. Examine the examples in Table 2.3 and decide from the descriptions which measurements seem more relevant and which less relevant.

TABLE 2.3. EXAMPLES OF MEASUREMENTS WITH VARYING DEGREES OF RELEVANCE

Question to be Addressed by the Evaluation	Description of the Measurement
1. Ms. Kofoed asks herself, "How well do the learning activities I plan and the test items I construct relate to the learning objectives I state?"	1. Ms. Kofoed has a peer teacher utilize the measuring instrument from Appendix C to examine one of her lesson plans. She then reads the peer teacher's responses to items 5, 6, 10, and 11.
2. An assistant principal for instruction raises the following question about one teacher's lessons: "Is there too much emphasis on simple recall and not enough on higher-level thinking?"	2. The assistant principal uses the instrument from Appendix A in observing three of the teacher's lessons. The ratio of high-level to low-level teacher-asked questions is computed for each of the lessons.
3. A principal worries that her school's biology program is in the hands of a first-year teacher, Mr. Palmer. She asks, "How effective has Mr. Palmer's teaching been during the five months he's been with us?"	3. The principal compares the science subtest scores of Mr. Palmer's classes from a standardized achievement test that they recently took to those of the biology students from the previous year.
4. A district mathematics specialist asks before deciding whether or not to recommend Mr. Eaton for a position teaching advanced placement (AP) calculus, "Does Mr. Eaton possess the competence to teach AP calculus?"	4. The mathematics specialist administers to Mr. Eaton a form of the district-mandated final examination for AP calculus students. Mr. Eaton's score is compared to the cutoff score for an A.

Based on the limited descriptions in Table 2.3, you can hardly be expected to make definitive judgments regarding the relevance of the four measurements. However, you can compare your opinion to the following one:

1. Assuming the peer teacher competently utilized Appendix C's instrument on a representative sample of one of Ms. Kofoed's lesson plans, the measurement should provide a relevant indicator of the answer to the question Ms. Kofoed raised.

2. If based on an expert administration of Appendix A's instrument, the ratio of high-level to low-level teacher-asked questions appears to be relevant to whether or not too much emphasis is on simple recall and not enough on higher-level thinking, at least for the questioning portions of the teacher's lessons. However, this measurement fails to provide data relevant to the high-level versus low-level variable for aspects of the lessons (e.g., lectures, homework, and small group discussions) in which the teacher does not ask questions.

3. Two factors make the relevance of the measurement in the third example suspect. First, if the standardized achievement test is typical, it focuses on knowledge-level skills and samples only a very limited range of content (Cangelosi, 1990b, pp. 178–84). So, if Mr. Palmer teaches for higher cognitive objectives as most science education specialists recommend, the test items probably do not cover his learning objectives. Second, a comparison of last year's scores to this year's is not likely to yield information about Mr. Palmer's teaching, since it is untenable to assume that last year's students are comparable to this year's. Student achievement is simply too dependent on factors (e.g., motivation, prior achievement, and aptitude) that are out of Mr. Palmer's control (Medley, Coker, & Soar, 1984, pp. 33–41).

4. Surely there are skills, abilities, and attitudes necessary to teach AP calculus that are not measured by an AP calculus test designed for students. However, it can be argued that it is necessary, though insufficient, for a teacher to be able to score high on the test he or she is responsible for teaching students to pass. So, arguably, if Mr. Eaton's score is low, that's relevant to an evaluation that he does not possess the competence to teach the course. However, a high score should not be considered a sufficient indication that he is competent.

MEASUREMENT RELIABILITY

To be valid, a measurement must not only be relevant, it must also be reliable. *A measurement is reliable to the same degree that it can be depended upon to yield consistent, noncontradictory results.*

As you select or design measurements for use in evaluations of instruction, you should be concerned with three types of consistency: *internal*, *test–retest*, and *observer*.

Internal Consistency

Written-response tests, classroom observations, interviews, document examinations, and other types of measurements each consist of a number of measurement items. For example, Tom and Maxine discussed Mr. Brown's performance on the NTE in the scenario beginning on page 24; the reading section of the communication subtest of the NTE confronted Mr. Brown with 30 multiple-choice questions (i.e., items) (Scannell, 1985). For another example, Appendix C's instrument includes 11 observations about a written lesson plan to be recorded; thus, the measurement includes 11 items.

A measurement is *internally consistent to the same degree that the results from its different items are in agreement.* Consider the following example:

The Woodpine County Teachers Association charged a team of three teachers to recommend in-service programs for its membership. Aware that it is advantageous for teachers to use assertive, rather than passive or hostile, communications with students and their parents (Cangelosi, 1988a, pp. 30–31, 200–202), the team wants to determine if the county's teachers would profit from an "assertiveness" workshop. Before making the decision, the team decides to evaluate the degree to which a representative sample of teachers display assertiveness.

Each teacher in the sample is administered an assertiveness test with ten items. *Items 1 and 6* present situations in which students ask the teacher to excuse them from doing homework. For each, the teacher describes how he or she would respond to the situation. A trained scorer classifies each of the teacher's responses as either "assertive," "hostile," "passive," or "indeterminable." Other items are similar, except that *items 2 and 4* relate to situations in which the teacher is conferring with parents of students who display disruptive behavior patterns; *items 3 and 10* relate to situations in which the teacher is asking parents to supervise their children's homework; *items 5 and 8* relate to situations in which the teacher wants a student to participate in a group discussion; *items 7 and 9* relate to situations in which students refuse to take tests.

The results from items 1 and 6 for four of the teachers is given in Table 2.4. The individual item results suggest that for situations in which students ask to be excused from doing homework, Ms. Ferney would be assertive and Mr. Holdaway passive. However, the results are contradictory for the other two. Item 1 indicates Ms. Wilkinson would be assertive, but not Mr. Bailey; item 6 suggests the opposite.

Measurement results that are dominated by contradictions, such as Mr. Bailey's and Ms. Wilkinson's on items 1 and 6, lack *internal consistency* and thus are unreliable. On the other hand, if the results do not contain a significant proportion of contradictions and are more in line with what items 1 and 6 yielded for Ms. Ferney and Mr. Holdaway, then the measurement is internally consistent.

Test–Retest Consistency

If the same sample of teachers from the Woodpine County Teachers Association took the same assertiveness test a second time, how closely would the second set of results agree with the first? Would teachers with high assertiveness scores the first

TABLE 2.4. RESULTS FROM ITEMS 1 AND 6 FOR FOUR TEACHERS ON AN ASSERTIVENESS TEST

| Teacher | Results from: | |
	Item 1	Item 6
Ms. Ferney	Assertive	Assertive
Mr. Holdaway	Passive	Passive
Mr. Bailey	Hostile	Assertive
Ms. Wilkinson	Assertive	Passive

time tend to score high again? Would those with low assertiveness scores the first time also give nonassertive responses the second time? If some of the teachers in the sample actually became more or less assertive between the test and the retest, then a *valid* assertiveness test *should* be sensitive enough to those changes so that there would be differences between the two sets of results. However, significant fluctuations or contradictions between the test and the retest that are not attributable to actual changes in assertiveness are a consequence of poor *test–retest consistency*.

The results of a highly reliable test will agree with those of a retest of the same subjects as long as the evaluation variable (e.g., some aspect of either teaching competence, teaching performance, or student outcomes) remains stable between the two administrations of the test. Even when the evaluation variable is stable, however, the results of a measurement that lacks test–retest consistency are unstable. Tom expressed concern over test–retest consistency of teacher competency tests when he remarked to Maxine, "Brown may have been having a 'good' day when he was tested and some of the others a 'bad' day."

Observer Consistency

Observer consistency, sometimes referred to as *scorer consistency*, is of concern for measurements that include items with scoring keys that require an element of judgment (e.g., classroom observation and essay). Consider, for example, the following three items:

1. *Written-response item on an assertiveness test for teachers.* It's Friday afternoon and you have just given your students about a two-hour homework assignment that is due Monday. You are planning to use their responses to the assignment to introduce a new lesson on Monday. But one student complains, "You can't give us homework this weekend! We have to go to the school fair!" Others agree with remarks such as, "Yeah, it would be your fault 'cause we couldn't go!" In less than five sentences, write out your verbal response to these students.

   Scoring key:
   Record Hostile if the response includes any retaliatory remarks to the students' assertions "You can't give us homework," "We have to go," or "Your fault" such as "I can give you homework anytime I want," "You don't have to go," or "It's not my fault."

Record *Passive* if (a) the response is not hostile and (b) the assignment is withdrawn, reduced, or postponed.

Record *Assertive* if the response is (a) not hostile and (b) communicates that the assignment is due Monday without modifications.

Record *Indeterminable* if the response does not clearly fit one of the aforementioned categories.

2. *Classroom observation item from Section II (Teacher Talk) of Appendix A's instrument.* Between 15 and 20 minutes into Betsy Yen's observation of his third-hour pre-algebra class, Aaron Wilkes comments to the group, "This class is full of smart mathematicians!"

   Scoring key: Record either D, J, S, N, H, L, X, or ? according to Appendix A's definitions for Section II.

3. *Multiple-choice item on a teaching competency test.* Which one of the following types of instruction provides the most effective means for helping students become skilled in the execution of a process (e.g., an arithmetic computation)?

   A. *Direct teaching*, in which expected step-by-step responses are explicitly communicated to students.

   B. *Inductive methods*, in which students are exposed to specific examples and asked questions leading them to draw a generalization.

   C. *Deductive methods*, in which students are confronted with a problem situation and asked questions leading them to select a means for problem resolution.

   D. *Synectic procedures*, in which analogies are used to help students see either familiar ideas in strange ways or strange ideas in familiar ways.

   Scoring key: +1 for "A" only, otherwise +0.

Measurement reliability is influenced by how consistently the measurement's items are scored. There are two types of observer consistency. The first type, *intra-scorer* consistency, depends on how well the observer's score on a response to an item one time agrees with that observer's score on an identical response a second time. The second type, *inter-scorer* consistency, depends on how well two different observer's scores on the same response agree.

Neither intra-scorer consistency nor inter-scorer consistency is an issue for measurements consisting of items (e.g., the third item in the above list) with scoring keys that leave no room for judgment. However, even items like the first and second above can be scored almost as consistently as multiple-choice items, provided the scoring key explicates very specific rules for what to record or how to award points; provided the observers are trained in how to score the measurement (for example, persons scoring the first item clearly understand the definitions of "hostile," "passive," and "assertive" communications); and provided the observers take special care to adhere faithfully to the scoring key (for example, the first item is scored for all teachers under similar conditions, such as when observers are alert, and different observers periodically score the same responses as a check for consistency).

MEASUREMENT USABILITY

No matter how valid a measurement might be for use in evaluating instruction, it is of no value to you if it is too time-consuming to administer or score, too expensive to purchase, jeopardizes relationships, or threatens the well-being of individuals. In other words, measurements must be practical for your needs. A *measurement is usable to the degree that it is inexpensive, is brief, is easy to administer and score, and does not interfere with other activities.*

MEASUREMENT COST-EFFECTIVENESS

A *measurement is cost-effective if it is both satisfactorily valid and usable.* The following illustrates cost-effectiveness:

For the past month, the administrative and supervisory staff of Van Buren Junior High School has been laboring over the problem of planning a system for making summative evaluations of their first- and second-year teachers' instructional effectiveness. Assistant Principal Inez Martinez has examined numerous options and is now presenting a proposal to the staff:

INEZ: I believe our department heads are in the best position to gather the most valid data on the instructional effectiveness of the beginning teachers in their respective departments. Better than anyone else, department heads understand the goals of the schools and their departments and they are in the best position to routinely administer observational and other types of measurements in these teachers' classes. However, I do not suggest we utilize department heads at all for summative evaluations, because to do so would jeopardize department heads' cooperative relationships with these teachers and make it more difficult for them to gather formative feedback for purposes of instructional supervision. In other words, measurements utilizing department heads or any other Van Buren personnel whom we expect to work hand-in-hand with these teachers will lack *usability*.

Looking for help from outside the school, I contacted BW Education Corporation. It's a consulting agency that for a nominal fee will utilize an instrument to observe each beginning teacher twice and provide us with data for our evaluations. We can afford their service, and the measurements they propose are relatively painless. But their measurements didn't seem relevant for our purposes and, after seeing their instrument, I doubt that only two observations could possibly produce reliable results. This option is usable, but I doubt that it would be *valid*.

Next, I checked with two specialists in the evaluation of instruction at the college. They proposed a rather elaborate process in which they acquaint themselves with our philosophy and curriculum goals and then design several measurements that include interviews, observations, and document examinations. It's all very impressive and I'm convinced that they would provide us with valid information for our evaluations. However, there's one problem. We can't afford them! They estimate they'll need 20 days at 250 dollars a day.

That takes me to the fourth option, which I propose we take. For about the same fee that BW Educational Corporation would have charged us, we can get the two guys at the college to teach our department heads and those over at Beaver County Junior High how to develop our own measurement devices. Then their department heads conduct the measurements for our teachers, and our department heads do the same for their teachers. The measurements may not be as valid as they would be if we did it ourselves or if those two specialists did it themselves, but the validity would probably be acceptable. Nor would this option be as usable as using BW, but we can afford it and it shouldn't jeopardize in-school relationships.

Table 2.5 depicts the relationship among measurement cost-effectiveness, usability, validity, relevance, reliability, internal consistency, test–retest consistency, and observer consistency.

DATA ANALYSIS

Statistical procedures are sometimes used to help interpret measurement results that are in the form of scores or numbers. Statistically manipulating scores can be helpful in the following situations:

- Multiple measurements relevant to the same teaching variable are made. For evaluation purposes, trends in those numbers need to be identified. For example, supportive to nonsupportive ratios for teacher replies using Appendix A's instrument have been gathered 20 times in the classes of a particular teacher. To obtain an indication of a typical ratio, an average or arithmetic mean for those 20 ratios is computed. To obtain an indication of how much those ratios vary from lesson to lesson, a standard deviation is also computed. In this example, a group of scores is reduced to two parameters, a mean and a standard deviation. *Descriptive statistics* (e.g., population means, standard deviations, variances, medians, and correlation coefficients) are used to summarize information from a large group of scores. Numerous references on descriptive statistics are readily available (e.g., Cangelosi, 1982, pp. 259–80; Kachigan, 1986, pp. 3–69).
- A research study is being conducted that requires an evaluation to be made regarding either the teaching competence, teaching performance, or student outcomes for a *population* of teachers. Measurements of the teaching of a sample from that population of teachers are made. Individual scores from

TABLE 2.5. QUALITIES OF COST-EFFECTIVE MEASUREMENT

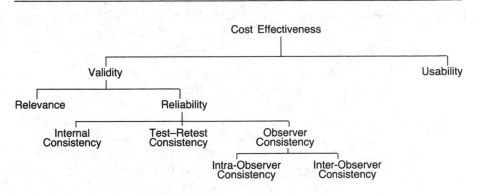

each member of the sample need to be combined into a group score (e.g., a sample mean or sample standard deviation) in order to make an inference regarding the population. In this situation, *inferential statistical procedures* (e.g., analysis of variance, Chi-square, sign test, t-test, multiple regression, and analysis of covariance) might be used with data from the sample to test hypotheses about the population. Numerous references on inferential statistics are available (e.g., Dowdy & Wearden, 1983; Kachigan, 1986, pp. 73–495; Keeves, 1988, pp. 501–781).

• The validity of a measurement used in the evaluation of instruction is assessed. Statistical procedures are normally helpful in such studies.

ASSESSING VALIDITY

Methods for assessing the *validities* of the measurements you use for evaluating instruction are addressed for different types of measurements (e.g., classroom observations and interviews) in Chapters 3 and 4. These methods generally involve three stages: examination of (1) relevance, (2) reliability, and (3) item effectiveness.

Examining Relevance

Numerous models for examining measurement relevance are offered by the scholarly literature on educational and psychological measurement and evaluation. Virtually all of these models provide some sort of systematic approach for analyzing how well a measurement's items relate to the variable the measurement's results are used to evaluate.

Some models employ statistical techniques (e.g., factor analysis and cluster analysis) that examine patterns of correlations among items. Judgments are then made as to whether these patterns tend to support or refute assumptions upon which the measurement is designed. The models presented in Chapters 3 and 4 emphasize systematic techniques that do not require sophisticated statistical procedures.

Information on how to assess relevance is scattered throughout a variety of sources (e.g., Cangelosi, 1982, pp. 243–53; Everitt, 1988; Hambleton, 1984; Kubiszyn & Borich, 1987, pp. 277–89; Nunnally, 1978, pp. 327–435; Spearritt, 1988; Zeller, 1988).

Examining Reliability

Assessing a measurement's reliability is typically easier than assessing its relevance. Statistical methods can be used to gauge consistency within measurement results, consistency between two administrations of the same measurement, and agreement among observers. Unlike assessments of relevance, examinations of reliability are not concerned with making judgments about the match between what items actually measure and what they are supposed to measure.

Assessment of Internal Consistency. In general, internal consistency is studied in one of two ways. First, *split-halves or odd-even methods* apply correlational statistics to gauge the consistency between the scores a measurement yields from one-half of its items with the scores from the other half of its items. For example:

A 40-item teaching competency test is administered to 50 teachers. To assess the internal consistency of the test, a score for each teacher is recorded for only the 20 odd-numbered items (i.e., 1, 3, 5, . . . , 39) and another score is recorded for each teacher for the remaining even-numbered items (i.e., 2, 4, 6, . . . , 40). The results for the first five teachers are given in Table 2.6.

TABLE 2.6. RESULTS FROM ODD AND EVEN ITEMS FROM 5 OF THE 50 TEACHERS WHO TOOK THE 40-ITEM TEACHING COMPETENCY TEST

Teacher	Results from:	
	Odd Items	*Even Items*
Ellen	14	15
Kern	7	5
Marvel	19	3
Melanie	19	20
Fred	0	13

A statistical correlation coefficient is computed from the 50 pairs of scores. The correlation coefficient is a number between −1 and +1 that indicates consistency between the scores from the odd items and those from the even items. If, for example, the vast majority of the pairs are closely aligned, such as Ellen's, Kern's, and Melanie's, then the correlation coefficient will be near 1 (e.g., .85). But, if the vast majority of the pairs are inconsistent, such as Marvel's and Fred's, then the correlation coefficient will be nearer to −1 (e.g., −.70). If there are about as many consistent as inconsistent pairs, then the coefficient will be near 0 (e.g., .15).

Correlation coefficients that are used to assess measurement reliabilities are referred to as *reliability coefficients*. Ordinarily, a reliability coefficient should be at least .80 before the measurement is judged reliable.

A second way to study internal consistency is through *Kuder and Richardson* (1937) *methods*. These accomplish basically the same thing as split-halves or odd-even methods. However, models based on Kuder and Richardson's work are easier to use. Instead of correlating two sets of scores that have been extracted from different halves of the same measurement, the reliability coefficient is computed directly from the measurement's one set of actual scores. Different formulas are used depending on characteristics of the measurement. For example, coefficient alpha (Ebel & Frisbie, 1986, pp. 78–79) would apply to a 30-point test consisting of four essay items administered to 15 or more subjects, and the Kuder-Richardson Formula 21 (Ebel & Frisbie, 1986, pp. 77–78) could be used for a 30-point test consisting of 30 one-point items administered to 15 or more subjects.

Assessment of Test–Retest Consistency. Theoretically, test–retest consistency is assessed by (1) administering the measurement to a group of subjects, (2) somehow preventing the evaluation variable from fluctuating relative to those subjects, (3) readministering the measurement to the same group of subjects, and (4) correlating the two sets of scores and thereby obtaining a reliability coefficient.

However, because of the difficulty of step 2 (maintaining the evaluation variable constant between the two administrations of the measurement), such a method is rarely practical. Fortunately, an argument can be made that a measurement with internal consistency will also have test–retest consistency (Ebel, 1965, pp. 308–43; Thorndike, 1988). Thus, assessments of internal consistency (e.g., Kuder-Richardson methods) tenably act as assessments of test–retest consistency.

Assessment of Intra-Observer Consistency. Acceptable methods for assessing intra-observer consistency vary. However, all of them contain features illustrated by the following example:

Betsy Yen has one of the class sessions that she observes with the aid of Appendix A's instruments videotaped. She puts aside the results from the observation. Two weeks later she observes the videotape of the same class session and, once again, completes Appendix A's instrument. Retrieving the results from her initial observation, she compares the consistency of each of the six ratios from the first observation with its corresponding ratio from the second observation.

Had Betsy conducted this experiment in which she observed and then reobserved numerous (15 or more) class sessions with the instrument, then she could have computed a correlation coefficient for each ratio to help her examine intra-observer consistencies.

Assessment of Inter-Observer Consistency. Inter-observer consistency is assessed similarly to the way Betsy assessed intra-observer consistency. However, instead of correlating the results obtained by the same observer at two different times, the results obtained by two different observers are correlated. In Betsy's example, inter-observer consistency could be assessed by having two different trained observers use Appendix A's instrument for the same class session, without conferring with one another. Each of the pairs of ratios is then compared for consistency.

Reference sources about methods for examining a measurement's reliability are readily available (e.g., Berk, 1984c; Brennan, 1984; Cangelosi, 1982, pp. 255–307; Ebel & Frisbie, 1986, pp. 70–88; Frisbie, 1988; Kubiszyn & Borich, 1987, pp. 291–301; Nunnally, 1978, pp. 225–55).

Examining Item Effectiveness

In addition to assessing relevance and reliability, measurement validation studies often examine the quality of each of the measurement's items. Data relative to individual items provide direction on how to improve the measurement by replacing or modifying faulty items. Procedures for collecting data on item quality are generally referred to as *item analysis*.

Many item analysis models exist. Some use advanced statistical routines; others require only fundamental arithmetic. Most focus on the consistency between the results yielded by an item and the results from the measurement as a whole. Chapters 3 and 4 should help you design items that would fare well under item analysis. The professional literature is replete with sources on assessing item effectiveness (e.g., Berek, 1984a; Cangelosi, 1982, pp. 309–40; Douglas, 1988; Hambleton & Swaminathan, 1985, pp. 1–52, 225–309; Lord & Stocking, 1988; Wright, 1988).

THE SELECTION AND DEVELOPMENT OF MEASUREMENTS FOR EVALUATING INSTRUCTION

Measurements should be designed to be cost-effective and should be selected for their cost-effectiveness. How do you go about designing, obtaining, and utilizing measurements that are both valid and usable for a given situation in which instruction is to be evaluated? The first step is to define clearly the specific purpose of the evaluation.

Defining the Purpose of the Evaluation

All evaluations of instruction include the three stages depicted in Table 2.2. For example:

Principal Lee Farmer speaks to Marie Caravello as she is entering her classroom at the beginning of a school day:

LEE: Since you're the lead kindergarten teacher, I need an evaluation of Vickie's instruction from you. It's required since she's been teaching kindergarten less than two years.

MARIE: When do you need it? I'll need time to observe her class.

LEE: It's due in a week.

MARIE: Okay, I'll have something on your desk by Friday.

LEE: Thanks. I knew you'd come through!

Marie arranges to visit Vickie's class and after a 45-minute observation, she completes a form similar to the one in Appendix B and leaves it for Lee.

Following Table 2.2's three stages:

1. Marie was confronted with a question about Vickie's teaching.
2. Her 45-minute observation and whatever prior knowledge she recalled served as measurements.
3. Marie made the evaluation and reported it on a form similar to the one from Appendix B.

Did Marie's haphazard process lead to an accurate evaluation of Vickie's instruction? That question cannot be addressed until we know specifically what Marie was supposed to be evaluating. What was the purpose of the evaluation? The fact that Lee mentioned that the evaluation is required for new kindergarten teachers suggests that the evaluation might be summative and used in determining if Vickie should be retained in her current position. Or maybe the evaluation is used to guide the instructional supervision of new kindergarten teachers. In any case, until Marie understands the exact purpose of the evaluation and just what evaluation variable should be addressed, she is in no position to choose measurements or to know what to judge.

Unlike Marie, the lead teacher in the following example clarifies the purpose of her evaluation before selecting measurements:

Principal Adonis Hebert speaks to Jan McDonald as she is entering her classroom at the beginning of a school day:

ADONIS: Since you're the lead kindergarten teacher, I need an evaluation of Ted's instruction from you. It's required since he's been teaching kindergarten less than two years.

JAN: This is something we have to talk about. How about 2:45 in your office today?

ADONIS: Can you make it 4 o'clock instead?

JAN: You got it. See you then.

At 4:09 p.m.:

JAN: Explain just what I'm supposed to evaluate.

ADONIS: Ted just has to go through the same thing you did when you started. He needs an evaluation from you and me and from Louise, the district's primary grade supervisor, before the board can tenure him at the kindergarten level.

JAN: I understand that. But, if I'm to make an evaluation, I need to know just what I'm to evaluate.

ADONIS: Ted's instruction; that's all!

JAN: That's not specific enough if you want this done well.

ADONIS: Okay, let's check the district guidelines for tenuring teachers. Hold on, it's right here. . . . Okay, it says, "Tenure is to be based on, one, *fulfillment of professional and civic responsibilities* and, two, *instructional effectiveness*." And then each is defined as, ahh—"

JAN: But the civic and professional business applies to what the board calls "general tenure." For Ted, aren't we just talking about retention as a kindergarten teacher?

ADONIS: You're right! Here it is. Our evaluations are only for instructional effectiveness for the level in question—kindergarten for Ted.

JAN: Let's see how "instructional effectiveness" is defined.

ADONIS: It lists "goal setting," "classroom management and discipline," "instructional methodology," and "assessment of student achievement."

JAN: Those appear to be teaching performance variables, rather than teaching competencies or student outcomes.

ADONIS: It really doesn't define those categories any further. I guess we're expected to plug in our own definitions.

JAN: I suggest we sit down with Ted and Louise and agree to just how we want to define "goal setting," "classroom management and discipline," "instructional methodology," and "assessment of student achievement" as variables that define teaching performance. Then, before we design an evaluation plan, choose data sources and such—

ADONIS: You mean measurements?

JAN: Right! As I was saying, before designing the plan, we should run our definitions of these variables by the district office to get their approval so they'll buy what we give them.

ADONIS: Louise will make sure the district agrees. But there's only one problem.

JAN: What?

ADONIS: The evaluation is due in a week.

JAN: I'm glad you're enough of a political genius to get us an extension. There's no way we can do this right within a week, or even a month! We have to specify the purpose by defining the evaluation variables, select or develop valid measurements for our purpose, use the measurements to collect the data, assess the validity of the measurements, interpret the data, make evaluations, and then communicate what we decide!

ADONIS: You're going to revolutionize the district's teacher evaluations!

JAN: You mean evaluations of *instruction*, not *teachers*!

Some weeks later, Ted, Louise, Adonis, and Jan finish clarifying the purpose of the evaluation and defining the evaluation variables. Table 2.7 displays the fruits of their work. Note from Table 2.7 that they expressed their collective judgment about the relative importance of the four areas and the subvariables by *weighting each as a percentage of the whole.*

TABLE 2.7 DEFINITIONS OF TEACHING PERFORMANCE VARIABLES FOR AN EVALUATION OF TED'S INSTRUCTION

The recommendation for tenure is to be based on an evaluation of teaching performance where teaching performance is defined by performance relative to a number of lessons (selected by the teacher in concert with the evaluation team) within the following areas:

1. *Goal Setting (25%)*

   Judgment regarding performance in goal setting will be based on the degree to which the teacher specifies learning objectives in lesson plans that:

   A. are congruent with curriculum goals (10%)
   B. reflect the individual needs of the students (15%)

2. *Classroom Management & Discipline (35%)*

   Judgment regarding classroom management and discipline during the lessons will be based on how well the teacher adheres to principles suggested by the agreed-upon references[a] when carrying out the following responsibilities:

   A. establishing a purposeful, businesslike learning environment (10%)
   B. orchestrating smooth, efficient transition periods (3%)
   C. obtaining student engagement for learning activities (7%)
   D. maintaining student engagement during learning activities (5%)
   E. efficiently teaching students to supplant off-task behaviors with on-task behaviors (10%)

3. *Instructional Methodology (30%)*

   Judgment regarding the efficacy of instructional methods during lessons will be based on how well the teacher demonstrates:

   A. teaching/learning principles applicable to the lessons' learning objectives, as suggested by the agreed-upon references[a] (20%)
   B. responsiveness to formative feedback based on student performance (10%)

4. *Assessment of Student Achievement (10%)*

   Judgment regarding performance in assessing student achievement will be based on:

   A. the validity of measurements used for summative evaluations of how well students achieved the lessons' objectives (3%)
   B. the efficacy of the formative feedback system (7%)

[a]The teacher is to select the references for the classroom management principles (e.g., Cangelosi, 1988a; Jones & Jones, 1986) and the teaching/learning principles (e.g., Arends, 1988; Joyce & Weil, 1986).

Jan added three more phases to those from Table 2.2. The enhanced process for *effectively* evaluating teaching is depicted by Table 2.8.

Using a Variety of Measurements

What types of measurements (e.g., in-class observations, document examinations, interviews with the teacher, student achievement tests, teaching competency tests, or student opinion questionnaires) are preferable data sources for evaluations of instruction?

TABLE 2.8 SIX STAGES NECESSARY FOR AN ACCURATE EVALUATION OF INSTRUCTION

1: Question arises about either teaching competence, teaching performance, or student outcomes.

2: The question is clarified, specifying the purpose of the evaluation and defining the evaluation variables.

3: Measurements are selected or developed that would appear to be cost-effective for the evaluation variables and for the specific situation.

4: The measurements are made.

5: The validity of the measurements is assessed (i.e., the measurement error is estimated).

6: An evaluation is made in light of both the measurement results and the measurement error.

In one of their meetings, Ted, Jan, Adonis, and Louise discuss possibilities for data sources relative to the variables defined in Table 2.7:

ADONIS: We need to decide how we're going to collect data for this evaluation. Before working on the details, let's see how close our thinking is by running through the list of variables and quickly giving our ideas on how to measure each.

JAN: We've got two under goal setting; the first is congruency with curriculum goals.

LOUISE: I say we examine Ted's lesson plans and devise a system for determining which ones fit under the state's core curriculum guide and which ones don't.

JAN: What if we just interview Ted and ask him to provide an argument as to why his objectives fit the core curriculum?

TED: I like that idea. Then I don't have to make sure everything is clear in writing and you don't have to look things up in the curriculum guide. I can just point it out for you.

LOUISE: What about a combination of the two. We look at the lesson plans, check off the objectives that obviously fit, and then ask Ted about the others.

ADONIS: I'd rather use mainly classroom observations and infer what Ted is trying to accomplish from what he does. After all, the goals targeted by his actions are more important than the ones Ted writes down on paper!

The conversation continues for another 15 minutes, and then the first variable under "instructional methodology" begins to be discussed:

TED: Okay that brings us to how well I demonstrate teaching and learning principles applicable to the lessons' learning objectives.

LOUISE: Now for that one, we should ask you to explain why your teaching strategies are appropriate for lesson objectives.

TED: In an interview or on paper?

LOUISE: Either way.

JAN: But that wouldn't be measuring teaching performance. That would be more teaching competence. We agreed we should evaluate how well Ted teaches, not his ability to teach.

ADONIS: Those two correlate. If you measure one, you've measured the other.

JAN: I thought you were the one who's big on in-class observations!

ADONIS: I am, and we surely should include items on our in-classroom observation instrument for the two variables under "instructional methodology."

The conversation continues in a similar vein.

Since one type of measurement (e.g., classroom observations) has its advantages (administered on the job in a realistic setting) and its disadvantages (occurs in a difficult-to-control, complex environment), why not utilize as wide a variety of measurements as is practically possible for a given situation? Having more than one type of measurement per variable may allow one data source's strength to compensate for another's weakness.

Chapter 3 focuses on ways of utilizing cost-effective classroom observations, while Chapter 4 is concerned with the cost-effectiveness of other types of data sources.

SELF-ASSESSMENT EXERCISES FOR CHAPTER 2

I. For each of the following multiple-choice items, select the one response that accurately answers the question or completes the statement:
A. During a classroom observation, an instructional supervisor records the number of questions asked by students. This is an example of _____.
   a. a formative evaluation
   b. a summative evaluation
   c. a measurement
   d. measurement results

B. An instructional supervisor heard 14 teacher-asked questions during a classroom observation. This is an example of _____.
   a. a formative evaluation
   b. a summative evaluation
   c. a measurement
   d. measurement results
C. An instructional supervisor decides to encourage a teacher to increase his ratio of teacher-asked to student-asked questions. This is an example of

   _____.
   a. a formative evaluation
   b. a summative evaluation
   c. a measurement
   d. measurement results
D. Appendix J displays _____.
   a. multiple-score measurement results based on an interview
   b. single-score measurement results based on an interview
   c. a formative evaluation displayed on a pseudo measuring instrument
   d. a summative evaluation displayed on a pseudo measuring instrument
E. A principal and a department head are discussing applicants for a teaching position. The principal remarks, "I would like to interview her simply because she's the only one that scored above the 80th percentile on the NTE." That remark reflected a _____.
   a. norm-referenced evaluation
   b. criterion-referenced evaluation
   c. use of data relevant to a student-outcome variable
   d. use of a pseudo measuring instrument
F. The relevance of a measurement depends on _____.
   a. the degree of both intra- and inter-observer consistencies
   b. its usability
   c. how well the evaluation variable is defined
   d. the degree to which the evaluation variable fluctuates between two administrations of the measurement
G. It is possible for a measurement to be valid but not _____.
   a. internally consistent
   b. relevant
   c. have observer consistency
   d. usable
H. Every evaluation _____.
   a. involves a value judgment
   b. is based on valid measurement results
   c. is based on invalid measurement results
   d. focuses on a clearly articulated variable
I. Which one of the following has the greatest influence on the relevance of a measurement?
   a. Its usability
   b. The internal consistency of its results

      c. The match between its items and the evaluation variable

      d. Whether the evaluation is formative or summative

  J. A measurement cannot be valid unless it is _____.

      a. cost-effective

      b. validated

      c. usable

      d. internally consistent

  K. A *relevant* measurement may not be valid because it _____.

      a. doesn't pertain to the evaluation variable

      b. lacks observer consistency

      c. lacks usability

      d. is not cost-effective

  L. Every usable measurement is _____.

      a. affordable

      b. relevant

      c. reliable

      d. cost-effective

Compare your choices with the following key: A-c, B-d, C-a, D-d, E-a, F-c, G-d, H-a, I-c, J-d, K-b, L-a.

  II. What, if any, role should statistical manipulations of measurement results play in the process of evaluating instruction? Express your answer in one or two paragraphs. Discuss your answer with another professional educator.

 III. What questions should be addressed by an assessment of the validity of a measurement to be used in an evaluation of instruction? Express your answer in one or two paragraphs. Discuss your answer with another professional educator.

 IV. You are part of an accreditation team that will spend a week at a middle school assessing its curricula, school organization, and quality of instruction. You and three colleagues are responsible for planning the evaluation of the "instructional quality" phase of the summative review. The week-long visit is scheduled two months from now, but your budget allows for about 12 planning days, a few of which could be spent at the school site in preparation for the visit.

  A. What questions relative to evaluating instruction should be addressed at the initial planning meeting with your three colleagues?

  B. In a page, describe one possible scenario in which you and your three colleagues go about selecting or developing measurements for use in this evaluation effort.

  C. Share and discuss what you have written with someone who has also read Chapters 1 and 2.

  V. Think back to a class of students you once taught. Suppose that at the time a summative evaluation was to be made of your instructional effectiveness with that class. How do you think the evaluation variable should be defined? Using a format similar to that in Table 2.7, define the variable with subvariables.

CHAPTER 3

Classroom Observations

Goal of Chapter 3

Chapter 3 suggests how to utilize cost-effective classroom observations as data sources for evaluating instruction. Specifically, this chapter is designed to help you:

1. Explain the advantages and disadvantages of using classroom observations for evaluations of instruction.
2. Given an evaluation-of-instruction variable, describe a process for selecting cost-effective classroom observation procedures and instruments relative to that variable.
3. Given an evaluation-of-instruction variable, describe a process for designing cost-effective classroom observation procedures and instruments relative to that variable.
4. In general terms, describe how to assess the validity of classroom observations.

FIVE TYPES OF CLASSROOM OBSERVATIONS

A measurement for which the primary data source is the viewing of and/or listening to what occurs in a classroom or other type of teaching/learning environment (e.g., playing field for a physical education lesson) is a *classroom observation*. The observer who conducts such a measurement views and listens to the classroom events and activities either on-site in the classroom or through a recorded medium (e.g., videotape). Medley, Coker, and Soar (1984, pp. 78–99) refer to four types of *formal* classroom observations: *structured observation systems, ecological observations, ethnographic observations*, and *in-class rating scales*. Classroom observations can also be *informal*.

Structured Observation System

With a structured observation system, the observer's attention is limited to a predetermined set of behaviors corresponding to items on a recording instrument (e.g., the one in Appendix D).

Ecological Observation

An ecological observation is an attempt to record virtually every event and activity that occurs in a classroom during a span of time. Ideally, the observer simply absorbs what happens without preconceptions as to what is important or what types of events and activities will be recorded. The goal is to obtain an exhaustive record. But unless the observation period is severely limited, an inordinate amount of time must be spent reviewing electronic recordings of classroom activities to obtain that exhaustive record.

Ethnographic Observation

Ethnographic observations arc similar to ecological ones in that the observations and recording are conducted without prior specifications. However, whereas ecological observers passively record all available information, the ethnographic observer responds to the classroom environment, selecting events and activities to be recorded as they occur. Ethnographic observers have the freedom to decide what is significant and worth noting: theoretically, however, those decisions should not be influenced by structure organized prior to the observation. Structure for the recording develops *during*, not prior to, an ethnographic observation. On the other hand, ecological observers are never free to impose structure at any time.

In-Class Rating Scale

In-class rating scales specify, prior to the observation, the *outcomes* of behaviors to be attended to by observers. Observers must record not what they see or hear, but their evaluations of what they see or hear. These classroom rating systems are pseudo measurements that are instruments such as the one in Appendix B. An in-class rating scale differs from a structured observation in this way: For an *in-class rating scale*, the observer records his or her evaluation about a performance or achievement, whereas for a *structured observation*, the observer records behaviors that are indicative of achievement or performance.

One of the principal drawbacks of in-class rating scales stems from observers' personal biases regarding what constitutes "effective teaching." From their experiences as students and teachers, virtually everyone has formed strong opinions about what teachers should and should not do. Results from in-class rating scales that have been colored by observers' biases are of little value unless they are accompanied by descriptions of those biases. For example:

As part of her responsibilities as mathematics supervisor for her school district, Chris Bowden uses the in-class rating scale from Appendix B in conjunction with an observation in one teacher's class. She circles " +1" ("mildly agree") for item 3 ("used effective methods") but also writes the following note on the form:

"The rating is based on the following belief about effective teaching methods: The teaching of mathematics can be effective only if the teacher uses (1) precision teaching techniques for knowledge level skills (e.g., executing algorithms), (2) inductive strategies for introducing new concepts and principles, and (3) deductive strategies for helping students apply what they know."

Informal Observation

Principal Steve Jones momentarily steps into Constance Daugs' classroom just as she tells her second graders, "We is about to start with art. So get your things." Steve thinks to himself, "Constance should model better use of grammar with her students."

Steve stepped into Constance's room for a purpose other than gathering data for an evaluation of her instruction. Possibly he only wanted to display his interest in the students' work or he was there to make an announcement. However, his unplanned observation leads him to make an evaluation about teaching performance.

Chance occurrences resulting in unplanned observations are referred to as informal measurements. Informal classroom observations are alluded to here, not because they should be part of a systematic evaluation process, but because, inarguably, these informal measurements occur with far greater frequency than do formal measurements. Consequently, they may be the most influential type of data sources on the evaluations of instruction made by supervisors, teachers, and even researchers.

ADVANTAGE OF CLASSROOM OBSERVATIONS

The instructional process can be organized into three phases (Jackson, 1966). The first is the *pre-interactive phase*, which involves determining students' needs, formulating objectives, organizing the learning environment, designing lessons, and preparing instructional materials. The second phase is the *interactive phase*, which involves conducting lessons, engaging students in learning activities, and managing student behavior. Third is the *post-interactive phase*, which involves evaluating student achievement.

Although all three of these phases are critical to effective instruction and each depends on the other two, it is the interactive phase that most people think of when they visualize teachers teaching. What teachers do before and after they enter the classroom largely determines how well they perform in the classroom, but the classroom is the stage for the most prominent phase of instruction. Thus, unlike other types of measurements, classroom observations are a data source that can be tapped *during* the paramount events of instruction.

DISADVANTAGE OF CLASSROOM OBSERVATIONS

"Even though classroom observations are almost universally regarded as the *sine qua non* of a complete teacher evaluation system, they are not without serious problems" (Popham, 1988, p. 277). The classroom with its social structure and activities is an incredibly complex environment. Far too much goes on in a classroom, much of which is influenced by unseen, unstable factors (e.g., whether or not a student argued with a parent the night before), for classroom observations to be the "direct" data source relevant to teaching competence, teaching performance, or student outcomes that they are sometimes naively thought to be. The number of people who possess the expertise to conduct cost-effective classroom observational measurements does not even begin to approach the number needed in schools for evaluations of instruction. Consequently, unless extensive efforts are undertaken to educate and train observers to use well-designed observational instruments, classroom observations will continue to be dominated by malpractice that produces invalid results.

APPROPRIATE USES OF CLASSROOM OBSERVATIONS

Relevant to Teaching Competence

Evaluations of teaching competence are concerned with what teachers are *capable* of doing. Classroom observations provide data only on what teachers do (i.e., teaching performance) and students do (i.e., student performance). Teaching competence (and, consequently, incompetence) cannot be seen or heard during classroom observations. Observations of what teachers do in classrooms *can* indicate some of their capabilities, but not their incapabilities. For example:

Walt Camparell is nearing the end of his student teaching experience at South High School. Walt's cooperating teacher, Kim Archibald, and Principal Walker Flyn are discussing the possibility of hiring Walt as a science teacher for the next school year:

WALKER: Do you think Walt is capable of helping students develop higher-order cognitive thinking abilities? I don't want another teacher who can only teach our students to memorize.

KIM: Well, I've used this classroom observation instrument in four of his lessons and all four times it showed extremely high ratios of high-level to low-level teacher-asked questions and also high ratios of high-level to low-level student-asked questions. I think anybody with those sorts of performance ratios must be getting the students to do more than memorize.

WALKER: If someone does something, they've proved they're capable of doing it!

KIM: (laughing) No one can argue with that logic!

WALKER: But is he competent to handle some of our tougher discipline situations? I'd like him to take over that ninth-grade earth science class; that's always a rough group to handle.

KIM: That's a good question. I can recall three different occasions on which he failed to respond decisively to fairly serious disruptive behaviors.

WALKER: But because he failed to tend to the disruptions during your observations doesn't mean he's incapable of doing so. Have you ever seen him respond decisively to misbehaviors?

KIM: No, but I haven't always given him a chance. When I'm observing, I tend to step in before things get out of hand.

WALKER: Well we need an evaluation of his competence in classroom management and discipline before considering him further for the job.

Teaching competence is a variable that cannot be directly observed, but indicators of competence to teach can be inferred from teaching performance. However, to tenably use classroom performance as an indicator of what a teacher is capable of doing requires frequent observations over an extended period of time. For example:

Dedra Lancy conducts ethnographic observations in David Chua's third-grade class every other day for six months. In that time, Dedra records detailed information on the unique characteristics of the class and patterns of David's behaviors and responses to students. The resulting case study report provides interesting insights about David's teaching competencies.

Lengthy ethnographic observations are hardly practical for evaluating instruction except for a few very limited research studies.

Relevant to Teaching Performance

Teaching performance variables are appropriately targeted by classroom observations. Here is an example in which Ted, Jan, Adonis, and Louise continue their efforts to develop cost-effective measurements for the teaching performance variables listed in Table 2.7:

ADONIS: We've got four areas—goal setting, classroom management and discipline, instructional methodology, and assessment of student achievement—for which we have to find or develop measurements.

JAN: We can forget trying to find existing measurements. Ted and I went through all the major references on data sources and quite a few test catalogues. We looked at dozens of instruments from other districts in the state and talked to several educational evaluation specialists at the university. We found nothing that appears to match our teaching performance variables that would be practical for our situation. This isn't going to be easy.

LOUISE: No, but there are people in the board office that want us to come up with data sources that are practical and valid so they can adopt them district-wide.

ADONIS: It would be nice if this stuff didn't have to be reinvented every time there's an evaluation of instruction.

LOUISE: I think we can come up with some basic procedures and instruments that can be easily tailored to fit other cases of summative evaluations of instruction.

JAN: Ted, you've got the notes from our last meeting. How far did we get?

TED: We agreed that if we didn't find existing measurements that satisfied our criteria, we would develop a combination of instruments to be used in concert with one another.

ADONIS: That's right! For goal setting, we favored a systematic way of examining the objectives the teacher states in the lesson plans.

TED: Right. And classroom observations for classroom management and discipline and for instructional methodology. Then a systematic analysis of tests students take and of descriptions the teacher writes for lessons' formative feedback systems takes care of area four, assessment of student achievement.

Having decided to measure Table 2.7's variables with intruments they develop themselves, the group turns its attention to the classroom management and discipline variable. First, they must operationally define the subvariables.

JAN: I think area two on classroom management and discipline is the most complicated one. Let's work on that one first, and we'll have the hardest one out of the way.

ADONIS: We agreed that classroom management and discipline should comprise 35 percent of the total weight of all the measurements. Is anyone opposed to starting there?

TED: Okay by me.

LOUISE: Fine. How do we begin?

JAN: Well, that area involves how well the teacher follows the agreed-upon principles for five subvariables of teaching: *establishing a businesslike environment, orchestrating smooth and efficient transition periods, obtaining student engagement, maintaining student engagement*, and *taking care of off-task behaviors*. Since we favor classroom observations for this part, we have to analyze each subvariable to determine just what to look and listen for in the classroom that would indicate something about the teacher's performance for that subvariable.

ADONIS: It sounds awfully complicated. Let's try the first one to see if we can come up with anything.

TED: It's how well the teacher adheres to principles from our references when establishing a purposeful, businesslike learning environment.

ADONIS: Let's look at the applicable principles from the reference.

TED: One has to do with preparation and quality of learning materials.

LOUISE: That's right! We agreed that by having learning materials organized ahead of time, teachers communicate something about the importance of the lesson and that class time is too precious to be consumed doing things that could have been done ahead of time.

TED: And by having intelligible displays like easy-to-see overheads, teachers show that they expect students to pay attention.

JAN: So, the subvariable *businesslike environment* includes at least two observable indicators related to learning materials: *one*, whether or not materials needed for the class are organized and ready to go in time for the learning activity, and *two*, whether or not the material is readily viewed and/or heard from all areas where targeted students are located:

ADONIS: I'm not so sure how those two are objectively observable.

JAN: At this point, I'm not all that sure either. But we've moved in the direction of observable indicators, so let's continue to narrow down the *businesslike environment* subvariable using the principles from the reference. Eventually, we'll get down to the level of measurement items.

ADONIS: But maybe not for all of the subvariables.

JAN: But some observable indicators would be better than none.

They continue to work until the subvariables for classroom management and discipline are narrowed down to the lists that appear in Table 3.1.

At their next meeting, the group undertakes the task of designing classroom observation items relevant to the *businesslike environment* subvariable as delimited in Table 3.1. Note, however, that during the process some broader issues surface, leading them to discuss the overall design of the classroom observation and to combine some of the subvariables from Tables 2.7 and 3.1:

ADONIS: I see a problem in trying to come up with items for this A-i-a and A-i-b on learning materials! Any teacher who knows these things will be observed will make sure to take extra care just for the observation periods. It won't necessarily reflect typical behavior for the teacher.

JAN: Research findings suggest you're absolutely right (Popham, 1988, p. 277). However, there are three reasons we should proceed with these indicators anyway. First, measurements of teaching performance should be consistently conducted from teacher to teacher. I think it's better to let the teacher know ahead of time just what will be observed; that way, we get data for all on their, so to speak, "best performances." Otherwise, we introduce the inconsistency of some teachers being forewarned and others not.

Second, if teachers fail to prepare the materials according to the criteria

TABLE 3.1. A DELIMITATION OF THE SUBVARIABLES UNDER AREA "2" FROM TABLE 2.7

---

2. *Classroom Management & Discipline (35%)*

Judgment regarding classroom management and discipline during the lessons will be based on how well the teacher adheres to principles suggested by the agreed-upon references when carrying out the following responsibilities:

A. establishing a purposeful, businesslike learning environment (10%)
  i. *Learning materials* are:
    a) prepared prior to when they are needed for learning activity,
    b) accessible and intelligible to the students.
  ii. *Nonlearning activities* (e.g., administrative matters and disruptions) are dispatched efficiently.
  iii. *Teacher, talk and actions* contribute to, rather than detract from, the purpose of the learning activity.
  iv. *Respectful behaviors* are modeled and motivated by:
    a) using descriptive instead of judgmental language,
    b) enforcing classroom rules of conduct that promote the freedom of students to engage in the business of learning without interference, intimidation, or fear of harm.
B. orchestrating smooth, efficient transition periods (3%)
  i. *The ratio of allocated to transition time* is maximized.
  ii. Transitions are continuous as opposed to flip-flopping.
  iii. Transitions are smooth as opposed to being jerky.
C. obtaining student engagement for learning activities (7%)
  i. At least 90% of the students are engaged during the initial stages of learning activities.
D. maintaining student engagement during learning activities (5%)
  i. At any point in a learning activity, 90% of the students are displaying engaged behaviors.
E. efficiently teaching students to supplant off-task behaviors with on-task behaviors (10%)
  i. Rules of conduct that promote respect among classroom participants are enforced.
  ii. At least 90% of the students are engaged during the initial stages of learning activities.
  iii. At any point in a learning activity, 90% of the students are displaying engaged behaviors.

---

when they're aware of an observation, that's a pretty reasonable indication that they don't ordinarily do it.

And third and most important, we're to gather data about specific lessons, not on the overall performances of teachers over a long period of time. The quality of the specified lessons is the issue.

ADONIS: Okay, let's try it.

LOUISE: The observer could list or describe instances when materials are used and then, maybe, just check "yes" or "no" for the item being available on time and "yes" or "no" if it's accessible and intelligible to all students who need it.

JAN: We could get fancier and time the interval between when materials are needed and when they're seen or accessed by all students.

LOUISE: That would be more trouble than beneficial.

ADONIS: And besides, that's getting away from this subvariable and into 2-b on orchestrating smooth, efficient transition periods.

JAN: You're right! I think Louise's "yes-no" check business is the route to go.

TED: Are we going to have one separate form for the businesslike variable?

LOUISE: Good question! I was thinking we'd have one observational instrument for the entire classroom management and discipline area and another for instructional methodology.

ADONIS: But that way you'd have to manipulate two forms during one observation.

JAN: Maybe not. We could videotape the lesson and use the recording for instructional methodology and the live observation for classroom management.

ADONIS: We're starting to get ahead of ourselves. The items have to be developed before we try to format the entire instrument.

LOUISE: Right! But, being aware of possible formats helps us know how flexible we can be in designing items.

TED: Okay, I've got an idea on items for 2-A-ii about how efficiently nonlearning matters are dispatched. Record how much of the lesson's allocated time is spent with the majority of students engaged in learning activities.

LOUISE: Remind me one more time what we mean by "allocated time."

TED: According to the agreed-upon classroom management references, allocated time is considered the part of the class period that the teacher plans for students to be engaged in learning activities.

ADONIS: In other words, any time except for transition periods between learning activities.

LOUISE: But that sounds more like it fits under subvariable 2-C or 2-D on obtaining and maintaining student engagement.

TED: I see it fitting either place.

JAN: As I look at these areas again (Table 2.7), there is a lot of overlap between 2-A-ii (Table 3.1) we're working on now and area 2-B orchestrating smooth, efficient transitions, and also with both 2-C and 2-D on obtaining and maintaining student engagement.

TED: Maybe we should fold 2-A-ii under those other areas.

ADONIS: I agree. Let's eliminate 2-A-ii and just make sure we cover it elsewhere.

TED: Yes, if transition time is used efficiently and students are remaining engaged during allocated time, then it's safe to assume that nonlearning matters are being efficiently dispatched.

ADONIS: That one is scratched, so we can turn to 2-A-iii, teacher talk and actions being purposeful.

TED: Here's my idea for this one: Suppose we do something like interaction analysis (Flanders, 1970) or like on this other instrument on communication style and level of questions (Appendix A) that Jan and I reviewed. The observer records a representative sample of teacher talk and classifies each instance as either purposeful or not according to criteria in our reference.

LOUISE: How would we quantify that?

JAN: A ratio of purposeful teacher-talk to total teacher-talk could be computed easily enough.

> LOUISE: Now that makes more sense to me for use in a formative evaluation where teachers can compare whether ratios are going up or down over time. But we have a summative evaluation problem here. Quality of teaching is the focus, not feedback for improvement.
>
> TED: True, but our agreed-to references tell us that purposeful talk contributes to the businesslike environment we associate with effective instruction, while nonpurposeful talk detracts from it.

That comment from Ted stimulates a discussion on criteria for interpreting results of the classroom observations:

> LOUISE: But I don't recall our references indicating what a "good" ratio of purposeful-to-total teacher talk should be, only the higher the better.
>
> ADONIS: That's something that's worried me throughout this process. We can get all the ratios and scores we want, but who is to say how high they need to be to indicate effective teaching?
>
> JAN: Ted and I talked about that and we've got a solution. We compare our scores to criterion-referenced standards available from the literature. For the ones for which we can't find standards, we conduct our own field tests to get norm-referenced standards.
>
> TED: Right! While we're field-testing our instruments we could obtain purposeful-to-total teacher-talk ratios on a sample of teachers' lessons. Then the ratio you get for my teaching or for any other evaluations could be compared with the average from the sample.
>
> JAN: For example, on that item, zero could be scored for a ratio that is less than a half standard deviation below the sample mean, one point for being within a half standard deviation of the mean, and two points if the ratio is more than a standard deviation above the mean.
>
> ADONIS: Seems complicated.
>
> JAN: Would we rather continue to use evaluation practices that became obsolete in 1935?

A week later, the group produces a draft of the instrument for the area of classroom management and discipline. It appears in Appendix E.

> As a preliminary field test, Jan tried out Appendix E's instrument in a colleague's class. The results of the experiment appear in Figure 3.1.

Relevant to Student Outcomes

Most of what students achieve as an outgrowth of their teachers' efforts is far too complex to be measured via periodic classroom observations (Cangelosi, 1990b, pp. 3–19). Ethnographic observations over an extended period can chart the progress of a limited number of students, but ordinarily such approaches are impractical. Structured classroom observations can be cost-effective data sources for some

Figure 3.1. Results from a Trial Run of Appendix E's Classroom Observation Instrument

TRAINED OBSERVER'S RECORDING FORM FOR THE CLASSROOM
MANAGEMENT & DISCIPLINE AREA
Part I (on-site) & Part II (videotaped)

Part I
On-site

Minutes from the beginning of class

1. Time line

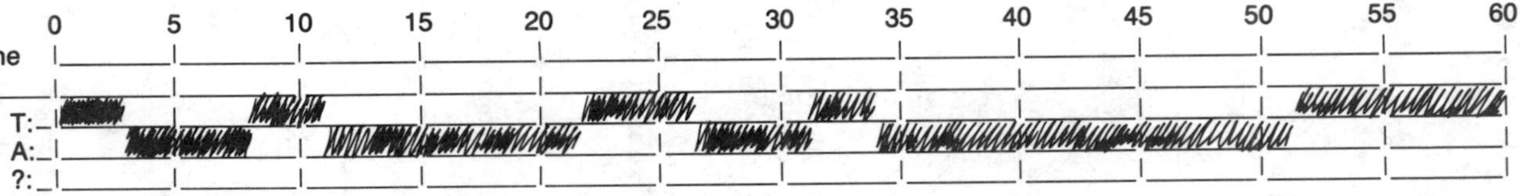

$Y_P = 9, N_P = 1$
$Y_V = 7, N_V = 1$
$Y_A = 8, N_A = 2$

2. Learning materials (Y, N, ?):

$V_1 = 4, R_1 = 2$

3. Classroom rules of conduct __ (Y, N, ?). If "Y," then (V1, V2, . . . & R1, R2, . . .):

$Y_O = 2$
$N_O = 3$

4. Obtaining student engagement for learning activities (Y, N, ?):

$Y_M = 6$
$N_M = 5$

5. Maintaining student engagement during learning activities (Y, N, ?):

Part II
Videotaped

Minutes from the beginning of class

0   5   10   15   20   25   30   35   40   45   50   55   60

1. Time line

T:.
A:.
?:.

$N_T=23$
$N_A=37$

2. Continuous vs. flip-flop transitions (C, F, ?):

C   C   F   C

$C_T=3$
$F_T=2$

3. Smooth vs. jerky transitions (S, J, ?):

J   S   J   J

$S_T=1$
$J_T=4$

4. Purposeful vs. non-purposeful teacher-talk (T, Ⓣ, ?):

⊘⊘T⊘⊘⊘   ⊘TT T ⊘TT⊘   ⊘⊘⊘   ⊘T⊘⊘⊘   TT   ⊘   ⊘T   ⊘T⊘TT

$⊘_T=19$
$T_T=8$

5. Descriptive vs. judgmental teacher-talk (D, J, ?):

?²TDDDT   D'?²   ?'²D'?TTD   JTDD ?DD   J?   DDJ   D????

$D_T=13$
$J_T=11$

$S_{I-2}=(.67)\left[(9/10)+(7/8)+(8/10)\right]=1.73$

$S_{I-3}=5\times(24)=5\times(.5)=2.5$

$S_{I-4}=10\times(7/6)=10\times(.40)=4$

$S_{I-5}=9\times(6/11)=9\times(.55)=4.91$

$S_{II-1}=37\div60=.62$

$S_{II-2}=3\div5=.60$

$S_{II-3}=1\div5=.20$

$S_{II-4}=3\times(19/27)=2.11$

$S_{II-5}=3\times(13/24)=1.63$

Total Score $=1.73+2.5+4+4.91+.62+.60+.20+2.11+1.63$

$=18.30$

narrowly defined student outcome variables that involve changes in overt classroom behaviors rather than academic achievement. For example, in the hands of a trained observer, BOCAS (see Appendix D) can provide data relevant to gains achieved by a student regarding overt cooperative classroom behaviors (Snyder, Messer, & Cangelosi, 1977). However, properly designed student-performance tests (e.g., those with written-response, performance observation, and product examination items) administered after, not during, lessons provide the most cost-effective data sources for student achievement of conventional curricula goals.

COMMON MISUSES OF CLASSROOM OBSERVATIONS

Classroom observations, along with listening to hearsay, are the most common data sources influencing evaluations of instruction in today's school (Bridges, 1986, pp. 7–12; Harris, 1985, pp. 146–64). However, most who routinely perform classroom observations have no formal preparation in how to evaluate instruction and are unaware of recent advances in systematic classroom observational procedures (Cooper, 1984b, pp. 80–84; Medley, Coker, & Soar, 1984, p. 80).

When classroom observers and observation instrument designers are inadequately prepared, informal observations become the primary data source for evaluations of instruction. Consequently, misinformation flourishes and teachers are unable to separate when they are being observed for formative purposes and when they are being observed for summative purposes. Furthermore, formal classroom observations are dominated by rating scales and other types of pseudo-measuring instruments.

There are other disadvantages of inadequate evaluation preparation. The purpose for classroom observations, focusing on specified variables, typically goes undefined. The procedures that Jan, Adonis, Ted, and Louise followed to develop the structured classroom observation measurement in Appendix E are foreign to most. Consequently, most classroom observations either provide data for *summative evaluations* that are too vague to be defended or *formative evaluations* that are not specific enough to influence teaching performance meaningfully.

Recognizing their need to evaluate instruction but unaware of state-of-the-art procedures for selecting or developing measurements, many supervisors, teachers, and researchers grasp whatever classroom observation instruments happen to be readily available. Consequently, the instrument determines what is evaluated, rather than the evaluation variable being the determining factor for what instrument is used.

INSTRUMENTATION

Single-Score Instruments

Jan, Adonis, Louise, and Ted designed the instrument in Appendix E to be relevant to one general variable: teaching performance in the area of classroom management and discipline. They defined this one variable by five subvariables (see Table 2.7) and each of the subvariables was delimited to a number of observable indicators (see Table 3.1). However, the measurement is still designed to reflect teaching performance regarding only the one general classroom management and discipline variable. Thus, the results from an administration of Appendix E's instrument are boiled down to a *single score* out of a possible 35 points.

Single-score instruments are typically more valuable for summative evaluations of teaching, in which a single decision regarding retention or promotion is in the balance, than they are for formative evaluations, in which detailed feedback about teaching performance is needed.

Multiple-Score Instruments

Appendix A's instrument is designed to produce formative feedback relative to (1) use of descriptive teacher-talk, (2) use of supportive teacher replies, (3) balance between teacher and student talk, (4) balance between teacher and student questions, (5) level of teacher-asked questions, and (6) level of student-asked questions. This instrument yields an *item score* for each of these six variables. The item scores are individually reported and, unlike the case in Appendix E's instrument, the item scores are not meant to be combined into a single overall score. Appendix A contains an example of a *multiple-score* instrument.

Items for Coding Specific Events

Some instruments for structured classroom observations contain items that require the observer to recognize and code each event within a predefined category. Item 2 of Part I in Appendix E, for example, requires an observer using this instrument to recognize each time the teacher introduces materials for students to see or hear and then code that occurrence according to item 2's directions (i.e., as either Y, N, or ? for each of three characteristics, P, V, and A). For these *coding-specific-events items*, the frequency of the observer's marks depends on the number of times a certain type of event occurs. Other examples of this type of item are item 3 of Part I in Appendix E, items 2–5 of Part II in Appendix E, and the items in Parts II and III in Appendix A.

Items for Categorizing Time Intervals

Some classroom observation items (e.g., item 4 of Part I from Appendix E and all of the items from BOCAS in Appendix D) have the observation period partitioned into time intervals. The observer is then required to categorize each time interval according to predetermined parameters. For example, Appendix E's item 5 of Part I requires the observer to code each predetermined two-minute interval according to whether or not a learning activity is in progress and, if so, whether or not at least 90 percent of the sampled students appear to be engaged. For categorizing time-interval items, the observer codes each predetermined time interval exactly once, no matter how many events occur during the classroom observation period. For Appendix E's item 5 of Part I, each of the predetermined two-minute intervals is coded one of four ways (i.e., either Y, N, ?, or left blank).

Items Requiring Narrative Descriptions

Some items for structured classroom observations require observations within specified parameters to be recorded as narrative descriptions. Appendix F contains an example.

SELECTION OF A COST-EFFECTIVE CLASSROOM OBSERVATION MEASUREMENT

Selection of a measurement should depend on an informed prediction about its validity (i.e., relevance and reliability) and usability. Such a selection process requires six steps:

1. The purpose of the evaluation is clarified by defining the evaluation variable with specific subvariables, each weighted (usually in terms of a percent) according to its relative importance as a component of the overall variable. (Jan, Adonis, Louise, and Ted completed this step by producing Table 2.7.) For most situations, it is advisable to utilize feedback from representatives of all those who will be affected by the evaluation process before finalizing the outcome of this step.

2. Standards for validity are established. Criteria should require:
   A. the measurement's items to relate to the subvariables listed in step 1.
   B. the results of the measurement to be influenced by each subvariable to a degree that approximates its weighting determined in step 1.
   C. field tests that suggest that the measurement can be trusted to produce reliable results.

3. Standards for usability are established. The cost in terms of money, time, and disruptions of other activities must be affordable for the given situation.

4. A survey of existing instruments is conducted utilizing library references (e.g., Educational Testing Service, 1986), publishers' catalogs, and contacts with institutions involved in evaluating instruction (e.g., school district offices, departments of education, and teacher preparation colleges).

5. Reasonably promising instruments emerging from step 4's survey are examined along with accompanying documentation. The examination includes:
   A. an item-by-item analysis comparing what the items actually measure with the targeted subvariables identified in step 1.
   B. other efforts to study how well the standards for validity and usability are met.
   For some situations, specialists in evaluating teaching should be engaged as consultants for this step.

6. If one or more of the examined measurements appears to meet the validity and usability standards, then the selection is made (possibly following negotiations with the providers of the measurements under consideration). If none meets the standards, then measurements need to be designed and developed.

DEVELOPMENT OF A COST-EFFECTIVE CLASSROOM OBSERVATION MEASUREMENT

The development of a usable classroom observation measurement that is likely to produce valid results depends on how well the following steps are accomplished:

1. The purpose of the evaluation is clarified by defining the evaluation variable with specific subvariables, each weighted (usually in terms of a percent) according to its relative importance as a component of the overall variable. (Jan, Adonis, Louise, and Ted completed this step by producing Table 2.7.) For most situations, it is advisable to utilize feedback from representatives of all those who will be affected by the evaluation process before finalizing the outcome of this step.
2. One or more observable indicators is determined for each subvariable identified in step 1. (Jan, Adonis, Louise, and Ted completed this step by producing Table 3.1.)
3. Specifications to be considered in the design of the measurement are formulated. (Appendix G contains the specifications formulated by Jan, Adonis, Louise, and Ted for Appendix E's measurement.)
4. In light of the specifications formulated in step 3, several items for each subvariable are developed and informally reviewed and field-tested in one or two classrooms to obtain feedback on (1) clarity of directions and procedures, (2) potential for validity, (3) and usability. The items are refined and rerefined until a promising pool of items for each subvariable is obtained.
5. A description of the subvariable (e.g., Table 3.1), the specifications (e.g., Appendix G), and the item pools are submitted to a panel for review and feedback regarding the relevance of the items. The panel is composed of representatives of persons who will be involved in using the measurement as well as specialists in the evaluation of instruction.
6. The item pools are modified in light of the results of step 5.
7. Adhering to the specifications and drawing from the item pools, the measurement is synthesized.
8. The instrument is informally field-tested with several classes. Feedback from the field tests is used to finalize the measurement.
9. Observers are trained.
10. A formal field test is conducted to assess reliability and, if appropriate, to establish norms and cut off scores.

TRAINING CLASSROOM OBSERVERS

For Ecological and Ethnographic Observations

Preparing experts in the art of conducting ecological and ethnographic observations for the complex environments of classrooms is a major undertaking. Because these types of classroom observations are impractical for all but a minute proportion of situations, the preparation of observers for ecological and ethnographic studies is not addressed herein. A number of references are available relative to the topic (e.g., Jacob, 1987; Patton, 1987; Stenhouse, 1988; Taft, 1988).

For Structured Classroom Observation Systems

In order for classroom observations to result in valid measurements, there must be available observers who conceptualize the subvariables targeted by the observation; who comprehend the instrument's terminology, symbols, codes, and directions; who conduct themselves unobtrusively during the classroom visit; who objectively focus their attention on the instrument's specific indicators; and who religiously adhere to the rules for marking and scoring the instrument. In the absence of such experts, classroom observations are, at best, useless, and at worst, sources of destructive misinformation.

A training program for observers should attend to four areas. First, observers may require *instruction on the pedagogical concepts, principles, techniques, and terminology that are critical to the evaluation variables.* Evaluations of instruction should be based on teaching/learning principles implied from research literature. Unfortunately, however, even when professional educators serve as classroom observers, it is unsafe to assume they will be familiar with the concepts, principles, techniques, and language associated with the pedagogical thought upon which the design of a particular measurement is based. Also, there is considerable debate in the professional literature regarding what constitutes effective teaching (Cangelosi, 1986). Thus there is a need for operational definitions and agreement on the school of thought and reference sources providing the foundation for the measurement items.

Second, the design of the classroom observation instrument dictates how the observers should conduct themselves during the on-site visit. Thus, for each instrument, observers must be taught a very specific set of directions regarding *where they station themselves, whether or not they move about the room, how, if at all, they should interact with students, and so forth.* Also, *general principles of classroom decorum* should not be neglected in the training sessions. For example, some observers may need to be reminded to arrive prior to the beginning of the observation period and take care of preliminary matters (e.g., setting up recording equipment ahead of time so as not to interfere with the progress of the class); to be sensitive to the fact that the teacher is in charge of the classroom (e.g., it would be rude to converse with students when the teacher expects them to be listening to a lecture); to comply with the teacher's wishes to postpone the observation because of unforeseen events; and to keep in mind that the observer is a guest in the teacher's domain but also that the observer has a professional responsibility to meet.

The third area involves the *technical aspects of conducting the measurement (i.e., how to observe, record, and score the particular instrument)*. This must be taught even to observers who are experienced with other instruments.

Finally, *exercises on how to use the instrument, practice using it, and feedback on how well it was used* are essential ingredients in the training. Without practice and feedback, there is little hope of obtaining satisfactory degrees of observer consistency.

Jan incorporated these four phases in the training session she conducted for observers planning to use Appendix E's instrument:

Jan's school district contracted 12 classroom teachers from a neighboring district to be trained to use Appendix E's instrument. These teachers would then be available to make classroom observations, producing classroom management and discipline scores to be used as one data source for summative evaluations about the instructional effectiveness of beginning teachers in Jan's district.

The plan is for Jan to conduct a workshop on two consecutive Saturdays for the 12 trainees. Over the course of the two weeks, the trainees are to engage in exercises and practice using the instrument.

During the first Saturday session the program is as follows. Jan first provides an overview of (1) the evaluation program that would be utilizing results from the classroom observations with Appendix E's instrument and (2) the instrument's history. This overview takes 20 minutes.

Next, using a variety of reference materials and audiovisuals, Jan instructs the group on pedagogical concepts, principles, techniques, and terminology germane to the measurement. The topics are (1) establishing a purposeful, businesslike environment, (2) orchestrating smooth, efficient transition periods, (3) obtaining student engagement for learning activities, (4) maintaining student engagement during learning activities, and (5) efficiently teaching students to supplant off-task behaviors with on-task behaviors. Terms such as the following are operationally defined: "descriptive language," "allocated time," "flip-flop transition," "jerky transition," and "indicator of student engagement." This section lasts 3 hours, including breaks.

Jan then engages the trainees in a discussion session on appropriate conduct of classroom observers. The session is quite lively and continues through the lunch break as the trainees, being teachers, stress an "observe-a-teacher-as-you-would-have-them-observe-you" attitude. The session takes 1 hour, including the lunch break.

Next, using a videotape of a classroom session, Jan explains and demonstrates the step-by-step process for utilizing both Part I and Part II of the instrument. This takes 3 hours, including breaks.

After distributing packets of materials including the instrument and accompanying documentation, Jan directs the trainees to practice using the instrument in colleagues' classes and to return the next week with the results and the videotapes. She asks some to volunteer to obtain their colleagues' permissions for the videotapes to be used in next Saturday's session. This final section takes 15 minutes.

The following Saturday the workshop continues. One of the videotapes brought by a trainee is viewed by all as they simulate on-site observations and complete Part I of the instrument. They then share their results and resolve discrepancies. From the discussion, the group clarifies the rules for coding the items. The viewing and discussion take 2.5 hours, including a break.

Again the trainees view the volunteer's videotape, but this time they complete Part II. Again the results are discussed and discrepancies resolved. This takes 2 hours, including a break.

Jan then arranges for each trainee to (1) use the instrument during one of Jan's class sessions over the next week and (2) review their techniques and results with her after the observation. This section takes 2 hours, including a lunch break.

After each trainee has observed Jan's class and met with her to discuss results and techniques, Jan judges 10 of the 12 trainees to be prepared to use the instrument for actual summative evaluations.

VALIDATION OF EXISTING CLASSROOM OBSERVATION MEASUREMENTS

An assessment of the validity of a structured classroom observation system should address questions about the measurement's relevance, reliability, and item effectiveness.

Assessing Relevance

Three questions are paramount in an assessment of relevance: (1) Is there a sound research or rational basis for assuming that the observable indicators reflect the evaluation variable? (2) Do the items provide opportunities for the observer to see or hear classroom events, behaviors, or activities that correlate with variations relative to the observable indicators? (3) If the measurement produces an overall score, to what degree is the relative influence of each subvariable on that score consistent with the weight assigned to the subvariable (e.g., in Table 2.7)?

These three questions were addressed and satisfied in the developmental stages of classroom observational measurements that were developed via the 10-step model outlined earlier in this chapter. Thus, simply documenting that the first nine steps of this model were followed when such measurements were developed serves as an assessment of relevance.

Assessing the relevance of classroom observational measurements that were not developed by the 10-step model can be more or less difficult depending on the complexity of the instrument and on whether relevance is examined informally or formally. *Informal assessments of relevance* are sufficient for routine classroom observations (e.g., ones commonly utilized by instructional supervisors) that are not for widespread use. Here is an example:

Oscar Gibbs, science teacher, and Kent Kenfield, science department chairperson, engage in the following conversation:

KENT: Yesterday, you mentioned that you're concerned about whether or not your lectures make any sense to the students.

OSCAR: Right.

KENT: Well, look at this classroom observation instrument buried in this thesis I checked out of the library.

OSCAR: The title is quite a mouthful: "Observation Scale for the Organization and Structure of Lecture Presentations"! Do you think it could give me some good feedback if you used it in my class?

KENT: I don't know. I haven't really examined it yet. But I've got a proposal for you.

OSCAR: I'm listening.

KENT: Tonight you draw up a list of questions you'd like answered about your lectures—you know, things you want to find out that might be picked up in an observation. While you're doing that, I'll go through this instrument item by item and list the things I think it actually measures.

OSCAR: I get it! Tomorrow, we see how well our two lists match. If there's a fair match, you'll use the instrument in my class.

KENT: And if not, we'll either find something better or develop our own from your list.

The next day, Oscar shows up with the list shown in Table 3.2 and Kent with the one in Table 3.3:

KENT: It says the instrument is designed to indicate how well a lecture is organized and structured along the three-phase advanced organizer model presented by Joyce and Weil (1986, pp. 70–88).

OSCAR: Looking at its eight subvariables suggests to me that the instrument is primarily relevant for lectures to help students acquire concepts.

KENT: Yeah, surely 2 and 5 are pointed at conceptual-level teaching.

OSCAR: And that's 25 percent of the score right there!

KENT: Your list of six questions isn't limited to conceptual-level learning, except maybe question 3 about examples.

OSCAR: Let's try to match them up. Is my first question on pacing addressed anywhere?

KENT: It's sort of related to subvariable 3. But that's not much of a match.

OSCAR: However, subvariables 1, 2, and 3 all relate to my question 2.

KENT: Yep. We may be able to apply part of this instrument to answer some of your questions. Your third question is not really addressed, but at least subvariable 2. . . .

The discussion continues as they compare what the instrument actually measures with what they want to evaluate.

Formal assessments of relevance are necessary for instruments intended for widespread use (e.g., the one in Appendix D). They are conducted in the same spirit displayed by Kent and Oscar. However, processes for formally assessing relevance include more systematic techniques for defining the evaluation variable, for determining what the instrument in question actually measures, for comparing the

TABLE 3.2. OSCAR'S QUESTIONS ABOUT HIS LECTURES

1. Is my pacing too fast or too slow?
2. Do I emphasize the main points or do they get confused with the trivial?
3. Do I use too many or not enough examples?
4. Does the lecture flow in some sort of logical order that allows the student to take coherent notes?
5. Are the students really paying attention (as they seem to me to be)?
6. Is my vocabulary too advanced, too low, or just about right for the students?

TABLE 3.3. SUBVARIABLES KENT LISTED AFTER ANALYZING THE OBSERVATION SCALE FOR THE ORGANIZATION AND STRUCTURE OF LECTURE PRESENTATION

Overall Variable:

Degree to which a lecture is organized along the lines of the three-phase advanced organizer model explained by Joyce & Weil (1986, pp. 70–88).

	Subvariable	Relative Weight
During the first phase of the lecture whether or not:		
	1. the aims of the lesson are clarified	15%
	2. the advanced organizer is presented including (a) defining attributes, (b) examples, (c) context, and (d) repetition	10%
During the second phase of the lecture whether or not:		
	3. material is clearly presented with its organization explicit	15%
	4. students appear to be attentive	10%
During the third phase of the lecture whether or not:		
	5. principles of integrative reconciliation are used	15%
	6. active reception learning is promoted	10%
	7. critical approach to subject is promoted	5%
	8. material is clarified and summarized	20%

evaluation variable with what the instrument actually measures, for utilizing feedback from both the persons to be affected by the evaluation and the evaluation specialists at critical decision points in the process, and for documenting the process followed. For example:

According to the published statement of philosophy of the Department of Teacher Education at Knight State College, summative evaluations of student teaching performance (upon which final grades and recommendations for employment are based) should address the following areas:

1. Preparation for effective instruction.
2. Use of teaching strategies appropriate to the objectives and learners.
3. Use of evaluations to improve instruction.
4. Effective use of classroom management strategies.
5. Involvement in professional leadership roles.

However, a number of faculty members express concern that neither the cooperating teachers nor college supervisors utilize or even have access to data relevant to making evaluations for each of these five areas. In response to this concern, the department faculty establishes a task force (consisting of two preservice teachers who have yet to engage in student teaching, two student teachers, two in-service teachers, one school principal, and two department members) to define each area's variables upon which summative evaluations of student teaching performance should focus.

A month later the variables recommended by the task force are finalized by the faculty. The variable and subvariables for area 2, "*use of teaching strategies appropriate to the objectives and the learners*," are listed in Table 3.4.

Five three-member teams, each consisting of two department members and the department's specialist in the evaluation of instruction, are assigned to locate (or possibly develop) measurements for the five areas. The team working on area 2 consists of Ruth, Julio, and Joseph. They locate the classroom observation instrument illustrated in Appendix H. By the following procedures, the team assesses how relevant Appendix H's measurement is to the evaluation of the variable defined in Table 3.4.

Independent of one another, each of the team members first analyzes Appendix H's instrument item by item to formulate a list of subvariables to which the measurement appears to be relevant and then indicates the relative weight each subvariable plays in the determination of the overall 10-point score.

Next, they share their list of weighted subvariables with one another and resolve discrepancies through debate and by consulting with other professionals. The collective judgments of the team and their consultants regarding what Appendix H's measurement actually measures is reported in Table 3.5.

Finally, the team juxtaposes Tables 3.4 with 3.5 to examine the match between the subvariable that should be evaluated and the subvariables that Appendix H's instrument actually measures.

The team's conversations include the following as they compare the two tables:

JULIO: There's some agreement between the two, but it's not even close to a perfect match.

RUTH: Let's identify the matches first, and then the mismatches.

JOSEPH: Our subvariable D [from Table 3.4] is as similar to the instrument's subvariable 3 [from Table 3.5] as we can ever expect to find.

JULIO: D is supposed to be 50% of what influences our evaluation.

JOSEPH: But subvariable 3, which is the instrument's equivalent of D, is only 30 percent of the measurement.

TABLE 3.4. THE VARIABLE AND SUBVARIABLES FOR AREA 2 TO BE TARGETED BY KNIGHT STATE COLLEGE'S EVALUATION OF STUDENT TEACHING PERFORMANCE

Area 2:
Use of Teaching Strategies Appropriate to the Objectives and Learners

Overall Variable:

the degree to which the student teacher's lessons are designed and conducted in accordance with the pedagogical principles enumerated in the goal statements of Knight State College's Preservice Teacher Professional Component of Core Courses. Specifically:

Subvariable	Relative Weight
A. The clarity of the communications (i.e., teacher talk, illustrations, printed materials, and media) utilized in the lesson	15%
B. Considering the comprehension and interest levels of the learners, the appropriateness of the communications utilized in the lessons	25%
C. Whether or not the purpose of the lesson is articulated for learners	10%
D. Whether or not learning activities are appropriate for the learning levels (i.e., behavioral constructs) specified by the targeted objectives. That is:	50%
1. Are direct teaching or drill and practice methods used for memory-level cognitive objectives?	
2. Are systematic inquiry methods used for higher-cognitive level objectives?	
3. Are direct teaching or drill and practice methods used for skill-level psychomotor objectives?	
4. Are methods based on strategies for examining alternatives or on reinforcement theory used for affective objectives?	

TABLE 3.5. THE KNIGHT STATE COLLEGE AREA 2 TEAM'S FINDINGS REGARDING THE SUBVARIABLES THAT APPENDIX H'S INSTRUMENT ACTUALLY MEASURES

Subvariable	Relative Weight
1. The degree to which the learning objectives are made explicit during the lesson	20%
2. How well the teacher follows accepted principles from classroom management literature (e.g., Cangelosi, 1988a; Canter & Canter, 1976; Denham & Lieberman, 1980; Jones & Jones, 1986; Wolfgang & Glickman, 1986) for maintaining students engaged in lessons	20%
3. How well the methods practiced by the teacher follow accepted principles from the teaching/learning literature (e.g., Arends, 1988; Beyer, 1987; Joyce & Weil, 1986; Wittrock, 1986) for matching instructional strategies to the level of the learning objectives	30%
4. The variety of teaching methods modeled by the teacher during the lesson	30%

JULIO: It would have been 60 percent if we hadn't split the six points from item 3 [of Appendix H] into subvariables 3 and 4.

RUTH: We had to once we recognized how much item 3's score is influenced by how many different teaching methods are used in the observed lesson.

JULIO: Yeah, that's still something I don't like about the instrument.

JOSEPH: But maybe that doesn't create as much of a mismatch as it might seem.

JULIO: It doesn't if the lesson plan's objectives specify a variety of learning levels.

JOSEPH: If the plan includes at least one higher cognitive, one affective, and one skill- or memory-level objective, then 60 instead of 30 percent of the measurement relates to our subvariable D.

RUTH: We could report our findings on relevance two ways.

JOSEPH: Oh! I see what you mean. Use the 60 percent figure for subvariable D for when the objectives' learning levels vary and use 30 percent for cases when they don't.

RUTH: Or better yet, we report that between 30 and 60 percent of the measurement relates to subvariable D depending on how much variation there is in the learning levels of the stated objectives.

JULIO: I like that!

RUTH: Where else do the two lists match up?

JULIO: Our subvariable C is similar to the measurement's subvariable 1.

JOSEPH: C specifies that purposes actually be articulated for learners. But subvariable 1 doesn't quite go that far; the objectives only have to be explicit.

JULIO: But it's not a bad match. A student teacher who demonstrates C will score high on item 1 of the instrument.

JOSEPH: True, but getting the two points for item 1 doesn't ensure that the student teacher actually spelled out the purposes for the students.

JULIO: But you'll admit that performance on subvariable 1 will correlate very well with performance on subvariable C.

RUTH: And remember, in this business no measurement is exact. We do well to find measurement subvariables that simply relate to evaluation subvariables. Exact matches are virtual impossibilities.

JOSEPH: Okay, count 20 percent of the measurement as matching our subvariable C.

JULIO: But we only want 10 percent of the measurement to match C.

RUTH: That'll be made clear in our report. Any other matches between the two lists?

JULIO: The instrument's subvariable 2 is the only one we haven't addressed yet.

JOSEPH: In our stated goals that falls under "classroom management." That's area 4, not 2.

JULIO: That's at least somewhat related to evaluation subvariables A and B. Accepted principles of maintaining engagement emphasize the importance of clear communications geared to the comprehension levels of students.

JOSEPH: That's true, but let's be careful not to be too liberal in what we read into these variables.

JULIO: Ruth, you're also on the area 4 team on classroom management. Are strategies for student engagement being addressed there?

RUTH: They are. I agree that measurement subvariable 2 relates to our evaluation variables A and B. But I also see the other side of the argument Joseph makes. Since the area 4 team is dealing with the student engagement question, let's take the more conservative option and report that the 20 percent of the measurement related to subvariable 2 doesn't clearly match any of our evaluation variables.

JULIO: But the relation between measurement subvariable 2 and evaluation sub-variables A and B is worth at least a footnote in our report.

RUTH: That's a good idea. Eventually, our whole department faculty will have to pull together all the teams' reports into some coherent form so we can finalize one set of measurements.

JULIO: Maybe the scoring could be modified so that a piece of this instrument fills one of area 4's gaps and another instrument fills some of area 2's gaps.

JOSEPH: Like the gap we have for evaluation subvariables A and B.

The decisions from this discussion are reported in Table 3.6.

Given a classroom observational instrument, what is the most efficient (i.e., accurate and practical) method for formally assessing its relevance? That depends on the instrument's characteristics, on the evaluation variable or variables, and on just how much formal documentation is required by those to whom the findings will be reported. The science of assessing relevance is not exact. Often there is a need either to invent new methods or to tailor existing methods for unique situations. However, all methods should systematically examine the consistency between the subvariables measured by the instrument and the subvariables to be evaluated. Primarily, methods differ with respect to (1) *how input from both evaluation experts and those to be affected by the evaluation is gathered* (e.g., whether or not the opinions regarding what each item actually measures are solicited via a structured questionnaire), and (2) *the selection of statistical models for identifying measurement subvariables* (e.g., whether percentages are computed from the directions for scoring the instrument as Ruth, Julio, and Joseph did, or whether the scores gained from a field test of the instrument are subjected to factor analysis (Nunnally, 1978, pp. 327–435; Spearritt, 1988) or cluster analysis (Everitt, 1988; Kachigan, 1986, pp. 402–11).

Assessing Internal Consistency

If the score produced by a classroom observation measurement is based on the results of more than one item, then the reliability of that measurement depends on the correlations among the individual item results. To help yourself understand this

TABLE 3.6. RESULTS OF RUTH, JULIO, AND JOSEPH'S ANALYSIS OF THE RELEVANCE OF APPENDIX H'S INSTRUMENT RELATIVE TO TABLE 3.5'S EVALUATION VARIABLE

Subvariable Measured	Ideal Weight	Actual Weight on Instrument
A. The clarity of the communications (i.e., teacher talk, illustrations, printed materials, and media) utilized in the lesson	15%	00%*
B. Considering the comprehension and interest levels of the learners, the appropriateness of the communications utilized in the lessons	25%	00%*
C. Whether or not the purpose of the lesson is articulated for learners	10%	20%
D. Whether or not learning activities are appropriate for the learning levels (i.e., behavioral constructs) specified by the targeted objectives	50%	30%–60%†
Other subvariables not to be evaluated:		
1. Variety of teaching methods modeled by the teacher during the lesson	00%	00%–30%†
2. How well the teacher follows accepted principles from the classroom management literature for maintaining students engaged in lessons	00%	20%

*To some degree, subvariables A and B are related to the second subvariable listed under "other subvariables not to be evaluated." However, this subvariable falls within the domain of classroom management (i.e., area 4) in Knight State College's scheme.
†Depending on how much variation there is in the learning levels of the stated objectives.

phenomenon, examine Figure 3.1. Note that the overall score of 18.30 is the sum of the scores from items I-2, I-3, I-4, I-5, II-1, II-2, II-3, II-4, and II-5 (i.e., 1.73 + 2.50 + 4.00 + 4.91 + 0.62 + 0.60 + 0.20 + 2.11 + 1.63). The rationale for computing this instrument's overall score (35 point maximum) from these nine item scores is as follows:

The overall score is supposed to reflect teaching performance during the observation period regarding *classroom management and discipline*. According to Table 2.7, the designers of this instrument agreed to operationally define the overall evaluation variable of classroom management and discipline performance by five subvariables, listed A–E in Table 2.7, so that performance in classroom management and discipline is segmented into 35 equivalent parts: ten parts taken up by performance on subvariable A, three by performance on subvariable B, seven by subvariable C, five by subvariable D, and ten by subvariable E. Since the subvariables are component parts of the same overall evaluation variable, performance on each subvariable should correlate positively with performance on the overall variable. Thus, the subvariables should correlate positively with one another. If they don't, then something is amiss in the definition of *performance in classroom management and discipline*.

Utilizing the observable indicators identified in Table 3.1, the instrument's nine items were designed to be relevant to the subvariables. Therefore, if item scores are inconsistent with one another (e.g., one classroom observation produces a very high score for item II-2 and a very low score for item II-3), then the results contain contradictory information.

Thus, *internal consistency* should be assessed for any measurement in which results of individual items are reported as a single score. Here is an example in which internal consistency is *informally* assessed:

As a preliminary field test, Jan tries out Appendix E's instrument in a colleague's class. As she examines the experiment's results in Figure 3.1, Jan thinks to herself: I wonder if this instrument is going to prove internally consistent when we do the formal validation study. Let's see if it appeared to be internally consistent at least for this case. If not, then maybe we can work on the bugs before it's validated and used for real evaluations. At least the time lines for Parts I and II came out nearly the same. That's a positive note for internal consistency. Now for the hard part. Do the nine item scores follow a consistent trend? It's hard to tell, 1.73, 2.5, 4,—, they're not all on the same scale and I don't have scores from other observations to compare these to. How can I know what's high and what's low? I'll just convert them all to percentages to make rough comparisons.

Jan divides each item score by its maximum possible value to obtain the percentages in Table 3.7, which she compares with one another: Seven of the nine percentages are between 40 and 70. That's a pretty tight range considering how small the maximum point values are. A one-point difference creates a huge percentage difference. But items I-2 and II-3 are out of line with the others. I-2 deals with preparation of materials; as Adonis said, that one will probably always be high for teachers who know they'll be observed. I-2 may be a throwaway item that hardly discriminates. But why is II-3 so much lower than the rest? Four of the five transitions were jerky. I wonder if that was peculiar just to this one observation, or maybe this teacher tends always to have jerky transitions. A little check on test–retest consistency could help answer that. If it turns out that item II-3 tends to behave inconsistently from the other items during our major field test, then some modifications of the item could be in order. Actually, if everyone tends to have jerky transitions, then 20 percent on item II-3 may turn out to be high in a norm-referenced interpretation. More field tests will tell.

TABLE 3.7. DATA FROM FIGURE 3.1 USED FOR JAN'S INFORMAL ASSESSMENT OF THE INTERNAL CONSISTENCY OF APPENDIX E'S INSTRUMENT

Item	Maximum Points	Scores	% of Maximum Points
I-2	2	1.73	87%
I-3	5	2.50	50%
I-4	10	4.00	40%
I-5	9	4.91	55%
II-1	1	0.62	62%
II-2	1	0.60	60%
II-3	1	0.20	20%
II-4	3	2.11	70%
II-5	3	1.63	54%

To assess internal consistency formally, the instrument is field-tested in observations of at least 15 (preferably more) classrooms. Ideally, this sample is representative of the range of situations in which the instrument is intended to be used. Depending on the composition of the instrument and the format of its items, an appropriate formula is selected to compute an internal consistency reliability coefficient (Berk, 1984c; Cangelosi, 1982, pp. 279–303; Medley, Coker, & Soar, 1984, pp. 227–38). Reliability coefficients range between −1 and 1 inclusive. The nearer the coefficient is to 1, the more internally consistent the results of the measurement.

Here are two examples of formal assessments of internal consistency of classroom observations measurements:

Ruth, Julio, and Joseph discuss how they will assess the internal consistency of Appendix H's instrument:

JULIO: The measurement has three items, each worth more than one point. The sum of item scores equals the overall score.

RUTH: Those characteristics make it a good candidate for coefficient alpha.

JOSEPH: Coefficient alpha?

RUTH: Coefficient alpha (Cangelosi, 1982, pp. 284–87; Ebel, 1965, pp. 318–43; Medley, Coker, & Soar, 1984, pp. 227–32) is a reliability coefficient that's appropriate for virtually any type of multi-item measurement. To use it, we'll need scores from 15 or more observations of different teachers.

JOSEPH: How should we select our sample?

RUTH: Since we want to evaluate student teachers' performances, student teachers should be sampled. But we need a sample that varies on the subvariables to be evaluated. If the instrument is worth anything, it should detect differences among performance regarding instructional methods and techniques. But it doesn't have a chance to do that unless the sample contains subjects whose performances will range from low to high. So, what if we try it out on a sample of 20 composed of 10 subjects who are near the end of their student teaching experience, 5 who are just beginning to student teach, and 5 experienced in-service teachers? That way, our target group, student teachers near completion, comprises the average of our sample, but we also have representation from opposite extremes.

JULIO: That'll give us that range of performance we want.

JOSEPH: Should we get a cross sample for all grade and subject areas?

RUTH: I don't think so. That'll create more variation all right. But it's the wrong source of variation—variation because of differences in content and grade levels. I think we need to establish norms for each teaching specialty.

JOSEPH: Separate validations for lower elementary, upper elementary, middle school, or junior high by subject area, and high school by subject area.

JULIO: To compute this first coefficient alpha, let's go with middle school social studies teachers. We have more social studies student teachers right now than any other teaching specialty.

JOSEPH: What does this coefficient alpha look like?

Ruth writes the following on the board:

$$\alpha = \frac{k}{k-1}\left[1 - \frac{\sigma_1^2 + \sigma_2^2 + \sigma_3^2 + \ldots + \sigma_k^2}{\sigma_x^2}\right] \text{ where:}$$

α = the reliability coefficient, k = number of items, σ_1^2 = the variance of item 1's scores, σ_2^2 = the variance of item 2's scores, . . ., σ_k^2 = the variance of item k's scores, and σ_x^2 = the variance of the overall scores.

JOSEPH: Our instrument has three items, so k equals 3. Then we have to compute a variance for the 20 item 1 scores, a variance for the 20 item 2 scores, a variance for the 20 item 3 scores, and a variance for the 20 overall scores.

JULIO: That seems like a lot of trouble.

RUTH: It would be if you didn't have that sigma-squared button on your calculator that's programmed to do the variances for you.

JOSEPH: You don't even need to do that. Almost any decent computer statistical package can do coefficient alpha or any of the Kuder-Richardson formulas. SPSS (Norusius, 1988, pp. B203–4) has it.

Several weeks later the field test is completed and the team discusses the results as they appear in Table 3.8:

JULIO: So what does this .72 tell us about the internal consistency of the instrument?

RUTH: I really hate reliability coefficients that are between .65 and .80. I feel comfortable saying that below .65 indicates the measurement is not reliable and above .80 suggest reliability. But .72 is in between and difficult to interpret. For a classroom observation with only three items and items involving narrative descriptions, I'll admit to being surprised the coefficient is this high. More items usually mean higher reliability. And it's tougher to get decent reliability from classroom observations than, say, paper and pencil tests.

JOSEPH: So, what did you just say? What's your verdict?

RUTH: I was just thinking aloud, not really saying anything. Although I'm not comfortable with only .72, I can't help but think that for this kind of measurement, .72 is about as high as we should ever expect. The verdict is that the internal consistency is satisfactory for us to use this instrument. But we shouldn't depend as much on this measurement as we could if the coefficient turned out to be .95.

Pine County School District Office personnel are considering using BOCAS (see Appendix D) to gather student outcome data relative to how well certain behavior modification strategies used by teachers are working with students who habitually display uncooperative classroom behaviors. Jim, one member of the district's Evaluation Division, thinks to himself as he considers ways to assess the internal consistency of BOCAS:

TABLE 3.8. RESULTS FROM RUTH, JULIO, AND JOSEPH'S FIELD TEST TO ASSESS THE INTERNAL CONSISTENCY OF APPENDIX H'S INSTRUMENT

Subject	Item 1 Score	Item 2 Score	Item 3 Score	Overall Score
Teacher A	2	1	3	6
Teacher B	2	2	3	7
Teacher C	0	0	0	0
Teacher D	1	2	0	3
Teacher E	2	2	2	6
Teacher F	0	2	0	2
Teacher G	2	2	6	10
Teacher H	1	1	3	5
Teacher I	0	0	0	0
Teacher J	2	0	2	4
Teacher K	0	1	0	1
Teacher L	2	2	4	8
Teacher M	2	0	0	2
Teacher N	1	1	3	5
Teacher O	1	1	3	5
Teacher P	2	2	4	8
Teacher Q	1	1	1	3
Teacher R	1	0	0	1
Teacher S	0	0	0	0
Teacher T	2	2	3	7

$k = 3$, $\sigma_1^2 = 0.66$, $\sigma_2^2 = 0.69$, $\sigma_3^2 = 3.13$, $\sigma_x^2 = 8.63$

$$\alpha = \frac{k}{k-1}\left[1 - \frac{\sigma_1^2 + \sigma_2^2 + \sigma_3^2 + \ldots + \sigma_k^2}{\sigma_x^2}\right]$$

$$= \frac{3}{3-1}\left[1 - \frac{0.66 + 0.69 + 3.13}{8.63}\right] = 0.72$$

"For each student observed, BOCAS yields three overall scores: one for 'respect for authority,' one for 'respect for peers,' and one for 'respect for classwork.' So actually BOCAS is three different measurements, and I'll need a reliability coefficient for each one.

"Let's see, for Section I, 'respect for authority,' there are eight items, each worth 15 points. Is that right? No! BOCAS categorizes time intervals rather than coding specific events. So, each of the 15 columns represents a time interval to be categorized independently of the other 14. That makes each cell a separate one-point item. So, instead of Section I being eight 15-point items, it's 15 times 8 one-point items. That's 120 dichotomously scored items! Which means instead of the more complex coefficient alpha, I can apply the easier Kuder-Richardson 21 formula (Cangelosi, 1982, pp. 285–92; Ebel, 1965, pp. 318–26; Ebel & Frisbie, 1986, pp. 76–79)."

Jim locates the following form of the Kuder-Richardson 21 formula in an educational measurement text:

$$R = \frac{k\sigma^2 - \mu(k-\mu)}{\sigma^2(k-1)} \quad \text{where:}$$

R = the reliability coefficient, k = the number of items, μ = the mean of the overall scores, and σ^2 = the variance of the overall scores.

He thinks: "I could find a sample of 50 students to be observed. Fifteen of them should have no history of behavior difficulties, another 15 might be severe cases, and 20 or so could be typical of our target population. To use Kuder-Richardson 21, we'd need just the 50 overall scores for each section to compute the mean and the variance. k for Section 1 equals 120. Section 2 also has 120 cells, so k = 120 for 'respect for peers.' Section 3 has, let's see—10 rows and 15 columns—that makes k equals 150."

Three weeks later Jim muses over the following results from the experiment (more detailed results for Section 1 are provided by Table 3.9):

- R for Section 1 = 0.90.
- R for Section 2 = 0.81.
- R for Section 3 = 0.76.

He thinks: "That .90 is really high for a classroom observation instrument. Having so many items tends to enhance reliability—allows for consistent patterns to emerge. I'm not surprised that Sections 2 and 3 are lower. The 'respect for authority' items are easier for observers to pick up than the 'respect for peers' or 'respect for classwork' ones.

TABLE 3.9. RESULTS FROM JIM'S FIELD TEST TO ASSESS THE INTERNAL CONSISTENCY OF SECTION I BOCAS (APPENDIX D'S INSTRUMENT)

Subject	Score	Subject	Score	Subject	Score
Student A	65	Student R	79	Student II	65
Student B	53	Student S	33	Student JJ	99
Student C	55	Student T	65	Student KK	68
Student D	84	Student U	60	Student LL	44
Student E	71	Student V	41	Student MM	86
Student F	107	Student W	60	Student NN	46
Student G	77	Student X	62	Student OO	73
Student H	75	Student Y	61	Student PP	47
Student I	93	Student Z	45	Student QQ	80
Student J	74	Student AA	57	Student RR	96
Student K	59	Student BB	61	Student SS	61
Student L	71	Student CC	78	Student TT	51
Student M	40	Student DD	88	Student UU	79
Student N	51	Student EE	49	Student VV	46
Student O	90	Student FF	69	Student WW	54
Student P	49	Student GG	78	Student XX	93
Student Q	60	Student HH	57		

k = 120, μ = 66.10, σ^2 = 289.50

$$R = \frac{k\sigma^2 - \mu(k-\mu)}{\sigma^2(k-1)} = \frac{120(289.50) - 66.10(120 - 66.10)}{(289.50)(119)} = 0.90$$

Assessing Test–Retest Consistency

Before any examination of the *stability* of classroom observation scores is planned, the question must be answered as to which of the following is relevant according to the stated purpose of the evaluation:

1. The teacher's performance during the particular lesson observed
2. The teacher's accomplishments during the particular lesson observed
3. How well the teacher typically performs a particular task
4. How competent the teacher is in performing a particular task

If either 1 or 2 is the answer, then observations of lessons other than the one in question are irrelevant. In such cases, *test–retest consistency* is not an issue.

If either 3 or 4 is the answer, then variations in how well or how competently the teacher performs the task from one observation to another are very relevant to the evaluation. Thus, multiple observations are needed. However, to what degree are differences in the results from multiple observations a function of variations in the teacher's performances? And, to what degree are differences in the results from multiple observations a function of poor measurement test–retest consistency?

Evaluators can interpret the results from multiple observations in light of the answers to those two questions if they have access to findings from an assessment of the instrument's test–retest consistency. Here is an example:

Ruth, Julio, and Joseph continue their discussions regarding the validity of Appendix H's instrument:

JOSEPH: We'll be evaluating student teachers' performances in the area of teaching strategies.

JULIO: So, if we decide to actually use this instrument for real next year, we'll be using it several times for each student teacher.

JOSEPH: Right! For each, we'll need data from which we can generalize about how well that student teacher performs—not just performance in one lesson.

JULIO: That might be an atypical lesson!

RUTH: That's why we should be concerned about test–retest consistency.

JULIO: Oh, oh! That means we have to administer the instrument again to our field-test sample.

RUTH: Maybe not.

JULIO: But to assess test–retest consistency, we have to see if the higher scoring subjects from the initial round of observations will tend to have the higher scores again if the sample is reobserved. And similarly, do those with lower scores the first time, tend also to be low the second time? That's what score *stability* is all about.

RUTH: Theoretically, you're exactly right. But for this situation there's a more practical and accurate method of assessing test–retest consistency without having to reobserve our field-test sample (Berk, 1984c; Thorndike, 1988). We use the internal consistency reliability coefficient we've already obtained (see Table 3.8) to compute a standard error of measurement

(Cangelosi, 1982, pp. 292–300). The standard error of measurement, or SEM, provides an estimate of the amount of variability between two different observations of the same subject that is attributable to test–retest inconsistency.

JOSEPH: Show us what you mean.

Ruth writes what is illustrated by Table 3.10 as she continues her explanation:

RUTH: The formula for SEM is the standard deviation of the overall scores times the square root of the difference between one and the reliability coefficient.

JULIO: We can get the standard deviation by taking the square root of the variance.

JOSEPH: The variance (from Table 3.8) we know to be 8.63. So the standard deviation is 2.94.

JULIO: And we just plug in the alpha value of .72 (from Table 3.8) for the reliability coefficient and that gives us a standard error of measurement of—ahh. . . .

JOSEPH: Of 1.56. So what? What does that tell us about test–retest consistency?

RUTH: An SEM of 1.56 means that we can be about 67 percent confident that random test–retest measurement inconsistency accounts for about plus or minus 1.56 of the variation we'll get between an observation and a re-observation with this instrument.

JULIO: Sixty-seven percent confident is not very confident!

RUTH: By doubling the SEM you can be 95 percent confident. Tripling it gives you 99 percent confidence.

TABLE 3.10 THE ILLUSTRATION RUTH USES IN EXPLAINING THE APPLICATION OF SEM TO THE ASSESSMENT OF THE TEST–RETEST CONSISTENCY OF APPENDIX H'S INSTRUMENT

$SEM = \sigma\sqrt{1 - R}$ where σ = the standard deviation of the scores, and
R = the reliability coefficient.

Since the standard deviation is the square root of the variance,
$\sigma = \sqrt{\sigma^2}$. $\sigma^2 = 8.63$ (from Table 3.8), so $\sigma = 2.94$.
$R = \alpha = 0.72$ (from Table 3.11).

Thus, $SEM = \sigma\sqrt{1 - R} = (2.94)\sqrt{1 - .72} = 1.56$

Measurement error due to test–retest inconsistency causes a score of X from one observation to vary between $X - SEM$ and $X + SEM$ in about 67% of the reobservations, between $X - 2SEM$ and $X + 2SEM$ in about 95% of the reobservations, and between $X - 3SEM$ and $X + 3SEM$ in about 99% of the reobservations.

So, a student teacher who received a score of 6 the first time observed with Appendix H's instrument is about 95% certain of receiving a score roughly between 3 and 9 on a second observation, *provided the quality of the two performances does not actually vary.* Thus, any variation beyond this range is probably attributable to differences in the two performances rather than to test–retest inconsistencies of the instrument.

JOSEPH: How do we get 100 percent confident?

RUTH: That's impossible.

JULIO: Are you going to explain to us why this works this way?

RUTH: Not unless you enroll in my Measurement in Education and Psychology course. Otherwise, you'll have to just look it up in a measurement and evaluation text (e.g., Kubiszyn & Borich, 1987, pp. 305–14). It's all related to sampling error, normal curves, and the central limit theorem (Cangelosi, 1982, pp. 294–99; Marascuilo & Serlin, 1988, pp. 248–76).

JOSEPH: Let's walk through a hypothetical example where we would use this standard error of measurement.

JULIO: Suppose next year we have this student teacher named Mary. We observe her three times with the instrument and her scores are 7, 4, and 8. How does knowing that the SEM equals 1.56 help us?

RUTH: If we set the confidence level at 95 percent, we want to keep in mind that we expect measurement instability to account for a difference of about 3 between any two of the observations.

JOSEPH: Why 3?

JULIO: Because 3 is about twice 1.56.

JOSEPH: That's right. So, what you were about to say is that any difference between two of the scores that's greater than 3 is likely to reflect a difference in Mary's performance rather than only test–retest measurement error.

RUTH: Exactly. So, the scores don't indicate a difference in her performance between the first and third observation.

JOSEPH: But there is evidence that her second performance, for which she scored only 4, was markedly lower than the third one when her score was 8.

Assessing Observer Consistency

How much are the scores on a classroom observation instrument a function of *who* makes the observations and the *constancy* with which that observer follows the instrument's recording and scoring procedures? In other words, are two different observers of the same lesson likely to produce the same score, and to what degree does an observer vary in how he or she scores the instrument from one point in time to another? Assessments of *inter-observer consistency* and *intra-observer consistency* address these questions.

Educational and psychological measurement literature is replete with methods for assessing observer consistency (e.g., Frick & Semmel, 1978; Shavelson, Webb, & Burstein, 1986, pp. 59–86; van den Bergh & Eiting, 1989). The development of "newer" and "better" methods continues to be a popular pursuit of measurement specialists. In virtually all of these methods, for inter-observer consistency two or more observers use the instrument during the same classroom sessions; for intra-observer consistency the same observer uses the instrument twice for the same set of classroom sessions (e.g., with the aid of videotape). Two observations of the same session are spaced far enough apart to prevent the observer's memory of the first to influence the second observation. Then by some means (e.g., correlation coeffi-

Figure 3.2. Comparison of Results from Two Trained Observers Using Section I of BOCAS with the Same Student at the Same Time

SUBJECT _J. Mitchell_   OBSERVER _D. Chris_   LOCATION _Santee JR. (RM. II)_   TIME _10:15–11:05_   DATE _2/28_

1 RESPECT FOR AUTHORITY	1 m	1 m	1 m	1 m	1 m	1 m	1 m	1 m	1 m	1 m	1 m	Line Total
1 (1a) Cooperating in activities involving total class	✓	✓	✓	✓	✓	✓	✓	✓	✓	✓	✓	12
1 (2a) Volunteering to help (answer questions)		✓			✓	✓						3
1 (3a) Indicating agreement with auth. fig. (nodding, smiling, eye cont.)	✓	✓	✓		✓							3
1 (4a) Making supportive statements to or about the authority figure				✓								1
1 (5b) Talking back to the authority figure												15
1 (6b) Making mocking facial expressions, gestures												15
1 (7b) Ignoring/disobeying instructions	✓	✓							✓	✓	✓	9
1 (8b) Failing to answer when called upon												15

Positive Score _73_

78

SUBJECT _J. Michell_   OBSERVER _M. Shipley_   LOCATION _Santon, JR. PM. 11_   TIME _10:15 – 11:05_   DATE _2/28_

	1 m	1 m	1 m	1 m	1 m	1 m	1 m	1 m	1 m	1 m	1 m	1 m	Line Total
1 RESPECT FOR AUTHORITY													
1 (1a) Cooperating in activities involving total class	✓	✓	✓	✓	✓	✓	✓	✓			✓		11
1 (2a) Volunteering to help (answer questions)	✓			✓									3
1 (3a) Indicating agreement with auth. fig. (nodding, smiling, eye cont.)	✓	✓		✓	✓	✓		✓			✓		9
1 (4a) Making supportive statements to or about the authority figure					✓								1
1 (5b) Talking back to the authority figure													15
1 (6b) Making mocking facial expressions, gestures										✓			14
1 (7b) Ignoring/disobeying instructions									✓	✓	✓		12
1 (8b) Failing to answer when called upon													15

Positive Score _80_

Item	Agreement Frequency
1(a)	15
2(a)	13
3(a)	5
4(a)	15
5(b)	15
6(b)	14
7(b)	12
8(b)	15

$f = 104$ $n = 120$ $r = 104 \div 120 = 0.86$.

cients or a percent of agreement computation), the degree of agreement between the two sets of observations is quantified.

Consider, for example, how the inter-observer consistency of Section I of the BOCAS instrument (see Appendix D) might be assessed. BOCAS' items involve categorizing time intervals rather than coding specific events. This characteristic provides specific points where agreement or disagreement between observers can be detected and allows for the following procedure:

1. Two trained observers independently use Section I of BOCAS in observing the same student during the same classroom session.
2. The frequency of agreement, f, is tallied by counting the number of corresponding cells for which either (a) both observers checked or (b) both observers left blank.
3. The ratio of agreement, r, is computed by dividing f by the number of cells, k. For Section I of BOCAS, $k = 120$. (Figure 3.2 illustrates an example.)
4. Steps 1–3 are repeated with $n - 1$ other students.
5. If n is small (e.g., $n < 15$), the r values are "eyeballed" with the idea that *higher* r *values indicate better observer consistency than lower* r *values.* If n is somewhat large (e.g., $n \geq 15$) the mean and standard deviation of the r values are computed with the idea that the *higher the mean and the lower the standard deviation, the better the observer consistency.* If $n \geq 30$ and the selection of the students was random, then an inferential statistic (e.g., a z-test for proportions (Johnson, 1976, pp. 326–31) might be considered to establish a confidence interval relative to variation due to inconsistencies between observers.

For situations in which only an instrument's overall score for each subject (as opposed to individual item scores) is used in the evaluation, for inter-observer consistency, two trained observers independently use the instrument during the same class sessions for at least 15 subjects (e.g., Appendix H's instrument with 25 student teachers). A correlation coefficient (e.g., a Pearson product-moment correlation (Cangelosi, 1982, pp. 279–81; Dowdy & Wearden, 1983, pp. 229–39) is then computed from the pairs of overall scores produced by the two observers. Finally, the correlation coefficient (ranging between -1 and 1 inclusive) is interpreted with the idea that the nearer it is to 1, the better the observer consistency.

Unsatisfactory results from assessments of scorer consistency (e.g., a Pearson product-moment correlation coefficient $< .80$) typically suggest that observers are inadequately trained or directions for marking and scoring items are not clear or leave too much room for observer judgment.

Assessing Item Effectiveness

A measurement item is *effective* to the same degree that results from the item positively correlate with the results obtained from the measurement as a whole. In other words, an effective item enhances the internal consistency of the measurement of which it is a component part. The purpose of conducting an item-by-item effectiveness assessment is to identify faulty items. Such items can then be replaced or modified to improve the instrument's validity for subsequent use.

Item analysis refers to any of numerous methods for examining item effectiveness. However, the vast majority of formal, published item analysis methods (e.g., Berk, 1984a; Douglas, 1988; Ebel & Frisbie, 1986, pp. 223–42; Hoffmann, 1975) are not applicable to measurements with fewer than 15 items (Cangelosi, 1982, pp. 309–33). Because the vast majority of classroom observation instruments (e.g., those displayed in Appendices A, D, F, and H) do not have many items, conventional formal item analysis is not generally useful in identifying faulty classroom observation items. However, informal assessments of item effectiveness can be quite valuable, as it is in the following example:

Before conducting a major field test to assess the reliability of Appendix E's instrument, Jan, Adonis, Louise, and Ted try out the measurement in colleagues' classrooms. They discuss these preliminary experimental test results, which appear in Table 3.11:

ADONIS: The variability of the overall scores indicates that the instrument discriminates.

LOUISE: Yes, the scores range between 6.72 and 31.99.

JAN: Let's see how the items behaved.

TED: Just as Adonis predicted, all the results are high for I-2.

ADONIS: Yeah, the observation of Karchfield's class produced one of the lower scores, but he got two out of two for item I-2.

TED: But so did Romano, who had one of the higher scores.

JAN: There just doesn't seem to be much of a relationship between I-2's scores and overall scores.

LOUISE: If it's not discriminating, should we drop it?

ADONIS: I would if it correlated negatively with the overall score and gave misinformation. But it just gives no information, correlating neither positively nor negatively.

LOUISE: In other words, there's no reason to keep it.

ADONIS: There might be. It serves as a reminder to teachers that it's important to have quality learning materials. So what if they make special preparations for the observations? At least that's a bonus for the students!

JAN: Let's not start confounding in-service help for the teachers with summative evaluations.

LOUISE: And besides, item I-2 is one of the more difficult ones for the observer. Seems like a lot of trouble if it's not going to discriminate.

ADONIS: Okay, let's tentatively say we're going to either eliminate it, modify it, or replace it.

TED: We can come back to it later.

JAN: Look at item II-2; that's the one that really misbehaved! Compare its results with the overall scores.

TABLE 3.11. PRELIMINARY EXPERIMENTAL RESULTS JAN, ADONIS, LOUISE, AND TED CONSIDERED IN MODIFYING APPENDIX E'S INSTRUMENT

Teacher Observed	Item									Overall Score
	I-2	I-3	I-4	I-5	II-1	II-2	II-3	II-4	II-5	
Williams	1.73	2.50	4.00	4.91	0.62	0.60	0.20	2.11	1.63	18.40
Karchfield	2.00	1.10	0.50	0.33	0.51	1.00	0.00	1.78	0.67	7.89
Michelli	1.89	4.25	8.75	9.55	0.83	0.67	0.60	3.00	2.45	31.99
Samlo	1.90	2.37	3.41	4.80	0.62	0.76	0.16	2.13	1.07	17.22
Romano	2.00	4.00	8.62	8.33	0.76	1.00	1.00	2.49	0.73	28.93
Saidellu	1.79	3.35	6.44	6.71	0.69	0.48	0.50	1.90	2.06	23.92
Adams	1.80	1.27	0.00	0.70	0.46	0.92	0.11	0.88	0.58	6.72

TED: I see what's bothering you! Saidellu and Michelli got two of the three highest scores, but neither did nearly as well on item II-2 as Karchfield and Adams, who have the lowest overall scores.

LOUISE: That item has to go; it's contaminating internal consistency.

JAN: But what's wrong with it? We don't want to replace it with a worse one, or fix it incorrectly.

LOUISE: Maybe observing whether or not a transition flip-flops really isn't relevant to classroom management and discipline performance.

TED: According to our reference sources it should be.

ADONIS: Maybe our directions for the observers aren't clear and they're not accurately distinguishing between flip-flop and continuous transitions.

JAN: As I'm rereading these directions, I don't find that the distinction between clarifying previously stated directions and changing directions is all that clear. I think some examples would help.

TED: Let's rewrite. . . .

THE REALISTIC VIEW

Whenever most people think of evaluating instruction, they visualize an administrative supervisor engaging in a classroom observation armed with a rating scales (e.g., the one in Appendix B). Such practice is far more typical than the systematic and exacting efforts exemplified by Ted, Jan, Adonis, and Louise (see the example beginning on page 48 and by Ruth and her colleagues at Knight State College (see the example beginning on page 65). Is it realistic to expect supervisors, teachers, and researchers to acquire the ability and take the time to specify and operationally define their evaluation variables, systematically select or develop cost-effective classroom observation measurements for those variables, train observers, assess the validity of the measurement results, and interpret the results in light of the measurement error? That is a question you must answer for yourself. However, unless typical practice is supplanted by the exemplary efforts of educators such as Jan and Ruth, both formative and summative evaluations of classroom instruction will continue to be more a function of chance than a function of design.

SELF-ASSESSMENT EXERCISES FOR CHAPTER 3

I. Retrieve the work you did for Exercise V of the self-assessment for Chapter 2. For which of the subvariables that you listed do you think classroom observational measurements would be appropriate? For one of those subvariables, either select a classroom observation measurement via the six steps enumerated on pages 58–59 or develop one via the ten steps enumerated on page 59. Have a colleague critique your work.

II. Devise a plan for validating the classroom observation measurement you just selected or developed in response to Exercise I above. Have a colleague critique your plan.

CHAPTER 4

Additional Data Sources

Goal of Chapter 4

Chapter 4 suggests how to utilize cost-effective data sources, other than classroom observations, for evaluating instruction. It also examines the advantages and disadvantages of different types of measurements. Specifically, this chapter is designed to help you:

1. Describe processes for selecting, designing, and validating each of the following types of measurements for purposes of evaluating instruction: (a) interviews, (b) examinations of teacher-produced documents, (c) student achievement and aptitude tests, (d) teacher competency tests, (e) questionnaires, and (f) anecdotal records.
2. Explain the relative advantages and disadvantages of different types of data sources for use in evaluating instruction.
3. Given an example in which instruction is evaluated, distinguish between instances in which measurements and measurement results are used appropriately and instances in which they are misused.
4. Given well-defined evaluation-of-instruction variables relative to a situation that is familiar to you, design a plan for selecting or developing, administering, validating, and interpreting a variety of cost-effective measurements.

INTERVIEWS

Vicarious Observations

Classroom observations provide teachers (e.g., by viewing videotapes of their own class sessions), supervisors, and researchers with firsthand, empirical windows to events and activities. *Interviews* provide channels through which teachers, supervisors, and researchers gain secondhand information about events, activities, and even thoughts experienced by others. For example:

- A principal questions a prospect for a teaching position about the teacher's methods for handling certain classroom discipline problems, philosophy on how curricula should be determined, and experiences working in multi-ethnic schools.
- A teacher who is concerned about the pacing of her lessons queries several students regarding whether the lessons move too fast, too slow, or just about right.
- A graduate student studying the relationship among teachers' stated objectives, learning activities, and student achievement tests conducts one-to-one interviews with a sample of teachers to hear them describe their thoughts as they plan lessons and design achievement tests.

In an interview, an *interviewer* orchestrates an oral exchange with the interview subject or group of subjects by presenting a sequence of questions or directives to which the subjects respond. There is a distinction between an interview and a *conference*. Interviews are meetings conducted for the purpose of obtaining data to be used for evaluations (i.e., an interview is a measurement). Conferences, on the other hand, are meetings used to exchange ideas and communicate evaluations. The meetings in the following example are conferences, *not* interviews:

An instructional supervisor and a teacher meet to plan for a sequence of classroom observations. After each observation, they meet to discuss the results. During the last of these meetings, the supervisor communicates her formative evaluations relative to teaching performance.

Types of Interviews

Group. A group of subjects can be interviewed at the same session. For example:

Ms. Goldstein's ninth-grade health science class has just completed a unit on communicable diseases. According to the students' test results, two-thirds of the class achieved the unit's objectives to her satisfaction. However, Ms. Goldstein is searching for ways of doing an even better job with this class. As part of her data-gathering effort relevant to how she should conduct subsequent units, she holds a class meeting:

MS. GOLDSTEIN: What was the topic of the unit we completed Friday, Flo?

FLO: Communicable diseases.

MS. GOLDSTEIN: Now that the unit is over, ask yourself if you learned as much, less, or more than you expected to when it began. Raise your hand if you got less.—Okay, I see six hands up. Describe your expectations at the beginning of the unit, Tom.

TOM: Well, I thought we'd do more on stuff like how to not get sick. We spent all that time on AIDS and stuff. I'm never gonna get AIDS!

MS. GOLDSTEIN: Jocelyn, you also had your hand up. Do you agree with Tom's comment?

JOCELYN: Kind of. But, I'm glad we covered AIDS. My problem was. . . .

The group interview continues with Ms. Goldstein recording positive and negative comments as well as descriptions on how students prepared for the unit test, the way they completed homework exercises, impromptu discussions the unit stimulated, and thought processes they engaged in as the unit progressed.

Group interviews are convenient mechanisms for hearing a variety of perceptions about the events or activities in question. However, group settings, with their variety of complex social structures, hardly lend themselves to the in-depth probing that expert interviewers can often accomplish interviewing one person at a time in private settings.

One-to-One. Unlike group interviews, privately conducted one-to-one interviews afford opportunities to pursue questions in depth and allow a subject to "think aloud."

Closed Structure. In closed-structure interviews, interviewers faithfully follow predesigned scripts and limit their recordings or coding of subjects' responses to prespecified topics. Closed-structure interviews are virtually always one-to-one and utilize an instrument for coding and scoring responses. Here is an example:

In an attempt to determine whether or not the Woodpine County Teachers Association should recommend that the district office offer in-service workshops for teachers on being assertive with parents, a study is undertaken addressing the following question: What proportion of the district's teachers display an assertive, as opposed to a hostile or passive, style in their communications with students' parents?

Part of the study includes conducting closed-structure interviews with a sample of the teachers. Each interview utilizes Appendix I's instrument. Here is a portion of one of the interviews, conducted by Vinnie Mason with a teacher, Gwen O'Hare:

VINNIE: Within the last six weeks, about how many individual conferences with parents of your students have you had?

GWEN: I talk to parents every day. Do you mean just the ones that are prearranged, or do you want to include the chance meetings?

VINNIE: Let's limit this to the prearranged ones.

GWEN: I'll have to think about this for a minute.

Vinnie notes on the copy of Appendix I's instrument: "Distinguishes between prearranged and chance conferences. Only prearranged to be included herein." Vinnie discreetly marks the instrument throughout the interview without revealing what he writes to Gwen. Later, after all teachers have been interviewed, Vinnie will send Gwen a copy of the form completed during her interview.

GWEN: Roughly 50.

VINNIE: Without revealing the identify of any of the parties involved, recall two of those conferences. First, the one that in your judgment was the least successful. Second, the one that was the most successful. When you have both cases in mind, just say, "okay."

GWEN: Wow! There have been so many, some wonderful, some awful!—Okay, I have 'em.

VINNIE: First let's talk about the conference that did not go as well as the other. As you began this conference, what did you hope to gain from it? Please explain without revealing identities.

GWEN: I had this one student whom I saw throwing food in the lunch room. Later the same day, during reading, I caught him jabbing his partner in the ear. I gave him a note asking for his Mom to call me to set up an appointment. My purpose was twofold; to elicit her help in discouraging this kind of behavior and to communicate to the boy that I didn't plan to tolerate such misbehaviors.

Under item 2 of Appendix I's instrument, Vinnie summarizes Gwen's comments and scores +1 on the **A** scale.

VINNIE: Describe what happened during the conference that prevented it from going as well as it could have gone.

GWEN: Gracious! What didn't go wrong? Okay, first of all she showed up a half hour late and that threw my schedule way off. I had other things to do, and I just wasn't as enthusiastic about speaking with her as I was at the appointed hour.

VINNIE: But you held the conference anyway.

GWEN: Right! I couldn't tell her to reschedule after she was at school.

Under item 3, Vinnie marks +1 on the **P** scale.

VINNIE: Please continue.

GWEN: I expected her to apologize for being late. Instead she told me that the boy hadn't thrown the food and that I must have been mistaken. I asked her how I could have possibly been mistaken. And then she had the gall to say that her son only patted the other student to congratulate her for doing a good job! I thought we'd really work out a constructive plan. Instead I spent all my time convincing her that I wasn't mistaken!

Vinnie summarizes Gwen's response and adds the following to item 3's score: $+1$ on the **A** scale for alluding to the unfulfilled purpose, $+1$ on the **P** scale for failing to control the direction of the conference, and $+1$ on the **H** scale for competing with the parent. Vinnie then presents item 4's directive and the conference continues.

Open Structure. Open-structure interview items are designed to stimulate subjects to speak on specified topics, virtually without interruption from interviewers. In the following example, the open-structure interview items listed in Table 4.1 are used:

The Department of Curriculum and Instruction of State University is collaborating with a consortium of several local school districts to plan a beginning teacher induction program to be implemented at the start of the next school year. To help identify problem areas for beginning teachers on which the program should focus, 30 of this year's beginning teachers are interviewed.

In a pre-interview conference with each beginning teacher, the trained interviewer explains (1) the purpose of the study, (2) how the interview results will be used, (3) that confidentiality regarding any individual's responses will be maintained (i.e., aggregate results only will be made known, but "who said what" will not be reported), (4) that interviews will be audiotaped, but the tapes will be destroyed after results are compiled from them, (5) how the hour-long interview will be conducted, and (6) that a $30 stipend will be paid for submitting to the interview. If the beginning teacher agrees to participate, the interview is scheduled for a time and place that ensures privacy and minimizes interruptions.

During the interview, the interviewer presents the items listed in Table 4.1, allowing the beginning teacher to speak uninterrupted on each. If the teacher's response is short, the interviewer asks for elaboration without influencing *what* is said. For each item, the interviewer's task is to clarify the question and encourage the teacher to express his or her thoughts, but not to make an impact on those thoughts.

After the interview, the interviewer uses the recording of the responses to conduct a *content analysis* (Patton, 1987, pp. 149–50) classifying problems raised by the teacher according to Table 4.2's categories.

TABLE 4.1. OPEN-STRUCTURE INTERVIEW ITEMS USED IN THE STATE UNIVERSITY AND SCHOOL DISTRICT CONSORTIUM STUDY OF BEGINNING TEACHERS' NEEDS

1. When you think back on your experiences teaching this year, what things stand out in your mind as having gone particularly well?
2. When you think back on your experiences teaching this year, what things stand out in your mind that did not go well?
3. Tell me about some particularly troublesome problems you faced.
4. What were some other factors that made it difficult for you to teach effectively?
5. List the teaching and professional responsibilities that you feel you were most qualified to fulfill during the first month of this school year.
6. List the teaching and professional responsibilities that you feel you were least qualified to fulfill during the first month of this school year.
7. Talk about any other aspects of your teaching experiences this year that might help us plan a program to help next year's beginning teachers.

TABLE 4.2. CATEGORY SYSTEM FOR CONTENT ANALYSIS OF RESPONSES TO TABLE 4.2'S OPEN-STRUCTURE INTERVIEW ITEMS

Classify each problem identified in the interview by the following:

I. Professional relationships with:
  A. Administrators
  B. Supervisors
  C. Teaching colleagues
  D. Students' parents
  E. Others

II. Organizing for teaching relative to:
  A. Acquisition and management of supplies and equipment
  B. Time management and scheduling
  C. Obtaining information
  D. Obtaining counsel and advice
  E. Other

III. Managing outside-of-classroom administrative and school governance tasks:
  A. Nonroutine
  B. Routine, recurring
  C. Other

IV. Managing classroom administrative tasks:
  A. Nonroutine
  B. Routine, recurring
  C. Other

V. Developing curricula and teaching units that are:
  A. Consistent with school, district, and state requirements
  B. Relevant to students' needs
  C. Practical to implement
  D. Other

VI. Planning for instruction:
  A. Long-range planning (beyond a single unit)
  B. Unit planning
  C. Short-range planning (lesson or daily)
  D. Other planning

VII. Conducting lessons for:
  A. Knowledge-level objectives
  B. Higher cognitive objectives
  C. Affective objectives
  D. Psychomotor objectives
  E. Other

VIII. Managing student behavior and classroom activities relative to:
  A. Efficiently using transition time
  B. Motivating students to become engaged in learning activities (including homework)
  C. Maintaining student engagement during learning activities
  D. Dealing with nondisruptive off-task behaviors
  E. Dealing with disruptive off-task behaviors
  F. Individualizing for varying student needs and learning rates

IX. Evaluating:
  A. Student achievement for summative purposes
  B. Student achievement for formative purposes
  C. Student aptitude
  D. Teaching performance or effectiveness

X. Other

TABLE 4.3. AGGREGATE RESULTS FROM 30 INTERVIEWS RELATIVE TO TABLE 4.2'S CATEGORY VII-B

x	f
0	5
1	7
2	7
3	6
4	0
5	2
6	1
7	1
8	0
9	0
> 9	1

x = the number of examples fitting Category VII-B in a single interview.
f = number of interviews with exactly x examples fitting Category VII-B.

For each of Table 4.2's categories and subcategories, a frequency distribution patterned like the one in Table 4.3 is reported at the conclusion of the 30 interviews.

Informal. Unfortunately, chance occurrences that result in unplanned interviews, such as informal classroom observations, loom large among data sources commonly influencing many evaluations of instruction. For example:

Principal Segaloff hears an unusual amount of noise emanating from Jerome Eaton's seventh-grade classroom as he walks down the hall. He steps inside the room but does not see Jerome. Holding up his hand to signal for silence, he asks one of the students, "Daryl, where is Mr. Eaton?"

DARYL:	He said he'd be back soon and for us to manage ourselves.
MR. SEGALOFF:	How long has he been gone?
BRENDA:	Not more than 20 minutes.
DARYL:	Oh, it hasn't been that long! More like 10 minutes.
DOMINIQUE:	Hey, Mr. Segaloff, is Mr. Eaton gonna be in trouble?

MR. SEGALOFF: If he's been called out of class, maybe I can help him. Does anyone know where I might find him?

BRENDA: He just walked in behind you.

MR. EATON: Are they misbehaving?

MR. SEGALOFF: No, but is there something I can do to help you?

MR. EATON: No, thank you. It's just that Mrs. Willis sent me this note saying that Supply House phoned, so I called them back to check on my order of math materials.

As he leaves the room, Mr. Segaloff thinks, "Jerome displayed irresponsible behavior leaving his class like that. And what a stupid thing to ask me in front of the students! 'Are they misbehaving?' No, but he was. I'd better follow up on this."

Appropriate Uses of Interviews

Relevant to Teaching Competence. Teaching competence is primarily a function of the teacher's thought processes when approaching and attempting instructional tasks. Well-designed and well-conducted interviews provide vehicles for presenting teachers with hypothetical situations in which they have instructional tasks to perform and for probing their thoughts as they explain their approaches. Here is an example:

The faculty of the Department of Teacher Education at Knight State College evaluates the teaching competence of each preservice teacher before recommending that individual for a student teaching assignment. Those receiving unsatisfactory evaluations delay student teaching until a remediation program is completed. One data source for each evaluation is an interview such as the one Julio, a department member, conducts for Ken, a candidate for student teaching in secondary school mathematics. Here is a brief portion of the beginning of that one-to-one interview:

JULIO: Ken, I assume you understand that this interview is just one of the ways the faculty gets information that we use to evaluate your readiness to student teach. Am I correct?

KEN: Yes, sir. The process has been explained to me.

JULIO: I'm going to present you with situations not unlike ones you might encounter as a student teacher. For each, I'll ask you to explain how you would handle your responsibility in that situation. Now, keep in mind that since this is an interview, I'll be a bit more stoic than I would be if we were just having a nice social exchange.

KEN: That's scary!

JULIO: It's natural to be nervous. I'll keep that in mind as we get into the interview. Like you, I'm a teacher. And as a teacher, I'll be tempted to display satisfaction with your insightful responses and disappointment with others. However, I'm going to resist that temptation. So, don't look for feedback from me. I do encourage you to ask me for clarifications and explanations of what I mean. If you have a question and aren't sure if you should ask it, go ahead and ask away, and I'll decide if it's in the rules for me to answer it. Okay?

KEN: Okay.

JULIO: I'll also ask you to elaborate from time to time, and explain to me what you mean when I don't understand. Are you ready?

KEN: Yes.

JULIO: It's your first day as a student teacher. You are about to observe your cooperating teacher conduct a lesson for the first time. Some students are talking to the cooperating teacher about a mathematics problem as you wait for the period to begin. The cooperating teacher asks you to take two of the students into an office adjoining the classroom for about 10 minutes and help them settle a mathematical argument. As the cooperating teacher starts the class, one student tells you that the square of any number is greater than the number. The other disagrees. They ask you, "Who is right?" Describe for me what you would do.

KEN: I've got 10 minutes, right?

JULIO: Right.

KEN: Okay. Let's say the one who thought the square is always greater is Mary and the other one's Joe. Is that okay?

JULIO: Sure.

KEN: First, I'd ask Mary to explain why the square will always be greater. Then I'd have Joe explain his position. If neither uses examples in their explanations, I'd ask Mary to illustrate why she's right by using a specific number. She'll probably pick a number like 3 to make her point. Then, I'd have Joe do the same. He'll probably choose a number like one-half. And, then—

JULIO: Why drag this out? Why not just explain why Joe is correct and let them get back to class?

KEN: Because that wouldn't help them understand the process for discovering mathematical relationships. They don't need another authority saying what's right. They need someone to guide their thinking.

JULIO: Aren't you afraid they'll think you don't know the answer yourself? After all, you're going to have to take over the class pretty soon and you don't want them thinking you don't know the answers!

KEN: In this situation, I'm not trying to teach them the answers. I want them to experience a reasoning process that'll help them discover answers for themselves. My job isn't to build my image; it's to teach them.

Inside himself, Julio is leaping for joy over Ken's response to this first item. Outside, he maintains his stoic expression as he moves on to the second item. Since Ken has responded so well to the first item, Julio *branches* to a more difficult item to ask next. Had Ken responded poorly to item 1, Julio would have selected a simpler situation for item 2.

Relevant to Teaching Performance. Interviews are valuable for filling information voids not covered by classroom observations. When used in concert with classroom observations, interviews can provide reports on occurrences between the on-site observations as well as explanations regarding what was observed during a class-

room visit. Do not confuse the following example with a post-observational conference in which evaluations are communicated and ideas exchanged; data gathering is
the purpose of this interview:

As part of the instructional supervision program that Principal Nelson provides the
teachers at Malaker Middle School, Amy Naquin, social studies department head, uses
periodical classroom observations and interviews for formative evaluations. Amy is
interviewing Byron Johnson just after observing one of his civics classes:

AMY: When I observed the class on Thursday, you assigned students to locate
publications on gun control and bring them to class on Monday. That's
today, and no one did. I was really disappointed.

BYRON: Oh, yeah! Friday I postponed that assignment, when I found out I needed
to work first on two of their skills before taking on such a hot issue.
Friday's formative feedback indicated that most of them don't know how to
go about locating articles on a topic, nor are they ready to engage in
productive debates. That's why you saw us discussing less controversial
topics today. I'm going to work on those skills before we debate gun
control.

AMY: Okay, update me on what else went on between Thursday's and today's
observation.

BYRON: I deviated from Thursday's lesson plan because. . . .

Relevant to Student Oucomes. Although formal interviews are not commonly used
to measure student outcome variables, they could be used to probe opinions (e.g.,
from the teacher, parents, and students themselves) about what students have gained
from classroom experiences. Also, a well-designed interview can provide a valuable
means for measuring the *depth* of students' achievements (Cangelosi, 1990b, pp.
129–31). However, interviews are not very usable for measuring the achievement of
more than a small sample of students.

Common Misuses of Interviews

Formal interviews are commonly used in the hiring of new teachers. Too often,
results of those interviews are used to evaluate potential teaching effectiveness.
However, such interviews are often relevant only to evaluating the likelihood that the
candidate is a cordial, easy-to-talk-to person who is pleasant to interact with
socially; they are not relevant to the candidate's teaching competence. For example:

Blaine Swenson, Cliffview School District Associate Superintendent for Instruction, is
screening candidates for teaching positions. After looking over Joyce Blureor's application file for a position as an upper elementary school teacher, Blaine interviews Joyce:

BLAINE: Thank you so much for coming. It's very nice to meet you, Mrs. Blureor.
Did I pronounce that correctly?

JOYCE: Yes. Most people don't get it right the first time.

> BLAINE: Tell me something about yourself.
>
> JOYCE: I received my B.A. in education about nine years ago, but I've waited until my youngest reached school age before starting my teaching career.
>
> BLAINE: So, how many children do you have?
>
> JOYCE: Two. Now, I'm ready to start working with other people's children.
>
> BLAINE: What a wonderful attitude! . . .
>
> After another 10 minutes conversing along these lines, Joyce leaves and Blaine completes the rating form as it appears in Appendix J. However, virtually none of the areas relevant to the items on the rating form were raised in the interview.

As with classroom observations, misuse of interviews that fail to provide valid data stem from a failure to clearly define and clarify the purposes of the evaluations and from poorly prepared interviewers.

Selection, Development, and Validation

The principles upon which classroom observation measurements should be selected, developed, and validated also apply to collecting data via interviews. As with classroom observations, assessments of relevance depend on how well items match clearly defined evaluation variables. Assessments of reliability depend on: consistencies of subjects' responses (i.e., the more a subject contradicts him- or herself, the less reliable the interview), and on how closely the results from two different interviewers' recordings from the same interview agree.

Training Interviewers

Just as Jan held a workshop to train observers to use Appendix E's instrument, so interviewers must learn to stimulate subjects to "open up," without influencing what they say or coaching them in one direction or the other; and learn to follow faithfully the specific procedures for presenting items, probing, and recording responses.

Effective interviewing requires concentration, mental acuity, sensitivity, interpersonal understanding, and discipline. Numerous references on how to conduct interviews are available (e.g., Goetz & LeCompte, 1984, pp. 119–42; S. Jones, 1985; Patton, 1987, pp. 108–43).

EXAMINATIONS OF TEACHER-PRODUCED DOCUMENTS

By-Products of Teaching

Teachers' efforts to help their students attain learning goals create by-products that sometimes serve as data sources for evaluations of instruction. Examining by-products in the form of *documents* can be particularly useful. For example, an analysis of a teacher's *lesson plans* may provide a measure of teaching performance in the areas of determining objectives, designing learning activities, and giving attention to preparation. Reading a *teacher's journal* may help an instructional supervisor remain aware of what students and the teacher are doing between classroom observations. Also an analysis of a *teacher-made achievement test* can reflect the levels (e.g., memory or higher cognitive) at which student achievement is being assessed.

Types of Document Examinations

Information Retrieval. The most straightforward use of an existing document as a data source is simply to read it for the purpose of comprehending its author's message. For example:

Nora and Sheldon are both third-grade teachers at Eugene Street Elementary School. It is the beginning of the school year and they have just agreed to begin providing formative evaluations of one another's teaching performances. They are in the midst of a discussion about their plans for providing each other with this service:

NORA: I'll be able to observe your class once a month, but I could be more helpful if I could stay apprised as to what's going on almost every day. Classrooms are such dynamic environments, things change so quickly, that once a month seems inadequate! There's no way we could meet often enough. It's too hectic around here before and after school!"

SHELDON: You've just given me an idea! For the last couple of years I've been in the habit of keeping a daily journal to keep track of what goes on in my classroom. I refer to it when I need to remember when I did what. And then at the end of the year I go back and look it over to plan for the upcoming year.

NORA: And you're going to leave your journal somewhere where I can read it every now and then!

SHELDON: Don't you think that would solve the problem?

Analytical. More systematically focused and difficult to conduct than information retrieval examinations are *analytical document examinations*. Analytical techniques are used to identify prespecified relationships embedded in documents. For example:

Aware of the renewed interest in teaching mathematics at the conceptual and application cognitive levels (National Council of Teachers of Mathematics, 1989), Sheldon would like Nora to evaluate the cognitive levels at which his mathematics lessons are directed. Sheldon and Nora are cognizant of research findings indicating that students tend to achieve at cognitive levels no higher than the levels measured by their teachers' achievement tests (Stiggins, Conklin, & Bridgeford, 1986). Therefore, Nora examines several of Sheldon's mathematics tests to determine the cognitive levels of the items. To do this, she utilizes a two-way table of specifications (Cangelosi, 1982, pp. 243–51; 1990b, pp. 42–45; Cunningham, 1986, pp. 126–32; Gronlund, 1985, pp. 120–27). The results of those analyses as Nora presented them to Sheldon for discussion are contained in Figure 4.1.

Typically, analytical document examinations utilize instruments designed to focus the examiner's attention on the particular relationships or variables to be inferred. Appendix K contains an example of such an instrument. It was developed for the Tennessee Career Ladder Better Schools Program (Tennessee Department of Education, 1985) for the purpose of inferring data about teaching performance from an analytical examination of lesson plans.

Informal. Like informal classroom observations and interviews, informal document examinations are unplanned, almost accidental, measurements. Here is an example:

Tom Yamasaki has just dismissed his fourth-period English class when his department chair, Ory Banker, steps into his room:

ORY: Well how's your first week here going?

TOM: Hey, I love it! But some of the kids are a little nervous right now; they're taking their first test from me tomorrow.

ORY: Testing so soon?

TOM: Yep, here's a copy of the one I'm giving tomorrow.

ORY: May I keep a copy for my test files?

TOM: Sure, go ahead.

ORY: Thanks.

Later, Ory looks over Tom's test and thinks to himself, "This test is way above the students' capabilities. Tom must not be very realistic about the level he's working with. I'd better monitor the situation."

Appropriate Uses of Examinations of Teacher-Produced Documents

Relative to Teaching Competence. Be careful not to confuse *examinations of teacher-produced documents* with *teacher competency tests*. The former uses documents that are natural by-products of instruction. The latter also involves documents (e.g., a written-response test instrument), but with teacher competency tests, the teachers respond to situations *contrived* by test designers. Using Appendix K's instrument to analyze a lesson plan a teacher writes as a natural function of instruction is an example of *document examination*. Analyzing the lesson plan a teacher developed in response to a hypothetical situation described in a measurement item is an example of *teacher competency testing*.

Cognitive Level

Content Area	Simple Knowledge	Algorithm Skill	Compre- hension	Concept- ualization	Application	Points /Wt.
+ with whole nos.		〲 ////			/	10
	0	9	0	0	1	11%
− with whole nos.		〲〲 /			/	12
	0	11	0	0	1	13%
× with whole nos.		〲 〲 〲 / 〲 /	/		//	24
	0	21	1	0	2	27%
÷ with whole nos.		〲 //	//		/	10
	0	7	2	0	1	11%
+ & − with rationals	//		〲 /		///	11
	2	0	6	0	3	12%
× & ÷ with rationals	//		////	//	/	9
	2	0	4	2	1	10%
geometric relations	〲 //	/				8
	7	1	0	0	0	9%
measure- ment	/	//	//		/	6
	1	2	2	0	1	7%
Points /Wt.	12 13%	51 57%	15 17%	2 2%	10 11%	90 100%

Figure 4.1. Results of Nora's Analytical Document Examination of the Cognitive Levels of Sheldon's Third-Grade Mathematics Tests

With that distinction in mind, it seems that examining teacher-produced documents would *not* ordinarily be a cost-effective approach to measuring teaching competency.

Relative to Teaching Performance. As is exemplified by Nora's examination of Sheldon's tests and the use of Appendix K's instrument in the Tennessee Career Ladder Program, systematic examinations of teacher-produced documents can provide cost-effective measurements for the evaluation of teaching performance in the areas of *assessment of student achievement* and *planning for instruction.*

Nora also examined Sheldon's journal to complement her classroom observations. Teachers maintain journals as an ongoing, integral part of their efforts to improve their work with students (Healy, 1983; Kaplan, 1987). The practice facilitates reflective thinking about one's teaching (Arends, 1988, pp. 60, 70–71). Thus, examinations of journals as a data source should be limited for use with *formative, never* summative, evaluations. There are two reasons for this. First, teachers should be encouraged to write journals; unless they are assured that their words will not influence summative evaluations, they will not feel free to make open, honest entries in their journals. Second, journals provide an important data source for teachers to make formative evaluations about their own instruction. For reasons explained in Chapter 1, distinct separation should be maintained between formative and summative evaluative processes.

Relative to Student Outcomes. The use of teacher-produced student achievement test results is dealt with later in this chapter. Examinations of other teacher-produced documents are not generally cost-effective measurements of student outcomes. One possible exception may be the use of teachers' journals, provided the journal entries include descriptions of students' performances. The journals may be a particularly important source of information about unanticipated student outcomes that are not prescribed by lesson objectives. Here is an example:

As Sheldon skims through his journal from last year, he detects a trend in the chronological accounts of students' behaviors. The entries indicate that integration between the sexes during both work and play activities dramatically increased as the year progressed. He notes higher proportions of girls choosing science and athletic activities near the end of the year than at the beginning. Similarly, there was an increase in the number of boys choosing domestic activities (e.g., cooking and sewing) toward the latter half of the school year. The following day Sheldon discusses the finding with Nora:

SHELDON: I'm really pleased with these apparent changes in attitudes. But I'm curious as to what caused them. Was it just a maturing process or did I do something right I'm not aware of?

NORA: It doesn't have anything to do with their maturing. If you'd just observe yourself with the kids you'd see how you effect such changes. You don't refer to them as "boys" and "girls" like so many of our colleagues. You use nonsexist language. You. . . .

Common Misuses of Examinations of Teacher-Produced Documents

Because examinations of teacher-produced documents are not as commonly used as data sources for evaluations of instruction as are classroom observations, teacher competency tests, student achievement tests, or even interviews, their misuse is not as widespread as it is for these other sources.

One cause of misuse is *a misinterpretation of an information retrieval examination*. For example:

To help Artie Kinyo's principal understand what Artie has been doing for the past week in her home economics class, the principal reads the week's lesson plans that Artie passed on to him. He notes that virtually every one of Artie's objectives make some reference to "increasing students knowledge to. . . . " Consequently, he thinks, "Artie puts much too much emphasis on knowledge-level learning; there's hardly anything on understanding or application!"

Actually, Artie uses the word "knowledge" far more liberally than it is conventionally used in the educational literature. She wrote those objectives with what is conventionally called "conceptual" and "application" learning in mind, but she is unaccustomed to that vernacular.

Misuse can also stem from *an analytical examination with an ill-defined purpose and a poorly prepared examiner*. For example:

Margo Atwater is told she should analyze the cognitive levels of her tests with a two-way table of specifications (similar to Figure 4.1). She does so, but confuses *cognitive level* with *item difficulty*. Consequently, she categorizes items that students find "hard" as higher cognitive (e.g., "application") and easy items as low on the cognitive scale (e.g., "simple knowledge").

Third, *an informal examination can result in misleading, incomplete information*. For example:

To keep parents apprised about their children's activities in his health science class, Trevor Gall sends his students' parents a monthly newsletter (Cangelosi, 1988a, pp. 104–5). The newsletter is discussed in this conversation with Trevor's department head, Judy Fullerton:

JUDY: Apparently your newsletter is working out super.

TREVOR: Yeah, parents are showing more interest in what we're doing. Homework has improved. It's been great! The only problem is it's beginning to get expensive. Maxine [the principal] left me a note last week telling me I've exceeded my postage and duplicating allotment.

JUDY: But you're doing something special here. Does she know about the newsletter?

TREVOR: I don't know.

JUDY: Would you like me to make a pitch for you, get her to increase the allowance?

TREVOR: I'd appreciate that.

JUDY: Give me a newsletter to show her.

TREVOR: Here's the rough draft of the next one. But I haven't proofed it yet or even run it through my spell-check.

JUDY: That's okay, I'll explain that when I show it to her.

Judy goes to Maxine's office, but the principal isn't available. Judy leaves the following note attached to the draft of the letter for Maxine: "Maxine, call me so we can discuss the attached newsletter and how we can help Trevor foot the bill for sending them to parents.—Judy" Upon reading the note and its attachment, Maxine thinks, "Gracious! This newsletter is full of misspelled words and grammatical errors. I thought Trevor was more competent. He should know to be more careful with his communications for parents!"

A fourth misuse stems from *the use of the same results for both summative and formative evaluations.* For example:

In one of his undergraduate methods courses, Kohn Johnson learned to maintain a teacher's journal as a data source for making formative evaluations about his teaching. He mentioned this to his university supervisor when they first met at the beginning of Kohn's student teaching experience. At the time, the supervisor said, "Great! Reading your journal will help me determine your final grade for student teaching."

Now, in the midst of student teaching, the formative feedback intent of the journal is subverted. Kohn writes his journal for the purpose of impressing the university supervisor.

Selection, Development, and Validation

Information-retrieval document examinations involve no instruments or technical procedures requiring formal selection, development, and validation processes. Of course, informal examinations are, by definition, unsystematic and unplanned. However, you should keep fundamental principles of measurement validity in mind whenever determining how a document examination will impact an evaluation of instruction.

The instruments and processes used in analytical document examinations should be selected, developed, and validated via basically the same procedures that apply to structured classroom observation systems and structured interviews. However, documents are not dynamic as are classroom environments and interview subjects. Because they are stable and unaffected by the examination process, test–retest consistency is of no concern. But attention should be paid to relevance and to inter- and intra-examiner consistencies.

Training Examiners

Over a two-week period, Jan trained 12 teachers to use Appendix E's classroom observation instrument (see page 61). Ordinarily document examiners can be trained to focus on the relevant variables and follow the directions for an analytical examination with much less effort. For example, a teacher who is familiar with third-grade mathematics curricula and schemes for classifying cognitive learning levels (e.g., Bloom, 1984; Cangelosi, 1990b, pp. 8–13) can readily learn to analyze Sheldon's tests as Nora did when she produced Figure 4.1's results. The teacher would have to be provided with directions for (1) categorizing each test item according to its content area (e.g., + with whole numbers), (2) categorizing each test item according to its cognitive level (e.g., application), (3) tallying the number of items that fit each cell (e.g., the number of items testing students' conceptualization of ÷ with whole numbers), and (4) expressing the emphasis on each content area and cognitive level as a percent. In other words, educators who are familiar with fundamental pedagogical and evaluation principles need only specific directions and operational definitions to be able to conduct such an analytical document examination.

STUDENT ACHIEVEMENT AND APTITUDE TESTS

Types of Student Tests

Single-Score Achievement Tests. An achievement test is supposed to provide data relevant to students' standings with respect to a particular learning variable. The learning variable may be broad (e.g., how well students comprehend what they read) or more focused (e.g., how well students can apply the Pythagorean relationship to solve real-life problems).

The complexity of any learning variable necessitates that it be defined in terms of component parts. The variable *reading comprehension level*, for example, is dependent on a set of subvariables (e.g., how well students (1) decode, (2) recall word meanings, (3) identify main ideas, (4) make literal interpretations, (5) make inferential interpretations, and (6) make critical interpretations). For another example, the learning goal of *students being able to apply the Pythagorean relationship to the solution of real-life problems* may be defined in terms of specific objectives (e.g., students being able to (1) explain why $a^2 + b^2 = c^2$ for any right triangle with dimensions a and b for the legs and c for the hypotenuse, (2) recall that $a^2 + b^2 = c^2$, (3) determine whether or not solving for the length of the side of a right triangle is pertinent to the solution of a given real-life problem, and (4) use the Pythagorean relationship to compute the length of the third side of a right triangle when the lengths of the other two sides are known).

Although each individual item on an achievement test is designed to be relevant to a particular subvariable, a student's results from a *single-score achievement* test are summarized as a single number computed from item scores. It is hoped that the number reflects that student's standing in relation to the overall learning variable.

Diagnostic Achievement Tests. Diagnostic achievement tests are used to supply data relevant to students' progress regarding each individual subvariable subsumed by an overall learning variable. Thus, for each student, a diagnostic test produces a set of scores that may be used in identifying the specific objectives that need to be emphasized in subsequent learning activities.

Aptitude Tests. Student aptitude tests are used for predicting how well students can be expected to achieve goals in a particular area if they are provided with appropriate learning opportunities. Some aptitude tests are used to predict achievement in a single content area (e.g., *Test of Mathematical Abilities*, Mitchell, 1985, pp. 1578–79). Others are used to predict general school performance (e.g., *Otis-Lennon School Ability Test*, Mitchell, 1985, pp. 1106–12), and still others *claim* to measure general learning ability (e.g., *Wechsler Intelligence Scale for Children*, Mitchell, 1985, pp. 1707–22).

Teacher-Produced Tests. The vast majority of student achievement tests are designed and constructed by classroom teachers. Although most teachers appear inadequately prepared in the art of test development and the science of evaluating their students' achievements (Stiggins, 1988), teacher-produced tests are the most valid data sources available for assessing student achievement of classroom learning goals. Those teachers who are adept at measuring student achievement adhere to test-design principles (Cangelosi, 1990b, pp. 41–177) that are increasingly being introduced in preservice teacher preparation programs. Thus, there may be some cause for optimism regarding the future role of teacher-developed tests in processes for evaluating instruction.

Commercially Produced Tests. Achievement tests for general content areas (e.g., history and biology) at every grade level can be purchased from commercial publishers. Some of these tests accompany textbook series or are produced as part of curricula packages that can be purchased by school systems. Also there are the "big event" tests administered on a school-wide or district-wide basis once or twice a year. Although capable of providing some evidence of student achievement relative to broad general areas, big-event commercially produced tests are not designed to be relevant to the specific learning goals targeted by individual classroom teachers.

Standardized Tests. The more commonly known big-event commercially produced tests (e.g., *Stanford Achievement Tests, Metropolitan Achievement Tests*, and *California Achievement Tests*) are *standardized*. A standardized test is one that *has been field-tested for the purpose of assessing its reliability and establishing norms for use in interpreting its scores.*

The principal advantage of standardized tests is having these norms (e.g., means and standard deviations computed from the field-test results) to provide a uniform mechanism for comparing the scores of one group of students with those of another. Typically, scores from standardized test results are reported in terms of *derived scores* (e.g., percentiles, stanines, and scaled scores), which depend on how many items a student responds to correctly in comparison with the average number of correct items obtained by the field-test, comparison group.

Criterion-Referenced Tests. In the mid-1970s many school districts began supplementing their standardized testing programs with big-event criterion-referenced tests. Whereas standardized test scores are interpreted in light of norms established by scores from field-test groups, criterion-referenced test standards are based on operational definitions of "success" and "failure" independent of test takers' performances. For example:

In response to a State Office of Education mandate for local school districts to implement the "Core Curriculum Goals" that had been recently adopted by the State Board of Education, the East City School District's Evaluation Division undertook the task of developing criterion-referenced tests aimed at those state-mandated goals. The division hired teams of teachers, working with measurement specialists, to develop a test for each subject area included in the core curriculum (i.e., language arts, mathematics, science, social studies, and physical education) by grade level. Over the course of a year, each team completed the following for its assigned subject and grade level:

1. Clarified each of the assigned core curriculum goals and agreed to the following criteria for students' levels of achievement of that goal:
   a. "Mastery" is defined as having responded correctly to at least 80 percent of the items pertaining to the goal.
   b. "Partial-mastery" is defined as a correct response rate of between 50 and 80 percent to those items.
   c. "Nonmastery" is defined as a correct response rate of 50 percent or less to those items.
2. Developed an item pool for each goal.
3. Reviewed, field-tested, and refined the item pools.
4. Synthesized the test.
5. Established a scoring and reporting format so that for each goal each student receives a score labeled "mastery," or "partial-mastery," or "nonmastery."
6. Field-tested, assessed the reliability of, and refined the test.

The tests are now in place. Some teachers fear the test results will be used for summative evaluations of teaching while others embrace the test as an opportunity for obtaining formative feedback useful to them and their instructional supervisors.

Appropriate Uses of Student Tests

Any uses of student achievement or aptitude test results for evaluating instruction are obviously limited to *student outcome* variables. The drawbacks of focusing on student outcomes as a basis for *summative* evaluations of teaching were alluded to in Chapter 1 and are summarized here:

1. Student outcomes are significantly influenced by factors that teachers cannot control.
2. Often student achievement tests lack satisfactory levels of validity.
3. Often-used statistical methods either for computing gains between post- and pre-achievement tests or for comparing results from different tests are untenable.
4. Teachers are encouraged to limit their curricula to the student performances upon which their instruction will be evaluated.

On the other hand, measures of student outcomes in the form of student achievement tests, especially diagnostic, criterion-referenced tests, can be valuable data sources for *formative* evaluations of instruction. For example:

Nora and Sheldon are discussing the results of a diagnostic test recently administered to Nora's third graders:

SHELDON: Most of them really did well on the items on distinguishing plant life from animal life.

NORA: I'm not surprised; we've been hitting that hard lately. But, do you see how much better they did with the comprehension-level items than they did with the application ones?

SHELDON: That surprises me. For this kind of material, application learning usually follows right along with comprehension! What do you think went wrong?

NORA: I don't know. Maybe I need to use more of a deductive structure once we get by comprehension.

SHELDON: Could be. But I see where Margo and Casey got all of the application-level items.

NORA: Those two are going to achieve the higher cognitive-level objectives with or without help. On the other hand, . . .

Common Misuses of Student Tests

Unfortunately, misuse of student achievement and aptitude test scores in instructional evaluation programs is widespread (Cangelosi, 1982, pp. 346–49, 356–60; Popham, 1982; Soar, Medley, & Coker, 1983). The following scenario includes examples of the more common types of abuse:

The Oil County School District Office selected a standardized achievement test battery and a standardized aptitude test for its long-range, system-wide testing program. Initially the tests were used only for monitoring progress and as an aid in identifying students for special programs (e.g., gifted or Chapter I). However, recent demands for school accountability and productivity reports by both local and state-level politicians led the Oil County School Board to extend use of the tests into the process for evaluating instruction. The board passed a policy mandating that teachers' merit raises and decisions regarding retention of teachers be dependent on the standardized achievement test scores of their students.

The local teachers' union contested the policy as being unfair because of the extreme variance existing among the students of different teachers. A compromise was worked out so that the achievement test score gains upon which each teacher's effectiveness would be judged would be adjusted by a measure of that teacher's students' aptitudes.

A procedure was ultimately implemented for each teacher: At the beginning of the school year, the teacher's students are administered both the achievement test battery and the aptitude test. Achievement test results are reported in the form of grade-equivalent scores (Cangelosi, 1990b, pp. 191–92; Hills, 1986, pp. 2, 8). Aptitude test results are reported in terms of deviation IQ scores (Cangelosi, 1982, p. 356) that a district office statistician/computer programmer converted to "expected gain in grade equivalent months" scores. The mean of this pretest of student achievement (μ(pre)) and the mean of the students' "expected gain" scores (μ(exp)) are then computed. Near the end of the school year, the teacher's students are re-administered the standardized achievement test. The mean of this post-test is computed (μ(post)). The teacher's "effectiveness" score (*TE*) is computed as follows:

$$TE - [\mu(pos) - \mu(pre)] \div \mu(exp).$$

The greater *TE*, the more likely the teacher is to receive a merit pay raise or be retained in the district. Moreover, if $TE \geq 1$, the teacher's effectiveness is considered highly satisfactory.

After two years, the school board rescinded the policy after a number of knowledgeable teachers, supervisors, and, surprisingly, high school students publicly demonstrated several facts. First, some teachers had been subverting the process by discouraging students from scoring high on the achievement pretests and the aptitude tests, then teaching to the post-tests and limiting their curricula to material covered by the test. Second, the validities of both the achievement and aptitude tests are questionable. Finally, the method for computing *TE*s violates fundamental principles of sound measurement and statistical practice (e.g., because of the way the scores are scaled, subtracting two grade equivalents leads to distorted results and consequent misleading information, Cangelosi, 1982, pp. 356–61; Medley, Coker, & Soar, 1984, pp. 36–39).

Selection, Development, and Validation

Unlike classroom observational, interview, and document examination measurements, student tests are not ordinarily selected, developed, or validated specifically for purposes of evaluating instruction. As was illustrated by the example of Nora and Sheldon and the Oil County School District example, evaluating instruction is only a secondary use of tests of student achievement or aptitude. Therefore such tests have already been selected or developed for other purposes (e.g., for decisions about student placement) before they are used in an evaluation of instruction. For purposes of evaluating instruction, the question is not which student test to use or how to develop it; the question is whether or not existing student test results are valid for use in the particular evaluation of instruction that is to be conducted.

Numerous references are available that describe how to assess the validity of a student achievement or aptitude test (e.g., Berk, 1984a, 1984b; Cangelosi, 1982, pp. 243–53, 255–307, 309–40; Ebel & Frisbie, 1986, pp. 70–88; Everitt, 1988; Hambleton & Swaminathan, 1985, pp. 1–52, 225–309; Kubiszyn & Borich, 1987, pp. 243–53, 291–301).

TEACHER COMPETENCY TESTS

A Historical Caveat

Between the seventeenth and twentieth centuries, teacher competency tests were the dominant mechanism for preventing "illiterates" and "fools," but hardly anyone else, from becoming teachers (Vold, 1985). In the first few years of the 1900s, educational reformers urged that professional preparation in quality normal schools should supplant teacher competency tests as the primary means by which people become teachers (Cubberley, 1906, p. 76). The shift in emphasis from testing to preparation appeared complete by the end of the first quarter of the century. However, as Vold (1985, pp. 6–7) states:

> In 1940, the American Council on Education established the *National Teacher Exam* (NTE). In what appears to be the second verse of an old song, Evan Collins (1940) welcomed this development in an editorial in the *Harvard Educational Review*, noting, "such examinations should do much to indicate those academic illiterates who too often become 'teachers,' and should . . . supply a crying need for an effective bulwark against the persistent meddling of petty local politicians" (p. 4).
>
> With the introduction of the NTE in 1940, teacher testing had come full circle. Whereas teacher exams had once been eliminated in the name of reform, now they were reintroduced in the name of reform. This record ought to serve as a flashing yellow light to the teacher testing movement. On the one hand, the competency test will cut out illiterates and fools, but it does not guarantee that all who pass are competent. Moreover, it might cut out some who, far from being incompetent, are just different.

Virtually all states either have teacher competency testing programs in place or are having such programs considered by legislators or state office of education officials. Since 1980, there has been an increase in the number of states where one or more of the following are dependent on the results of teacher competency tests (Lehman & Phillips, 1987; Rudner, 1988):

- Admittance of individuals into teacher preparation programs
- State approval of college and university teacher preparation programs
- Certification of individual teachers
- Contract renewals of certified teachers

Types of Teacher Competency Tests

Standardized Tests. Typically, state-mandated teacher competency tests are standardized (i.e., they have been field-tested for the purpose of assessing reliability and establishing norms for interpreting scores). Both nationally distributed (e.g., The *National Teacher Examinations* [NTE] [Mitchell, 1985, pp. 1063–70], *Pre-Professional Skills Tests* [Mitchell, 1985, pp. 1187–89], *California Basic Educational Skills Test* [Dimock, 1985], *California Achievement Tests* [Mitchell, 1985, pp. 242–48]) and locally developed (e.g., in Florida, Oklahoma, and Georgia [Flippo & Foster, 1984; "Testing for Teacher," 1982]) standardized tests are used. The best known of these, the NTE, is described by Cross (1985, p. 7):

> The NTE tests include a Core Battery of three tests plus a series of 26 Specialty Area tests, 18 of which focus on entry-level teaching specialties requiring no graduate studies. Educational Testing Services (ETS) describes these tests as objective, standardized measures of knowledge and skills developed in academic programs for the preparation of teachers. The Core Battery, introduced in the fall of 1982 as a replacement to the common examinations, contains three tests: Communication Skills, General Knowledge, and Professional Knowledge. Because NTE tests were not specifically constructed as certification tests, any state wishing to use them for that purpose must conduct a state-wide validity study. Using scores from these tests for certification decisions without conducting a validity study would constitute improper use of these tests, according to the NTE Policy Board, and would likely be challenged in court.

In the face of the increasing use of standardized teacher competency tests is the unnerving fact that studies examining the validities of these instruments do not support their use as bases for evaluating the abilities of individuals to teach (Ayers, 1988; Cross, 1985; Popham, 1988, pp. 278–79; Smith, 1984). The NTE have consistently failed in predictive validity studies relative both to teaching performance as measured via classroom observations and to student outcomes as measured by standardized achievement tests (Soar, Medley, & Coker, 1983).

Basic Literacy and Arithmetic Skills Tests. The publicizing of instances in which teachers appeared unskilled in the use of basic language arts and arithmetic (e.g., "Help! Teachers Can't," 1980; Williams, Howard, McDonald, & Renee, 1984) has hastened a return to the seventeenth-century purpose of teacher competency testing: screening "illiterates" and "fools." Basic skills testing (e.g., *The Texas Examination of Current Administrators and Teachers* [Shepard & Kreitzer, 1987]) comprises a major part of the majority of state-mandated teacher competency testing programs (Dimock, 1985, pp. 2–9).

Teacher Attitude and Personality Tests. "Competency" is typically associated with one's ability to perform. "Attitudes" (i.e., affective behaviors) and "personality traits" are associated with what one feels, believes, appreciates, desires, and is willing to try. So ordinarily, *competencies* (i.e., what people are capable of doing) do not include attitudes (i.e., what people value doing). However, the complex art of teaching is inextricably dependent on personality traits, beliefs, desires, and motivations of teachers (Fox & Peck, 1978; Levis, 1987). Thus, competency testing for teachers subsumes attitude and personality testing.

Standardized tests (e.g. *A Teacher Attitude Inventory* [Conoley, Kramer, & Mitchell, 1988, pp. 212–26], *Minnesota Teacher Attitude Inventory* [Cook, Leeds, & Callis, 1951], *Educational Attitudes Inventory* [Bunting, 1981], and the *Minnesota Multiphasic Personality Inventory* [Mitchell, 1985, pp. 995–1011]) that are designed to measure some of the attitudes and personality traits thought to be associated with effective teaching (e.g., enthusiasm, concern for children, and decisiveness) are data sources incorporated into the hiring processes of some school districts. Some teacher preparation programs also factor the results of such tests into evaluations about preservice teachers' readiness to student teach. Unfortunately, teacher attitude and personality tests are dominated by self-report items and tend to fare poorly in validation assessments (Levis, 1987).

Nonstandardized Tests. Nonstandardized tests dominate measures of teaching competency in teacher preparation programs. Such tests often require preservice teachers to respond to hypothetical situations in which they are assigned instructional tasks. For example:

To test her preservice teachers' competencies to utilize alternative learning activities in response to students' misbehaviors during first-option learning activities (Cangelosi, 1988a, pp. 202–3), an education professor includes the following items on a test:

1. Within the domain of your teaching specialization, write one learning objective that you conceivably might target for a class of 25 students.
2. In a paragraph, describe an appropriate learning activity you might use for helping those 25 students achieve that learning objective.
3. In another paragraph, describe an alternative learning activity you might conceivably turn to when a significant portion of the 25 students choose not to cooperate with you during the original learning activity.

To test their competencies to utilize high-level questioning strategies (Arends, 1988, pp. 289–91), an education professor directs preservice teachers to prepare either a conceptual or application-level 10-minute microteaching lesson (MacLeod, 1987; Perlberg, 1987) for a group of peers. The professor scores the lesson according to criteria for conducting effective high-level questioning sessions.

Appropriate Uses of Teacher Competency Tests

Teacher competency tests obviously do not apply to evaluations of instruction that focus on either teaching performance or student outcome variables. Results of validation studies of currently available standardized teacher competency tests should discourage anyone from using them as a tool for summative evaluations of the competency of an *individual* teacher. However, work is under way that one day may lead to competency tests that will provide cost-effective data sources for use in concert with other types of teacher competency measures (Cangelosi, 1988b; Carlson, Pecheone, Stanley, & Popham, 1989; Cole, 1987; Haertel, 1987). Presently, the uses of teaching competency tests should be limited to certain situations. For example, specific competencies of preservice teachers (e.g., ability to use high-level questioning strategies) should be assessed during teacher preparation programs and as a precondition for progressing to the next stage of the program (e.g., for approval to student teach); nonstandardized tests, designed specifically for the targeted competencies of teacher preparation programs and often employing performance items (e.g., microteaching), are necessary for such assessments. Further, although standardized tests have not proven to be valid for the evaluation of the teaching competency of *individual* teachers (Popham, 1988, pp. 278–79), they may provide tenable data sources for research studies comparing the general competence of one *group* of teachers to that of another (Nelson, 1985).

Another example can be seen in one of the career ladder programs in Utah, in which teachers have the option of taking standardized teacher competency tests as one mechanism for demonstrating their abilities. Peterson (1987, p. 20), in a report on these programs, argues:

> Teacher evaluation systems that use multiple and variable lines of evidence of teacher performance (Peterson, 1984; Peterson & Mitchell, 1985) create an opportunity for optional use of individual lines of evidence. This innovation in teacher evaluation enables districts to use controversial sources of data. Multiple judges or sources of information have been acknowledged as a way of increasing fairness in decision making (Epstein, 1985). In optional use systems, teacher tests are not used for minimal protection, but for acknowledgment of quality in certain teachers. Legal precedent also suggests the optional use of tests as one source of source of information about teacher quality.

The Master Teacher Program in Florida (Fisher, Fry, Loewe, & Wilson, 1985) is among merit-play plans that have utilized standardized teacher competency tests as one of several data sources.

Common Misuses of Teacher Competency Tests

A cost-effective test for overall teacher competence would be the ideal data source for use in decisions regarding the hiring and retention of teachers. Not only is such an instrument nonexistent, however, but research does not clearly indicate what constructs should be measured by a test of competency to teach. In spite of test invalidity and lessons of history, standardized teacher competency test results nevertheless continue to influence decisions regarding teacher certification, hiring, and retention. Current trends suggest that this misuse will spread before further research and development efforts offer relief.

Selection, Development, and Validation

Cost-effectiveness is the basis upon which any test should be selected and is the attribute it should be designed to exhibit. Models for selecting and developing cost-effective tests are presented in the educational and psychological measurement literature (e.g., Berk, 1984b; Cangelosi, 1990a; Kubiszyn & Borich, 1987). Reference sources for validating tests were given near the end of the previous section on student achievement and aptitude tests.

QUESTIONNAIRES

Written-Response Interviews

Questionnaires, like interviews, are designed to elicit information and opinions from individuals. Questionnaires tend to be more usable than interviews in that they can be concurrently administered to a large group of persons and do not depend on the availability of expert interviewers. However, in the hands of an expert interviewer, interviews tend to be more valid because during interviews it is easier to use probing questions, use branching items, clarify questions, and clarify responses. Because questionnaires do not provide these opportunities, questionnaire items tend to address more superficial questions and require greater attention to wording in order to reduce ambiguity.

Types of Questionnaires

Examiner Opinion. Examiner-opinion questionnaires are used to focus the communication of an evaluation. Here is an example:

As part of Hillyard School District's summative evaluation program for beginning teachers, teachers from neighboring school districts are hired and trained to utilize measurement instruments (e.g., ones similar to those appearing in Appendices C, E, and H) in classroom observations, interviews, and document examinations for Hillyard's first-year teachers. After making a number of these measurements, each examining teacher communicates his or her summative evaluation regarding the respective beginning teacher's performance by completing the questionnaire appearing in Appendix L.

Student Opinion. A teacher can hardly keep from being influenced by the informal, unsolicited feedback provided by students. But should the opinions of those whom instruction is supposed to serve also be formally solicited for use in evaluations of that instruction? At the college level, *student-opinion questionnaires* are the most commonly used data source for summative evaluations of instruction (Franklin, 1989; Marques, Lane, & Dorfman, 1979; Marsh, 1989). Results from carefully designed questionnaires consistently correlate positively with measures of college student achievement and classroom observations of college teaching performance (Aubrecht, 1981; Marsh & Overall, 1980). If student-opinion questionnaires prove to be a cost-effective data source in the evaluation of college instruction, it can be argued that they should be used at least as one of a number of data sources at the elementary and secondary levels (Haefele, 1980).

Any argument favoring the use of such questionnaires depends on the existence of cost-effective instruments that are administered so that neither students nor teachers feel threatened by the process. Appendices M and N contain examples of student-opinion questionnaires that were systematically developed for use at two universities.

Descriptive. Particularly useful for formative evaluations are questionnaires that elicit information about events, circumstances, and activities rather than opinions. Here is an example:

Byron Johnson engaged his civics students in a lesson in which they searched for and reviewed publications and videotaped news programs relative to the issue of gun control, presented information and points of view on the issue to the class, and debated the issue. The goal for the activity was for the students to learn how to locate information, how to use systematic argumentation, and how controversial issues are addressed in political arenas. To help him evaluate how well the activity involved students in the experiences in which he hoped it would, Byron administered the descriptive questionnaire appearing in Appendix O.

Appropriate Uses of Questionnaires

Relevant to Teaching Competence. Questionnaires should hardly be considered a primary data source for evaluating teaching competence. However, examiner-opinion questionnaires can provide a vehicle by which expert judges communicate evaluations of teaching competence that they based on measurement results from classroom observations, interviews, document examinations, tests, and other data sources.

Relevant to Teaching Performance. Designing and developing cost-effective questionnaires require creativity, skill, and appropriate field-testing. Questionnaires that have been properly developed (unfortunately, most are not) can be extremely valuable tools in certain situations. For example, suppose a number of evaluations regarding specific aspects of teaching performance are to be factored into single, broad evaluation of teaching performance. Examiner-opinion questionnaires can be used to record and communicate evaluations about the specific aspects. Then the questionnaire results influence the broad evaluation as if they were measurements. In a previous example, Appendix L's instrument is used in this way in Hillyard School District's summative evaluation program for beginning teachers.

Another example is found in Appendix O, which shows an instrument by which students provide their teachers with formative feedback. Similarly, students provide teachers and supervisors with summative feedback using instruments such as the ones in Appendices M and N.

Relevant to Student Outcomes. Conventional data sources for student outcome variables (i.e., written-response achievement tests and observations of student performances) can be supplemented with questionnaires soliciting students' descriptions of what they learned. Such questionnaires are especially valuable as indicators of student outcome variables exclusive of achievement of stated learning goals. For example:

As she embarks on the beginning of another school year, Ann Givens-Bell thinks to herself, "Every year I collect data on how well my first graders learn to read, communicate, think mathematically, get along, and other academic stuff from curricula. But I wonder if I tend to turn these little folks *on* or *off* to school."

To help her address this question, Ann administers Appendix P's questionnaire to her first graders in the first week and again in the twelfth week of school. She uses the differences in the two sets of results in evaluating whether her students' attitudes toward school are improving, degenerating, or remaining about the same.

Common Misuses of Questionnaires

Relative to evaluating instruction, the more common misuses of questionnaires occur because questionnaire items are ambiguously worded, because subjects do not conscientiously respond to items, because the evaluation variables are not well-defined and consequently the questionnaire does not fit the purpose for which it is being used, or because evaluators overrely on the questionnaire results (especially at the college level).

Ambiguously Worded Items. The bane of questionnaires is the varying ways respondents interpret an item. Words that have not been operationally defined are a major source of ambiguity. For example:

An examiner-opinion questionnaire includes the following item: "Did this teacher display *professional* behavior in his/her contacts with you?"

In response to this item, one respondent thinks, for one teacher, "Yes, he always dressed neatly with a tie in front of the students. He always stood erect, spoke politely, and was very respectful to me."

Another respondent interprets the term "professional" quite differently and responds to the item with these thoughts, "She behaved professionally alright, focusing on the needs of students, describing their activities and behaviors to me without ever labeling or characterizing anyone. She conscientiously maintained confidences and she's intently interested in advancing the causes of teachers."

Ill-defined standards are the source of ambiguity in the following example:

Embedded in an examiner-opinion questionnaire is a rating scale in which examiners are to classify the instructional strategies displayed by a student teacher as either "well above average," "somewhat above average," . . . , "well below average." One respondent visualizes "average" to be typical of in-service teachers. Another uses the strategies of other student teachers' behaviors as the standard.

Unconscientious Respondents. Having words like "professional" and "average" operationally defined relieves respondents from the burden of reading meanings into items. However, some are unwilling to take the time to read the explanations and carefully follow directions. Frankly, they are used to thoughtlessly filling out poorly designed instruments and are unmotivated to deal with the detail of unambiguously worded items. A college student who feels positive toward an instructor may quickly circle all the 5s on Appendix M's instrument without even bothering to read the items. A disgruntled student may circle all 1s without paying attention to the items' wording.

Some may respond dishonestly. For example, a nonassertive supervisor may rate a teacher's performance high on an examiner-opinion questionnaire either to avoid having to defend a negative evaluation, to gain the favor of the teacher, or to protect the feelings of that teacher. Or, on Appendix O's questionnaire a student might exaggerate the amount of time spent on the assignment in an attempt to win Mr. Johnson's favor.

Ill-Defined Purpose and Irrelevant Questionnaires. Unfortunately, the following example is not uncommon:

A university's Faculty Senate and its Student Government Association issue a joint position paper arguing that instructors should be held accountable for the quality of their teaching. Peter Minahan, Dean of Academic Affairs, responds by assembling a task force (consisting of a faculty representative from each college, an undergraduate student, and a graduate student) to develop a "student evaluation questionnaire" to be used university-wide. Here is a portion of the conversation from the task force's initial meeting:

MARGO: I think we should have a question about availability of the instructor. I hear a lot of students complaining that they can never find instructors when they need them!

WILMA: I agree, but let's not forget fairness of tests; that's another one we always hear about.

PETER: Okay, so we'll ask those two questions. How do you want to word them?

BRIMLEY: I favor Likert (1932) scale items. They're easily quantified and lend. . . .

After a lively start, the construction of the questionnaire bogs down by the fifth meeting. A questionnaire is eventually developed but the question of what evaluations were to be influenced by its results was never addressed in the process. The instrument could never be validated because the question, "Valid for what purpose?" was never answered.

What could a questionnaire possibly measure if those that designed it had no clearly defined evaluation variables in mind? The following anecdote occurred because a questionnaire failed to focus respondents' attention on prespecified variables:

Phil, a professor, and Elena, one of his former students, have the following conversation:

ELENA: I took only two courses this past semester.

PHIL: How did they go?

ELENA: Dr. Watkins' course was excellent! He's a wonderful teacher, so pleasant and organized. The class really enjoyed him.

PHIL: And what did you learn from Watkins' course?

ELENA: Gee!—That's a tough question.—I never really thought about that before.—I can't really pinpoint anything we learned, but I gave him the very highest possible ratings on the evaluation form.

PHIL: What about the other course you took?

ELENA: A real bore! Dr. Rainer taught that one. He's as dry as they come! I really gave him low ratings.

PHIL: I'm sorry to hear it was such a waste of time for you. Didn't you. learn anything?

ELENA: Oh, I found out a lot about contemporary literature. Actually, I've already used quite a bit from Rainer's class.

Overreliance. Reliance on student-opinion questionnaire results as the sole data source for summative evaluations of instruction spawn deplorable abuses. For example, instructors may feel compelled to court favorable student responses. One assistant professor remarked, "I'll be generous with grades and entertaining in class until I achieve tenure, then I'll start being an effective teacher."

Another problem is that student-opinion questionnaires are used for both summative and formative evaluations of instruction. Thus, as was indicated previously, the formative function is subverted. For example, a student may be reluctant to include constructive criticism among questionnaire responses out of fear that the comments will be used against the instructor whom he personally likes. Or, suppose the standard student-opinion questionnaire used at a university includes space for instructors to add their own items (e.g., at the end of Appendix N's instrument); one professor might like to include some questions that would help her gain some insights on improving her teaching, but she does not add them to the questionnaire out of fear that they could have a negative impact on summative evaluations of her instruction. Another danger involved in the use of student-opinion questionnaires is that some administrators and faculty members might take comfort in the fact that some evaluative process is in place and thus feel they can neglect developing and implementing a more comprehensive approach that includes other data sources.

Selection, Development, and Validation

A wide variety of student-opinion questionnaires used in evaluating instruction at the college level are available (e.g., see Weimer, Parrett, & Kerns, 1988). Selection of such instruments should be based on their cost-effective qualities which, most importantly, include the congruence between items and the prespecified variables to be evaluated. Virtually any other type of questionnaire for use in evaluating instruction will need to be developed.

Resource references for developing cost-effective questionnaires are available (e.g., Berdie, 1986; Converse, 1986; Sudman & Bradburn, 1982). In general, the stages of questionnaire development should be as follows:

1. The purpose of the evaluation is clarified by defining the evaluation variables. Typically, questionnaires are not single-score instruments, and thus there is no need to weight subvariables as would be done for a test or classroom observation that produces an overall score.
2. Characteristics of the respondents and the circumstances under which the questionnaire will be administered are considered. For example, the attention spans and reading and listening comprehension levels of first graders were taken into account when Appendix P's questionnaire was developed. The perceived threats to both college instructors and students of an end-of-the-course questionnaire were considered when Appendix M's instrument was developed.
3. Specifications to be considered in the design of the instrument are formulated. The following are determined: (a) item format (i.e., (i) what combination of short-answer, multiple-choice, rating scale, checklist, ranking scale, or essay features will be incorporated in the items and (ii) how items will be presented, e.g., orally or in print); (b) number of items per variable to be measured; (c) whether or not individual responses are to be confidential; (d) how the instrument will be administered (e.g., individually, in a group setting, or by mail); and (e) how the results will be compiled and reported.
4. For each variable, a pool of several items is drafted.
5. Informal field tests of the items are conducted by administering them to several subjects comparable to targeted respondents, asking subjects to share their thoughts as they respond to the items, and then interviewing them regarding item clarity and usability.
6. The item pools are revised in light of the informal field tests.
7. A list of the variables, the questionnaire specifications, and the item pools

are submitted to a panel consisting of representatives of persons who will be involved in using the questionnaire and specialists in the evaluation of instruction for review and feedback regarding the relevance of the items.
   8. Again, the item pools are modified.
   9. Adhering to the specifications and drawing from the item pools, directions are written and the questionnaire is synthesized.
   10. The instrument is administered to a field-test group for the purpose of discovering ways to improve cost-effectiveness. Consistency between responses to items from the same item pool is examined and field-test subjects are interviewed regarding clarity of directions.
   11. The questionnaire is finalized.

   The principal threats to the validity of questionnaires are mismatches between items and evaluation variables, ambiguously worded items, and unconscientious respondents. Mitigating these weaknesses during questionnaire development is the goal of the 11 aforementioned stages. Validating a questionnaire typically involves documenting how it was developed.

ANECDOTAL RECORDS

An *anecdotal record* is a written account of an extraordinary event, often placed in a personnel file. Here are two examples:

With the leadership of their teacher, Len Rice, fifth graders organize a school-wide mock election of community officials. The activity holds the interest of students throughout the school for two weeks. Recognizing benefits derived from Len's efforts, the principal writes a description of the project and, with Len's permission, inserts it into Len's personnel file.

Just as Principal Allison Heinemann glances into Edmond Krause's social studies room she hears a student, Josh, say to Edmond, "I'm not doing this work; you can just stick it!" She then sees Edmond grab Josh by the back of the neck, stand him up, and, still holding on, say, "You want me to stick it! Well what if I stick you right through that window? You don't seem so tough right now! What have you got to say now? . . . Nothing, eh? I didn't think you would, tough guy!"

Josh sheepishly sits down as Edmond lets him go and then sees Allison at the door. He walks over to her, and they step into the hall just out of the room and have the following conversation:

   EDMOND: Josh mouthed off in front of the class, but I think he's learned a lesson.
   ALLISON: Would you please stop by my office to talk about this during your planning period today?
   EDMOND: Sure, just as fourth period begins.

Allison goes directly to her office and describes in writing exactly what she observed during the exchange between Edmond and Josh.

The conversation during their fourth-period meeting includes the following:

ALLISON: Here's an account of what I observed going on in your room today. Please read it and tell me if it's accurate.''

EDMOND: (After reading) That's exactly what happened and I'm sorry it did. But I can't allow a kid to challenge me like that in front of the class.

ALLISON: Now that you've had some time to think about it, do you think you handled it well?

EDMOND: I don't know, I guess I could have. . . .

The conversation continues for another 22 minutes and then concludes on this note:

ALLISON: Because I'm confident that you understand you have no right to grab a student like that and that you will work with me on how to defuse conflicts, I'm not going to censure you. However, I'd like you to write a note at the bottom of this anecdotal account of what I observed, either attesting to its accuracy or indicating where it's in error. I'll place this in your confidential file. It'll be removed at the end of the school year provided no similar incidents occur in the meantime.

Anecdotal records are inherently unsystematic and thus should be interpreted as incomprehensive, unreliable data sources for evaluations of instruction. However, having written accounts of extraordinary events may prevent overreliance on what is remembered from informal observations.

TRANSLATING MEASUREMENT PRINCIPLES INTO PRACTICE

Having examined principles for selecting, designing, and validating measurements, it is time to attend to the business of applying those principles to specific situations in which instruction needs to be evaluated. Models applicable to formative evaluations of instruction are presented and illustrated in Chapters 5 and 6. Chapters 7–10 deal with applications for summative evaluations relative to the status of beginning teachers, the advancement of expert teachers, the retention of marginal teachers, and research studies.

SELF-ASSESSMENT EXERCISES FOR CHAPTER 4

I. Explain in one or two sentences the advantages and disadvantages of each of the following types of data sources for summative evaluations of the subvariables you identified in your response to Exercise V of the self-assessment for Chapter 2:

   A. Structured classroom observations
   B. Ethnographic classroom observations
   C. Closed-structure interviews with the teacher
   D. Open-structure interviews with the teacher
   E. Examinations of teacher-produced documents
   F. Student achievement tests
   G. Standardized teacher competency tests
   H. Student-opinion questionnaires
   I. Anecdotal records
II. For the teaching situation you recalled for Exercise V for Chapter 2, what is one area of your teaching on which you would have most welcomed formative feedback? Design a cost-effective measurement that would have provided formative feedback relative to that area. Design a plan for validating that measurement. Have someone who has also read Chapters 1–4 critique your measurement and validation plan.

PART II
Formative Methods

CHAPTER 5

Analyzing a Complex Art

Goal of Chapter 5

Chapter 5 suggests how *formative* evaluations of instruction can be divorced from *summative* evaluations so they can be used for instructional supervision without threatening the cooperative relationships and openness of communication between teachers and instructional supervisors. Chapter 5 also presents a model for subdividing teacher responsibilities into manageable components for the purpose of providing teachers with formative feedback. Specifically, this chapter is designed to help you:

1. Describe some practical methods for maintaining separation between formative and summative evaluations of instruction.
2. Explain the futility of addressing overall teaching performances with formative evaluations, and thus the necessity for formative evaluations to focus on specific aspects of instruction.
3. Categorize examples of instructional responsibilities according to the following scheme: (a) organizing for instruction, (b) managing resources, (c) managing time, (d) developing curricula, (e) determining learning goals, (f) designing lessons, (g) managing student behavior, (h) conducting lessons and engaging students in learning activities, and (i) assessing student achievement.
4. Originate and describe examples in which specific teacher-controlled variables are targeted for formative evaluation purposes.

INSTRUCTIONAL SUPERVISION

Cooperative Partnership

Instructional supervision is the art of helping teachers effectively instruct their students (Cooper, 1984a, pp. 1–2). People unfamiliar with current research-based instructional supervision principles (e.g., those forwarded by Acheson & Gall [1987], Glickman [1985], Harris [1985; 1989], Oliva [1989], and Sergiovanni & Starratt [1983]) tend to retain the outmoded view that supervisors should help teachers the way master artisans help novices ply their trade. The master–novice model casts supervisors in roles in which they not only hold some administrative authority over teachers but are also expected to be more knowledgeable about instruction than the teachers themselves. However, the complexities of teaching render such a model dysfunctional for purposes of instructional supervision. What constitutes effective instructional practice depends on a complex of factors unique for each teacher and teaching situation. No supervisor can understand these factors and the teacher's thinking well enough to be helpful unless a cooperative, non-threatening teacher–supervisor partnership has been established.

Openness

The principal in the following example serves as an effective instructional supervisor because he and his teachers cooperatively share responsibility for improving instruction:

Lynn Smith is beginning to realize that she needs to emphasize application-level learning with her sixth-grade mathematics students to a far greater degree than she has in the past, but she feels ill-prepared to do so. She is unsure how the curriculum's topics (e.g., rational numbers, inequalities, and polygons) can be applied in real-world situations. She approaches her principal, Ron O'Connell:

LYNN: All the mindless textbook computations and word problems we do seem to be turning my students off. I'm really worried that I'm losing them; they're learning to hate math!

RON: Give me an example of what you're talking about.

LYNN: You should have seen the bored looks on their faces today when I was showing them how to find the least common multiples of two whole numbers. I need to excite them with real-life situations where this stuff applies, but I just can't come up with any!

RON: Math isn't my field, but there are bound to be some resources we can call on. Isn't there a professional organization for math teachers that publishes materials addressing concerns like yours?

LYNN: Oh! You mean the one that. . . .

Lynn and Ron go on to work out a plan in which she will identify pertinent reference materials (e.g., booklets and videotapes available from the National Council of Teachers of Mathematics) for the school district to add to its resource library and also will use one of her "professional-leave" days to observe and visit with teachers at other schools who may be conducting application-level lessons in their classrooms.

But many teachers and administrators would argue that Ron's relationship with his faculty is atypical because principals' roles in *summative* evaluations of instruction preclude the kind of open exchange enjoyed by Lynn and Ron. The following may better reflect what occurs in most schools:

Julie Hanks is beginning to realize that she needs to emphasize application-level learning with her sixth-grade mathematics students to a far greater degree than she has in the past, but she feels ill-prepared to do so. She is unsure how the curriculum's topics are applicable in real-world situations. Concerned that her position at the school might be compromised if Principal Leona Hoefeinheimer found out about this inadequacy, Julie does not share her concern. Rather, she adds this to her list of private worries.

Freedom to Make Mistakes

Effective instructional supervision is unlikely wherever teachers feel compelled to appear "perfect" and are reluctant to risk making mistakes. The teacher in the following example is unlikely to improve his instruction as long as he feels that trying new approaches places his reputation at risk:

Bob Griffith's classes have the reputation of being "very well behaved." His principal openly compliments Bob's classroom management skills. Recently Bob has been considering inserting small-group learning activities into his lessons but, not having tried that approach before, he fears the students may get out of control. Thus, rather than risk his reputation as an effective disciplinarian, he decides not to attempt anything different.

DIVORCING FORMATIVE FROM SUMMATIVE EVALUATIONS

The value of cooperative partnerships between teachers and supervisors where instructional supervision takes place in an atmosphere of openness and freedom to innovate is unquestioned. But because school administrators (e.g., principals) are responsible for both summative and formative evaluations of instruction, skeptics argue that the independence between the two cannot be maintained well enough to allow for such an atmosphere. If you are unwilling to give up on instructional supervision as a lost cause, then consider some of the practical strategies for separating the two functions.

Partitioning Time

Teachers need ongoing formative feedback, but summative evaluations need to be made only infrequently (e.g., for retention, tenure, promotion, and merit-pay decisions). Administrators took advantage of this difference when they implemented the evaluation policy of the school district in which the following example takes place:

Lydia Gustafson, Northside School District personnel director, explains the district's evaluation procedures to new teachers at the annual orientation meeting:

LYDIA: We consider instructional evaluation vital to our continuing efforts to improve instruction, encourage professional growth, and maintain high quality-control standards. As our faculty handbook explains, Northside's policy stipulates procedures for two *distinct* types of evaluations of your classroom instruction.

First of all, we have ongoing *formative* evaluations, the sole purpose of which is to provide you with helpful feedback. We believe strongly that teaching is too complex an undertaking for *anyone*, even the most experienced teachers, to go it alone. Your supervisors as well as other teachers will be responsible for providing you feedback. Now, I can just hear you saying to yourself, "Northside District is going to be a wonderful place to teach! I'll have colleagues who feel responsible for helping me work with my students!" Well you're absolutely right, but there's a price you're expected to pay for all that help. You too will be expected to play a role in the formative evaluations of the instruction of other teachers. In other words, we all have a stake in the success of each other's students.

The second type of evaluations are called *summative*. They are checks on the overall quality of instruction. Summative evaluations take place only twice each year—for a week in mid-January and again for a week in early April. Obviously, whether or not you are offered a continuing contract and the amount of merit raise you receive depend largely on the Examination Board's judgment of your instructional effectiveness. The *only* evaluations that the Examination Board will access for judging that effectiveness will be those conducted during the two summative evaluation periods.

Yes, Ross, you have a question.

ROSS: I know this was all explained before I signed my contract, but I'm still bothered that 10 months of teaching is judged on the basis of two one-week periods.

LYDIA: It bothers me too—and a lot of other people as well. We're still debating the issue. When these procedures were developed three years ago, we compromised on that point. Although summative evaluations are absolutely necessary, we don't want them to subvert our formative evaluations—which most of our faculty find immensely helpful. We limited summative evaluations to those two time periods so that teachers would feel free to seek formative feedback without worrying that mistakes might haunt them later.

JUANITA: But is that realistic? My principal is going to form opinions about me all year long. Those are bound to influence her summative evaluations.

LYDIA: That's certainly a real concern. But we've built some safeguards into the system. First, personnel from your own school are essentially responsible for formative evaluations, whereas data for summative evaluations are gathered by a team from other schools and the district office. Second, summative evaluations must be justified by documented measurement results gathered only during the two designated periods. And, finally, the policy is public. That's one reason we review it at this open meeting. This provides somewhat of a hedge against a supervisor sneaking in information gathered during a formative evaluation.

ROSS: But as I understand it from the handbook, instructional effectiveness isn't the only factor considered for judgments about things like contract renewal. Principals are supposed to look at things like contributions to developing school programs.

LYDIA: That's right. And, unlike instructional effectiveness, the bases for judging those other variables are not limited to the two one-week periods.

Differentiating time periods for summative and formative evaluations solves some but not all of the problems of keeping the two separate. To maintain truly independent formative evaluation procedures, evaluators themselves also need to be separated.

Differentiated Evaluators

Examination Board. Ideally, teachers can depend on the services of instructional supervisors who are not involved in the summative evaluations of their instruction. This differentiation of personnel may be achieved through the constitution of an *examination board* responsible for conducting summative evaluations throughout a school district. Representatives of the district's teachers, instructional supervisors, and administrators, in consultation with specialists in the evaluation of instruction, might define the board's role and establish guidelines for how it operates, how its members are selected, prepared, and compensated, and how its activities are monitored. The board would then be required to demonstrate that its judgments of instructional effectiveness are based on data resulting from measurements conducted within the designated guidelines. Serving on such an examination board for an average-size school district might well be a full-time job. There are various possibilities for contracting professionals to serve on the board. Teachers, supervisors, and administrators from the district might be selected for staggered terms, with members being provided full or partial release time from their regular responsibilities while they serve on the board. Or, teachers, supervisors, and administrators from outside the district can be hired to serve while they are on leave (e.g., sabbatical) from their own districts.

Most school boards would need to increase their allotment of funds for instructional evaluation to undertake this kind of system, but a well-designed and implemented plan may in fact prove cost-effective. Instructional supervision and formative feedback will become a reality, thus making in-service and staff-development programs more efficient. Supervisors will be freed from the burden of conducting summative evaluations, and such systematically constituted summative evaluation procedures will not be as vulnerable to legal challenges as those that are now typical in most districts.

Individualized Committees for Teachers. A single examination board provides some uniformity among district-wide evaluations of instruction. On the other hand, tailoring an examination committee for each teacher may lead to summative evaluations that are more responsive to that teacher's unique situation. In cooperation with the principal and department head, a teacher might, for example, select a four-person committee to be responsible for designing and conducting a summative evaluation of that teacher's instructional effectiveness. The committee might consist of another on-site teacher, two teachers from other schools, and a district-level administrator. Guidelines should ensure that teachers have ready access to instructional supervision that is totally independent from the activities of their individual committees.

Financial costs for such an operation would be at least as great as those for a single examination board. Personnel would need to be compensated for serving on individual committees, and substitutes would have to be hired when teachers conduct summative evaluations. However, serving on these committees would contribute to professional growth and generate ideas for improving committee members' own instructional effectiveness (Cangelosi & Forsyth, 1985).

Formative Evaluations as Preparations for Summative Evaluations

The anticipation of an upcoming summative evaluation may motivate some teachers to seek formative feedback on their instruction. For example:

Assistant Principal Wilmo Stockton meets with history teacher Magdalene Leckner:

WILMO: Now that we have your evaluation committee in place, you need to set up a meeting with them to plan your January summative evaluation. Have you thought about the units you'll be teaching then?

MAGDALENE: That's less than two months away. I really need to get organized.

WILMO: You should be prepared to tell the committee your goals and plans for that time period. If you come to the meeting with a plan in hand, you'll set the agenda. That'll make their job easier and you more comfortable.

MAGDALENE: Okay, I'll make sure I have that ready. But I'm more bothered by a couple of my classes—they don't seem motivated.

WILMO: What's the problem?

MAGDALENE: That's just it—I'm not sure. The same approaches that excite my first- and third-period classes seem to bore my second- and fourth-

WILMO:

period students to tears. When my committee observes those classes, they're going to think I'm doing a terrible job!

We still have time to turn those classes around. Let's videotape all four classes for the next three days. Then you and I can analyze the tapes and see how the classes differ from one another.

Helping a teacher prepare for a summative evaluation provides an opportunity for an instructional supervisor to establish an open, cooperative partnership with the teacher.

Sharing Ideas among Peers

The examples on pages 95–96 illustrate two teachers, Nora and Sheldon, sharing ideas and providing one another with formative feedback. Teachers suggest that this type of nonthreatening interchange among colleagues provides them with the most productive type of in-service help and instructional supervision (Bang-Jensen, 1986; Brandt, 1989; Chrisco, 1989; Raney & Robbins, 1989). However, such idea sharing and formative evaluations will not become commonplace until administrators routinely allot time in teachers' schedules for this type of activity (Oliva, 1989, pp. 343–73).

Self-Evaluations

Teachers' ongoing formative evaluations of their own instructional activities do not threaten outcomes of subsequent summative evaluations. The teacher in the following example conducts an evaluation in the privacy of her own home:

Holly Jones videotapes a portion of one of her third-grade class sessions. That night she views the tape, taking notes furiously for use in planning subsequent sessions. She spends three hours going over one hour of tape, replaying some portions repeatedly in an attempt to analyze different aspects of the class.

She decides that next time she does this, she'll focus on only one aspect of her instruction at a time (e.g., her use of questioning). The experience leads her to realize that too much goes on in a classroom for anyone to examine all aspects during one observation.

Now that video cameras and recorders are generally available for classroom use and videotape players are household items, teachers can view themselves teaching in the privacy of their own home. However, to realize the potential of this resource as a means of obtaining formative feedback, teachers need to follow systematic procedures that focus on specific aspects of instructional behaviors (Harris, 1985, p. 149). Struyk (1990) demonstrated that teachers eagerly learn to do just that when provided with appropriate in-service opportunities. She developed and validated a classroom observation instrument, similar to that in Appendix A, which teachers utilized to obtain feedback efficiently from videotape recordings of themselves.

INFORMATION OVERLOAD

As with self-evaluations, formative feedback from instructional supervisors needs to focus on one variable at a time. Consider the following example:

Jacelyn Frank serves as mentor teacher to Leinka Borachek, a beginning fourth-grade teacher. Conscientious about this first assignment as a mentor teacher, Jacelyn attempts to "make the most" of her initial observation of Leinka's class. Their post-observational conference includes the following:

JACELYN: I'm really pleased with what went on in your class today! You really had your math groups moving. Tying the math to the science project really seemed to get them excited.

LEINKA: I'm so relieved to hear you say that! Do you really think I did okay?

JACELYN: Not just okay—great! Just keep doing what you're doing. Let me check my notes and we'll talk about some specifics. . . . Okay, I'll run through these quickly.

LEINKA: You mean I did some things wrong?

JACELYN: No, no—not *wrong*. I just have some suggestions. That's my job.

LEINKA: Anything you can suggest will be appreciated.

JACELYN: Okay. First, when you move them into math groups, you might consider having the directions already on their desks.

LEINKA: You mean the first time, when we were brainstorming, or when they were discussing their reports?

JACELYN: Umm, the second time, I think. When Tommy asked you if they were supposed to exchange papers.

LEINKA: Oh, right—so put papers out ahead of time. And that was when Evelyn said she was embarrassed about her project.

JACELYN: Oh, that's another thing. Instead of immediately telling her how great her project was, you might have used the active listening business—you know, a more supportive reply.

LEINKA: I didn't think of that. Do you really think that supportive talk stuff really works?

JACELYN: Absolutely. It's amazing how much better the kids listen. You just have to get used to doing it. Oh, I want to move on to your room arrangement. I'm not sure that group over by the north window could see the illustrations you used when you walked the class through the multiplication algorithm.

LEINKA: Do you mean the group with Eddie?

JACELYN: If he's the redhead, yes.

LEINKA: You know, I wanted to ask you about the way I presented that multiplication algorithm. Do you think it would have been better if. . . .

Understandably, Leinka's concern about the quality of his overall performance set an unfortunate tone from the beginning of the conference. Until Jacelyn began referring to her notes, the conversation focused on general summative evaluation questions rather than the formative feedback that was intended. Then Jacelyn began bombarding the communications with so many formative evaluation variables that no one was dealt with the specificity necessary to influence teaching practice efficiently.

Teaching is far too complex for anyone to be able to examine ways of improving all aspects at once. Thus, for purposes of providing formative feedback, an evaluation should focus on a limited number of specific variables.

ANALYZING THE TEACHER'S RESPONSIBILITIES

To narrow the focus of a formative evaluation, you need to subdivide instruction into component parts. The professional literature, especially in instructional design, provides myriad schemes for conceptualizing the components of instruction (e.g., Cangelosi, 1988a, pp. 4–6; Dick & Carey, 1985, pp. 2–7; Jackson, 1966; Merrill, 1983). Categorizing instructional responsibilities as follows can prove particularly useful:

1. Organizing for instruction
2. Managing resources
3. Managing time
4. Developing curricula
5. Determining learning goals
6. Designing lessons
7. Managing student behavior
8. Conducting lessons and engaging students in learning activities
9. Assessing student achievement

Of course, questions regarding the interactions among the components of instruction also need to be addressed by formative evaluations. As Dick and Carey (1985, pp. 2–4) suggest:

> A . . . contemporary view of the instructional process is that instruction is a systematic process in which every component is crucial to successful learning. This perspective is usually referred to as the systems point of view. . . . A system is technically a set of interrelated parts, all of which are working together toward a defined goal. The parts of the system depend on each other for input and output, and the entire system uses feedback to determine if its desired goal has been reached. . . .
>
> The result of using the systems view of instruction is to see the important role of all the components in the process. They must all interact effectively. . . . And it is clear that there must be both an assessment of the effectiveness of the system in bringing about learning, and a mechanism to make change if learning fails to occur. . . . In the broadest system sense, a variety of sources provides input to the preparation of instruction. The output is some product or combination of products and procedures that are implemented. The results are used to determine if the system should be changed, and, if so, how.[1]

---

[1] From *Systematic Design of Instruction* by W. Dick and L. Carey. Copyright © 1985 by Scott, Foresman and Company. Reprinted by permission.

Teaching success within each of the nine areas in the list above depends on a complex of variables. The *appropriateness of the learning goals determined by the teacher* (area 5), for example, depends on variables such as curriculum guidelines, prior achievements of the students, student aptitudes, student interests, student needs, availability of resources, capabilities of the teacher, school policies, cultural backgrounds of the students, prior experiences of the students, and time allotted for learning activities.

Note that the teacher can control only some of these variables. Instructional supervision, and consequently formative evaluations, should target variables *over which the teacher can exercise control*. Measuring some variables that teachers *cannot* influence (e.g., student aptitude) can sometimes help in better understanding how controllable variables should be manipulated.

The next nine sections of this chapter identify teacher-controlled variables that might be targeted by formative evaluations.

ORGANIZING FOR INSTRUCTION

Teacher preparation programs typically provide preservice teachers with field experiences working in classrooms organized by other teachers and conducting learning activities that fit within existing instructional systems (Lanier & Little, 1986). Student teachers may design, plan, and conduct entire units of instruction, but the classrooms, curricula, and resources are usually organized by their cooperating teachers before student teachers ever appear at the schools. Consequently, beginning teachers typically struggle to overcome a plethora of difficulties that stem from their inexperience in organizing classrooms, materials, and curricula prior to the start of a school year (Duke, Cangelosi, & Knight, 1988). Thus, *organizing for instruction* is a concern of instructional supervision and an area to be examined in formative evaluations. For example:

Part of Abbie Wagner's responsibilities as chairperson of the upper-grades department at Westview Elementary School is to coordinate the instructional supervision of the department's teachers. Just before the start of the school year, Abbie asked first-year teacher Mary Tinsely if she needed help pulling together materials and making plans for the year. Mary indicated that she had everything under control and would call on Abbie if she "ran into trouble." Now it's November and the two are in the midst of a conversation:

MARY: I'm really frustrated; I just can't put my finger on the problem!

ABBIE: I didn't see any problems with the way you presented that lesson yesterday.

MARY: I don't have a problem with any one lesson. It's that when I look back on a bunch of lessons, they don't seem to be getting the class anywhere. Each lesson teaches them something, but the lessons don't work together. I can't really explain what I mean. . . . I get the feeling that each day the kids are wondering, "What in the world is she going to have us do today?" It's not like they don't enjoy what we do, but there's no feeling of continuity from one day or week to the next. Also, I'm getting to where I'm having trouble developing activities. I used up my file of activities from my college days a month ago.

ABBIE: Are you working from some sort of master plan?

MARY: What do you mean?

ABBIE: Here, let me show you mine. . . . Everything I do plugs into this outline.

MARY: You made this back in August?

ABBIE: Right. I tried to anticipate what I'll need for the whole year, so the lessons are sequenced into a coherent whole. I prepare my materials and schedule my time well in advance.

MARY: If I'd have done this, I wouldn't be getting my supplies a month after I need them!

ABBIE: Let's work through a plan that'll take you through the next couple of weeks anyway. . . .

Over the next few months, Abbie helps Mary to organize for teaching and develop her own master plan. Abbie also decides to initiate a program for providing teachers with formative feedback on how they organize for instruction prior to the next school year.

Sometimes teachers lose control over variables that have an impact on the effectiveness of their instruction because they fail to organize for instruction in advance. In the example, one of Mary's lessons may not have related to a previous one because she had not thought about the subsequent one before designing the first. In addition, Mary's learning activities may have been limited to those for which materials were available. Had she anticipated the learning activities far enough in advance, she might have been able to obtain the materials by the time they were needed.

Organizing-for-instruction variables that can be targeted by formative evaluations include the following:

- how, if at all, the teacher formulates a long-range master lesson plan for the upcoming school year
- how the teacher arranges and equips the classroom
- how, if at all, the teacher establishes beginning-of-the-year classroom administrative procedures and classroom movement patterns
- how well the teacher anticipates the need for supplies
- how, if at all, the teacher schedules long-range student and teacher time

Chapter 6 provides a model for designing formative evaluations of instruction. Focusing those evaluations on teachers' efforts to organize for instruction requires an understanding of principles of long-range classroom planning and management. Numerous references on those principles are contained in the professional literature (e.g., Arends, 1988, pp. 86–121, 159–201; Cangelosi, 1988a, pp. 51–81, 165–75; Dick & Carey, 1985; Emmer, Evertson, & Anderson, 1980; Emmer, Evertson, Sanford, Clements, & Worsham, 1984, pp. 4–14, 69–88; Evertson, 1989;

Evertson, Emmer, Clements, Sanford, & Worsham, 1984, pp. 4–14, 665–85; Jones & Jones, 1986, pp. 31–55; Kauchak & Eggen, 1989, pp. 192–231; Levine, 1989, pp. 89–138; McNergney, 1988; Morine-Dershimer & Pfeifer, 1986).

MANAGING RESOURCES

Consumable supplies (e.g., paper, overhead transparencies, and computer disks), *instructional materials* (e.g., videotape programs, books, and computer software), *equipment* (e.g., computers, video recorders, and display calculators), *work space* (e.g., secure storage area, room for large group presentations, and room for small group work), and *personnel* (e.g., teacher aides, guest speakers, and resource professionals) can enhance teaching effectiveness. The availability of such resources depends on budget allocations, community attitudes, and administrative decisions that, unfortunately, are not typically controlled by teachers. However, teachers do control the management of resources that are made available to them. Resource management should sometimes be targeted by instructional supervision and, thus, by formative evaluations. For example:

Jeff Ziluski is a paraprofessional classroom aide to two middle school English teachers, Shirley Brown and Jill Goldberg. Although Shirley and Jill find Jeff helpful, they find "sharing" him difficult. Together they approach their principal, Dewanna Johnson, to ask if each might have her own aide:

SHIRLEY: Jeff does a great job, but Jill's schedule and mine are very similar, and we both tend to need him at the same time.

JILL: Tomorrow, for instance, I need Jeff to go over my classes' tests with them while I complete my student register—but Shirley's register is due too, and she needs him to work with several students who've fallen behind.

DEWANNA: Do I understand that you're using up your time to do clerical work while Jeff teaches?

SHIRLEY: Well, he's not really *teaching* for either one of us—just going over tests, doing some remediation, taking care of discipline problems. Actually, a lot of the time he's not doing anything.

JILL: It's just that when we do need him, we both need him at the same time!

DEWANNA: Listen to what you're both saying. You have Jeff carrying out responsibilities—going over tests, remediating students, dealing with discipline problems—that you are professionally educated to carry out. Why not have Jeff fill out your student registers instead?

JILL: But he doesn't know how—everything has to be so exact!

DEWANNA: You could teach him to do your registers more easily than he can learn to conduct lessons and handle discipline problems. And filling out registers is work that can be scheduled when time is available.

SHIRLEY: I see what you're saying. The clerical work can keep him busy in the

> off-times—and for that matter, he could write up instructional material
> we design, and. . . .
>
> Later, Dewanna decides to examine how all teachers are utilizing their aides and
> other available resources.

Management-of-resources variables targeted by formative evaluations might include the efficacy with which the teacher does the following:

- consumes available supplies
- selects instructional materials and equipment
- allocates available workspace
- utilizes available personnel

Professional literature emphasizes the pedagogical aspects of instruction but provides few ideas on allocating and managing resources. Suggestions on the use of instructional technology and media are available (e.g., Castle, 1988; Dick & Reiser, 1989, pp. 52–67, 86–101; Ellington, 1985; Kim & Kellough, 1987, pp. 233–48; Levine, 1989, pp. 139–94; Short & Lough, 1986), but references on other aspects of resource management are scarce.

MANAGING TIME

Time, like consumable supplies, is a resource. However, managing time is distinguished from managing other resources because it presents such a prominent problem for teachers. Are the following teachers' comments familiar to you?

- "I don't require my students to write essays because I don't have time to read them!"
- "I wish I had the time to develop item pools for my tests; it's a great idea. But there are only 24 hours in a day!"
- "Math *should* be taught at an application level, but if we took class time to do that, I'd never get through the book!"
- "Textbook classroom management theory is great, but who has time to deal with every problem that comes up?"
- "Sure I ought to communicate with parents, but how am I going to manage that when I deal with 160 students a day?"

Twenty-four hours per day is inadequate for teachers effectively to meet all the challenges their profession offers. The situation is further confounded by the fact that most teachers who support families supplement their teaching salaries by moonlighting during the school year (Biddle, 1987, p. 630).

In the following example, one teacher encourages another to be more assertive in his approach to allocating time:

BILL: There are so many things I ought to be doing but never get around to!

GRANT: Like what?

BILL: I need to develop enrichment materials for some of my kids who are way ahead of the rest of the class. And in this test development class I'm taking, I've learned to use item pools. It's a great idea, but I can't find the time to set up my computer to do it. And then there's the problem of—

GRANT: Okay, slow down! I know what you mean. The thing is, you have to realize that it's impossible to do everything you want to do or should do. You have to partition your time—make some difficult decisions. Prioritize from what you absolutely *have* to do—like sleep and eat and show up for class—then to what you really *want* to do, on down to what's not as important to do. I'd advise you to put a high priority on things that will help you save time down the road—like the item pool, for example. Neglect something else and get that organized; you'll save time putting together tests and your tests will be better to boot!

BILL: Yeah, you're right. Maybe a daily pocket calendar would help too. I keep track of things on my desk calendar, but then parents drop in and . . .

GRANT: Don't let it happen. You wouldn't drop in on your lawyer or doctor without an appointment. Don't let your clients do that to you.

BILL: What clients?

GRANT: Mainly your students, but also parents, colleagues, and administrators.

BILL: This is going to require a change in my attitude about myself.

GRANT: It's called "assertiveness."

BILL: But everything can't be scheduled. Unanticipated things have to be taken care of.

GRANT: Of course they do. Your schedule is an organizational tool for your convenience, not something you blindly follow. Sometimes you'll have to deviate from it, but that doesn't mean you throw the schedule out.

BILL: Like today, I needed to talk with Jackie's mother, but we were short one lunch room supervisor.

GRANT: Those are times when I take a "triage" approach. I decide where my time can be most efficiently spent. Some crises are beyond our reasonable control and others can wait.

BILL: But I don't have time to schedule my time! . . .

Management-of-time variables targeted by formative evaluations might include how the teacher does the following:

- determines when to design and prepare lessons
- partitions classroom time
- allocates time for students to engage in learning activities
- determines when to engage in the post-interactive phases of teaching (e.g., scoring tests)
- schedules professional development activities
- schedules noninstructional activities (including leisure, domestic, and school-related administrative duties)

The professional literature contains a few sources on how teachers can better manage time (e.g., Allen, 1986; Fisher & Berlinger, 1985; Halasz & Raftery, 1985; Richardson-Koehler, 1988).

DEVELOPING CURRICULA

Many teachers and administrators perceive a *curriculum* as "the textbook series adopted, mandated state or local curriculum guides, and/or content and skills appearing on mandated tests" (Zumwalt, 1989, p. 174). Definitions range from that very narrow one to the all-encompassing view forwarded by Brubaker (1982, p. 2): " . . . curriculum is defined as *what persons experience in a setting*. This includes all the interactions among persons as well as the interactions between persons and their physical environment. . . . "

Our definition of *curriculum* falls between the two extremes and is consistent with that most commonly presented in the literature on instructional supervision (Firth & Newfield, 1984; Oliva, 1989, pp. 262–66; Sergiovanni & Starratt, 1983, p. 241):

- A *school curriculum* is a system of the planned experiences (e.g., course-work, school-sponsored social functions, and contacts with school-supported services) designed to educate students.
- A *course curriculum* is a sequence of teaching units designed to provide students with experiences that help them achieve specified learning goals. A *teaching unit* consists of (1) a learning goal defined by a set of specific objectives, (2) a sequence of lessons each consisting of learning activities designed to help students achieve specific objectives, (3) mechanisms for obtaining and using formative feedback, and (4) a summative evaluation of student achievement of the learning goal.
- A *specialty-area curriculum* is a sequence of either courses or teaching units that is either limited to a particular content area (e.g., physical education or biology) or developed for a particular category of students (e.g., third grade or educable mentally handicapped).
- A *school-district curriculum* is the set of all the school curricula within that school district.

State-level, district-level, school-level, and specialty-area *curricula guidelines* are articulated in documents stored in the files of virtually every school. The consistency between official curricula guidelines and actual school curricula varies considerably. Obviously, a school's curriculum can be no more in line with stated guidelines than is the composite of the course curricula developed by its teachers.

Curriculum-development variables that might be targeted by formative evaluations include the following:

- consistency between a course or specialty-area curriculum and official curricula guidelines

- appropriateness of a sequence of units in light of student needs
- teacher's role in the development of the school curriculum

Three more important teacher-controlled curriculum-development variables, *the appropriateness of learning goals, how well lessons are designed*, and *how well student achievement is assessed*, are so complex that they are dealt with separately in subsequent sections of this chapter.

Many references are available that provide ideas on curriculum development (e.g., Firth & Newfield, 1984; Glickman, 1985, pp. 304–29; Hass, 1987; Oliva, 1989, pp. 261–301; Zumwalt, 1989). Also consider consulting references on curriculum development for the individual specialty areas of those teachers with whom you are working (e.g., health science or primary grade reading).

DETERMINING LEARNING GOALS

A major aspect of the curriculum-development phase of instruction is the design of teaching units. Each teaching unit focuses on a learning goal, with each goal being defined by a set of specific objectives (Cangelosi, 1990b, pp. 3–19). For example:

The social studies course curriculum developed by Waldo Little for his fourth graders includes 14 teaching units. Waldo defines the goal for each unit by a set of objectives so that each objective specifies both *subject-matter content* and a *cognitive, affective, or psychomotor level* at which students are expected to learn that subject-matter content.

For example, he defines the goal for his unit on the Constitution as follows:
   Goal: The students will be aware of fundamental aspects of the U.S. Constitu-
      tion, its history, and its influence on us today.
   Objectives:

   A. States that the purpose of the Constitution is to provide a general plan for governing the United States. (*Cognitive: simple knowledge*)
   B. Lists the general parts of the original Constitution as the Preamble and seven articles (with the subject of each article). (*Cognitive: simple knowledge*)
      •   •
      •   •
      •   •
   F. Explains at least four amendments that have been added since the Bill of Rights. (*Cognitive: comprehension of a communication*)
   G. Describes the general process for amending the Constitution. (*Cognitive: knowledge of a process*)
   H. Given a description of a well-publicized current issue, determines what, if any, bearing the Constitution has on the resolution of that issue. (*Cognitive: application*)
   I. Believes that the Constitution serves a valuable purpose. (*Affective: appreciation*)

The specific objectives Waldo uses to define each unit's goal provide him with direction in how the lessons should be designed. He uses one of the many schemes available from the professional literature to categorize the cognitive, affective, or psychomotor learning levels of his objectives (e.g., Bloom, 1984; Cangelosi, 1982, pp. 90–95; 1990b, pp. 7–15; Guilford, 1959; Harrow, 1972; Krathwhohl, Bloom, & Masia, 1964). Thus, for his first two objectives he knows to design learning activities appropriate for knowledge-level learning (e.g., according to the model presented by Joyce and Weil (1986, pp. 89–100). On the other hand, since Objective H targets application-level learning, he will design learning activities for that objective by applying principles for teaching higher-order thinking (e.g., Joyce & Weil, 1986, pp. 25–88).

Most teachers, however, do not define their goals so systematically without the benefit of expert instructional supervision. Formative evaluations might appropriately target *determining-learning-goal* variables, including the following:

- how well learning goals address student needs (e.g., Is the goal sufficiently ambitious without being unrealistic?)
- the consistency between the sequencing of the goals and teaching/learning principles
- how well objectives define learning goals (e.g., Is the set of goals comprehensive? Are they specific enough?)
- how clearly the subject-matter content of each objective is specified
- how clearly the learning level of each objective is specified

General and specialty-area instructional methods references, as well as references in the fields of teaching/learning theory and instructional design, provide an abundance of suggestions on how to determine learning goals (e.g., Dick & Carey, 1985, pp. 12–29; Dick & Reiser, 1989, pp. 8–35; Dubelle, 1986, pp. 23–28; Jacobsen, Eggen, & Kauchak, 1989, pp. 19–104; Kim & Kellough, 1987, pp. 73–153; Tenbrink, 1986).

DESIGNING LESSONS

Unfortunately, some teachers plan lessons simply by deciding how many pages from the prescribed textbook to "cover" (Jesunathadas, 1990). Others, fortunately, are more thoughtful in their approach to helping students learn. For example:

Parisa Triche's unit on "writing to report news" lists six learning objectives for her 28 second-period English students to achieve over the next two weeks. Parisa has already designed lessons for the first four objectives, and now she's thinking about how to teach for the fifth, which is stated as follows: The student edits and revises a news report he or she wrote utilizing feedback from a sample of readers. (*Cognitive: application*)

Parisa thinks to herself: "Since this is an application-level objective, I'd better have them work with a fresh piece of their own writing, something that hasn't been previously critiqued. That means I'll have to get them to write something in a hurry; we can't spend more than four days on this objective. Okay, I'll have each write a fairly short report on something newsy the first day. The second day, a panel of students reads and reviews it aloud while the writer silently listens and takes notes. Then the writer revises the piece for homework and explains the revisions and how feedback from the panel was used. I'll draw upon their explanations with questions to get them to induct the editing/revision principles I want them to apply. Then we can repeat the whole process, but this time they'll already be familiar with the editing/revision principles.

"It's a great idea, but there's no way we can do all that in four days! . . . I know! For the first round of writing, we'll split the class into 'writers' and 'reviewers.' Let's see, 28 in the class . . . How many reports will I need to have enough examples to induct the principles? Also how many reports can we realistically handle in the time frame? Probably six reports would be just about right. That leaves 22 students not reporting. Oh, I've got it! What a genius you are, Parisa! I'll pair up the writers so that we'll have 12 people writing six reports. Since this is the first time they've tried this, they'll need a partner for motivation and to bounce off ideas. Then, that'll give me 16 reviewers. I'll form three panels of five, five, and six. Each panel can review two reports. Everybody gets involved!

"Now, how should I assign the report topics? How should the pairs of writers be selected. Oh, what an idea! I'll make sure that I pair Mark and Willie to report on something to do with wrestling. Mark loves wrestling but hates to write. Willie has no interest in wrestling but loves to write. That way, Mark can provide the expertise in wrestling and it'll be a challenge for Willie to write about a topic he's not big on. Great idea, Parisa! They'll both be contributing and motivated for different reasons.

"Five more pairs to choose. But I wonder if. . . ."

Excitedly, Parisa continues to design the lesson, planning the learning activities for the five days. She also devises ways to keep the students engaged in the activities as well as ways to efficiently execute transitions between the lesson's learning activities.

As Parisa demonstrated, designing effective lessons is an extremely complex, creative, and exciting part of instruction. Only teachers are in the position to design lessons for their students, but instructional supervision plays a vital role in helping teachers carry out this most taxing aspect of curriculum development.

Designing-lessons variables that might be targeted by formative evaluations include the following:

- how well the content specified by a learning objective is addressed in the learning activities that are designed to help students achieve that objective
- whether or not the teaching/learning principles that apply to the learning level specified by an objective are utilized in the design of the learning activities (e.g., If the objective is at the conceptual cognitive level, will the learning activities engage students in inductive reasoning?)
- the appropriateness of the types of learning activities (e.g., lecture, discussion, questioning session, homework, and individualized seatwork)
- whether or not the lesson design includes a promising plan for obtaining and maintaining student engagement
- the practicality of the design considering such factors as the availability of resources, prior experiences of the students, and the classroom climate

The professional literature in specialty-area methods and in teaching/learning principles provides some very useful guidelines on how lessons, depending on the specified learning objective, should be designed (e.g., Cangelosi, 1988a, pp. 130–

65; Dillon & Sternberg, 1986; Ellis & Hunt, 1983; Joyce & Weil, 1986; McDiarmid, Ball, & Anderson, 1989; Phye & Andre, 1986; Weinstein, Goetz, & Alexander, 1988). Practitioner-oriented professional journals are especially helpful in providing ideas for lesson designs as well as other phases of curriculum development (e.g., *Art Education, Child Language Teaching and Therapy, Journal of Teaching Writing, Journal of Education for Business, Childhood Education, Elementary School Journal, Exercise Exchange, Journal of Reading, Journal of School Health, Arithmetic Teacher, Mathematics Teacher, Physical Education, Reading Teacher, School Science and Mathematics, School Shop, Science Activities, Science and Children, The History and Social Science Teacher,* and *Social Education*).

MANAGING STUDENT BEHAVIOR

Keeping students engaged in learning activities and on-task and effectively dealing with off-task, especially disruptive, student behaviors generally present teachers with their most perplexing challenges (Doyle, 1986; Steere, 1988, pp. 5–9; Weber, 1986). Overwhelmingly, teachers indicate that classroom management and student discipline problems cause their greatest difficulties and lead to feelings of inadequacy during their first two years of teaching (Cangelosi, Struyk, Grimes, & Duke, 1988; Evertson, 1989). According to studies conducted over the past 75 years, improper management of student behavior is the leading cause of teacher failure (Bridges, 1986, p. 5). Student behavior management must then be a paramount focus of instructional supervision.

Managing-student-behavior variables that formative evaluations target might include the following:

- the degree to which there is a purposeful, businesslike environment in the classroom
- how smoothly and efficiently transition periods are orchestrated
- how well student engagement is obtained at the beginning of learning activities
- how well student engagement is maintained during learning activities
- the efficacy of how nondisruptive off-task behaviors are handled
- the efficacy of how disruptive off-task behaviors are handled

In recent years a proliferation of references have provided practical and useful suggestions for teachers in the area of management of student behavior (e.g., Cangelosi, 1988a, 1990a, in press; Charles, 1989; Dubelle & Hoffman, 1986; Jones & Jones, 1986; Long & Frye, 1989; Wolfgang & Glickman, 1986).

CONDUCTING LESSONS AND ENGAGING
STUDENTS IN LEARNING ACTIVITIES

Well-designed lessons are of little value if they are not conducted as designed or if the teacher mishandles the activities. For example:

Assistant Principal Blair Eisenrich talks with fifth-grade teacher Faye Black after Blair has observed Faye conduct a 45-minute astronomy lesson:

BLAIR: How do you feel the lesson went?

FAYE: Not quite as I planned. I'd assumed their answers to the questions I asked would show them the paradoxes in their theories about life on other planets. When that didn't happen, I wasn't sure where to go next.

BLAIR: And that's when you went into that long monologue about how things aren't always the way they seem?

FAYE: Right. Do you think that went okay?

BLAIR: Well, frankly, I didn't think anyone was following you, except maybe Allison and Quai.

FAYE: Really? I guess I was so nervous about the lesson going off track that I didn't pick up on that!

BLAIR: They were sending you some clear signals that your words were wasted on them.

FAYE: Ouch! I had no idea.

BLAIR: Let's talk about some of the signals they were sending you and how you might have adjusted the activity in midstream. . . .

Traditionally, classroom observations focus on the performance of teachers *during* learning activities. Of course, the appropriateness of learning objectives, classroom and behavior management effectiveness, appropriateness of the lesson design, and how well the teacher implements the plan are inextricably interdependent. The success of even the best-designed lesson depends on the teacher's making in-class decisions.

Conducting-lessons-and-engaging-students-in-learning-activities variables that might be targeted by formative evaluations include the following:

- how faithfully the lesson designed is followed
- adjustments the teacher makes in light of formative feedback
- type of communications used by the teacher (e.g., descriptive versus judgmental, supportive versus nonsupportive, and assertive versus hostile or passive)
- teacher's body language and movement during the class
- teacher's responses to students' questions and comments
- how well the teacher includes all students in activities such as discussions and questioning sessions
- clarity of the teacher's communications
- wait time during questioning activities

References with ideas for conducting lessons and engaging students in learning activities overlap those for designing lessons and managing student behavior.

ASSESSING STUDENT ACHIEVEMENT

The number and variety of questions about which teachers must make judgments are unparalleled in other professions (Cangelosi, 1974; Clark & Peterson, 1986). For example:

- "What did my students really learn, if anything, from that lesson?"
- "Is Wilma ready to try that experiment?"
- "Should I increase the pace of this activity or slow it down?"
- "What grade should I assign Stephone?"
- "Chris' father wants a progress report. What should I tell him?"
- "Did that last assignment change any attitudes about homework?"
- "Does Laura possess the psychomotor skill to begin learning cursive?"
- "Can these students actually apply these principles or have they only memorized them?"

To address questions such as these, teachers must evaluate their students' achievements (i.e., what students have learned or are learning). Teachers spend between 20 and 30 percent of their time directly involved in data- or information-gathering activities (Stiggins, 1988). These include designing, synthesizing, selecting, administering, scoring, interpreting, and revising tests and other types of observations of students' performances and behaviors.

Tests and observations provide the information base for teachers' evaluations of student achievement. Unfortunately, studies examining the validities of tests commonly used in schools (both commercially prepared and teacher-prepared) and the evaluation methods of many teachers suggest that testing malpractice and inaccurate evaluations are widespread (Stiggins, Conklin, & Bridgeford, 1986). Consequently, assessment of student achievement for both formative and summative purposes should be a major focus of instructional supervision.

Assessing-student-achievement variables targeted by formative evaluations of instruction might include the following:

- the design of the system the teacher uses to make formative evaluations of student achievement
- the design of the system the teacher uses to make summative evaluations of student achievement
- how measurements (e.g., commercially produced tests) are selected
- how measurements are designed and constructed (e.g., whether or not item pools are utilized)
- how measurements are administered
- how measurements are validated
- the cost-effectiveness of measurements utilized by the teacher
- how scores are interpreted (including use of standardized test results and determination of cutoff scores)
- how measurement results are converted to grades
- how formative evaluations are communicated to students and their parents

- how summative evaluations are communicated to students, their parents, and *authorized* professional educators

The professional literature is replete with definitive suggestions on how teachers should develop, select, and utilize measurements to assess student achievement (e.g., Cangelosi, 1982; 1990b; Cunningham, 1986; Ebel & Frisbie, 1986; Gronlund, 1982; 1985; Keeves, 1988; Kubiszyn & Borich, 1987; Tuckman, 1988).

UNANTICIPATED OUTCOMES

For purposes of conducting formative evaluations, we divided instruction into nine overlapping, interdependent components: organizing for instruction, managing resources, managing time, developing curricula, determining learning goals, designing lessons, managing student behavior, conducting lessons and engaging students in learning activities, and assessing student achievement. However, the classroom is such a complex social environment that students are influenced in ways that cannot always be anticipated before lessons are actually conducted. Thus, formative evaluations also need to attend to outcomes other than achievement of stated learning goals. For example:

Rich Loyacono, Hillview Middle School physical education teacher, confers with his department head, Eva Allen:

RICH: Do you know Alma Kelly?

EVA: Oh, sure. She's a seventh grader in your fourth period. I was watching your class last week and was absolutely amazed at how you've got her participating. She's so shy. Last year Pauline couldn't get her to do anything in her class.

RICH: In the beginning, I had similar problems. But then, thinking she had an image problem, I gave her a little special attention—selected her as team leader more often than the others, used active listening techniques with supportive replies whenever she spoke.

EVA: And it worked?

RICH: Fantastically! But now I'm afraid she's too dependent on me. I think I may be the first man she's ever perceived as respecting what she has to say—of valuing her at all.

EVA: Knowing her and knowing you, I bet you're right. It's great what you've done for her!

RICH: But that's not my point. The problem is that she waits for my approval for everything. I can't give her the level of attention she expects without neglecting other responsibilities. But I'm afraid if I don't, she'll slide back into her shell.

EVA: That's a tough one. I don't have any suggestions for now. But why don't I observe your fourth period a few times. Pauline can cover my fourth period a couple of times; she's been wanting to return a favor.

RICH: So after you've observed, we'll confer again.

For purposes of providing formative feedback, unanticipated-outcome variables are *unanticipated* only until they have been identified. Then they fit one of the nine previously listed categories of instruction. In the example, once the problem regarding Alma was brought to light, Rich and Eva identified a student need and now can determine a learning goal (e.g., for Alma to become less dependent on Rich without damaging her newly acquired self-image) and can design a means for achieving the goal (e.g., one that applies the behavior modification principle of shaping [Cangelosi, 1988a, pp. 220–22; Garry & Pear, 1983, pp. 63–73]).

TRANSLATING IDEAS INTO A MODEL

In this chapter we examined ways of separating formative from summative evaluations and analyzing the complex art of instruction so that teachers can be provided with meaningful feedback. Chapter 6 presents a model for applying these ideas in realistic school settings.

SELF-ASSESSMENT EXERCISES FOR CHAPTER 5

I. Consider the problem of keeping summative evaluations of instruction from interfering with formative evaluations of instruction for the specific case of a school with which you are familiar (possibly one where you work or have worked). Now think about the suggestions presented in this chapter for divorcing formative from summative evaluations. Could those suggestions (e.g., ones under "partitioning time" or "differentiated evaluators") be implemented in the school you have just called to mind? If so, explain how in two paragraphs. Otherwise, take two paragraphs to explain why not. Share and discuss your paragraphs with another professional who has read Chapter 5.

II. In a paragraph, explain how the approach of the instructional supervisor in the following example might be changed to provide more useful feedback to the teacher:

Part of a post-observational conference between beginning teacher Ed Jones and his mentor teacher, Tamaria Michaels, goes like this:

TAMARIA: You were very poised in class; that's good. Now, your wait time after you asked questions was way too short. But the students did seem interested in the questions. They were good high-level questions.

ED: How do you think I handled Molina's interruptions? Did I come down on her too hard?

TAMARIA: Oh, no. You handled that just fine. Oh yeah, I just remembered! Try to move around the room a little more. You can control behavior better when you're right on top of them. And you could avoid turning your back to them if you used the overhead instead of the chalkboard.

ED: That's a good idea.

TAMARIA: And another thing, I liked the way you. . . .

Did any of your suggestions for Tamaria address the problem of "information overload"? Did you suggest that Tamaria should consider focusing on one aspect of instruction at a time?

III. Rewrite the previous scenario so that the conference focuses on a single formative evaluation variable that clearly falls under the area of management of student behavior. Compare your scenario with that of another who also completes this exercise.

IV. Categorize each of the variables listed below under one *or more* of the following aspects of instruction: (1) organizing for instruction, (2) managing resources, (3) managing time, (4) developing curricula, (5) determining learning goals, (6) designing lessons, (7) managing student behavior, (8) conducting lessons and engaging students in learning activities, (9) assessing student achievement.

   A. How student grades are reported to parents
   B. How a teacher determines what students need to learn next
   C. Whether or not a teacher acknowledges a student's question during a learning activity
   D. Whether or not a teacher unwittingly positively reinforces an off-task behavior during a learning activity
   E. Whether or not a teacher should utilize a portion of a budget allocation to rent a particular educational videotape program
   F. When a teacher decides to return students' test papers
   G. What should be assigned for homework tomorrow
   H. The clarity of a teacher's directions just before a learning activity begins
   I. Whether a teacher should try to teach a particular group of students the quadratic formula at the conceptualization level or only at the knowledge level
   J. How a teacher attempts to teach the quadratic formula at the conceptualization level

Compare your responses with these: A: 9; B: 4 and 5; C: 8; D: 7 and 8; E: 2; F: 3, 4, 6, and 9; G: 4 and 6; H: 7 and 8; I: 4 and 5; J: 4 and 6. Because of differences in interpretations (e.g., how broadly you define curriculum development), your responses are not expected to totally agree with the given ones. However, it is important for you to have these categories in mind so that you are better able to pinpoint variables to be targeted in formative evaluations of instruction.

CHAPTER 6

Analysis of Teaching Cycles

GOAL OF CHAPTER 6

Chapter 6 presents a model by which teachers in cooperation with instructional supervisors receive formative feedback at key points as they plan, design, prepare, implement, and assess outcomes of teaching units and lessons. Specifically, this chapter is designed to help you:

1. Describe examples of teaching cycles from your knowledge of a teacher's professional activities during some time period consisting of a day or more.
2. Describe the general process by which instructional supervisors and teachers follow the teaching-cycle analysis model to make formative evaluations of instruction.
3. Explain, relative to other approaches, the advantages and disadvantages of applying the teaching-cycle analysis model in a given situation.

TEACHING CYCLES

Effective instruction depends on formative feedback from instructional supervisors and teacher-conducted self-analyses (Harris, 1986, p. 7). With the *teaching-cycle analysis approach*, teachers and instructional supervisors collaborate to examine teaching performance variables relative to a particular teaching unit or lesson. Following are three examples of appropriate targets for this approach:

- The efficacy of the teaching unit on "selecting a domicile" that Terry Hives is planning to conduct for his home economics class.
- How Kristine Scott decides to deal with Tim's habit of interrupting his second-grade classmates when they are speaking.
- The efficacy of the lesson Byron Alley will use to help his sixth graders learn how to express fractions as percentages.

Each of these variables depends on how the teacher executes the steps in one complete *teaching cycle*. A teaching cycle is defined as the following four stages that teachers control each time they attempt to help students learn (Cangelosi, 1982, pp. 9–21; 1988a, pp. 4–13):

1. *Determination of either the goal of the unit or the objective of the lesson.* Learning goals and objectives should be dependent on the purpose of the curriculum and the needs of the students. Student needs are a function of what students have already achieved, what they are ready to achieve, their expectations, and societal expectations.
   - The efficacy of Terry's teaching unit depends on the appropriateness of its learning goal as defined by the objectives he formulates for the unit.
   - Should Kristine attempt to *teach* Tim to supplant his habit of interrupting others in the classroom with a habit of patiently waiting his turn to speak? If so, what would be a realistic objective for Tim to achieve?
   - Byron's objective dealing with converting fractions to percentages appears to have already been determined when the unit containing the lesson in question was designed.
2. *Designing lessons.* The design of lessons and the learning activities embedded in those lessons should depend on teaching/learning principles applicable for the content and learning levels specified by the objectives, students' interests and motivations, classroom management considerations, available resources, and the teacher's capabilities.
   - The efficacy of Terry's teaching unit depends on how well he plans practical lessons that will provide students with experiences leading them to achieve the unit's goal.
   - Kristine's intervention regarding Tim's disruptive behavior pattern is likely to succeed if it is consistent with research-based principles appropriate to Tim's case (Cangelosi, 1988a, pp. 183–231; Joyce & Weil, 1986, pp. 337–66).
   - Research reports in mathematics education provide clear guidelines on how a skill such as the one specified by Byron's objective should be taught (Cooney, Davis, & Henderson, 1983, pp. 174–201; Phye, 1986).
3. *Conducting lessons and learning activities.* The success of lessons depends on how well the teacher adheres to the lessons' designs and uses formative feedback to make adjustments during learning activities.

- Ultimately, Terry has to efficiently engage students in the planned lessons and orchestrate the activities if the unit is to succeed.
- If, for example, Kristine designs a strategy using the principle of shaping (Cangelosi, 1988a, pp. 220–22), whether or not Time actually learns to patiently wait his turn to speak will depend not only on the soundness of the design, but also on Kristine's own patience in consistently following through with the strategy.
- The success of appropriately designed lessons for the objective Byron determined for his students depends on such teaching performance subvariables as how well error patterns are detected during drill and practice activities and the clarity with which students' questions are answered.

4. *Assessing student achievement of the unit's goal or the lesson's objectives.* A teaching cycle is incomplete until the teacher has assessed student achievement for the purpose of, first, determining whether or not the goal or objectives have been achieved well enough to move on to a subsequent unit or lesson, and second, reporting summative evaluations of student achievement.

- Terry may need to assign grades for students' achievement during the unit.
- Kristine needs to determine when she can safely begin scaling down the intervention.
- Byron won't want to move on to another lesson that depends on students' skill in converting fractions to percentages until he is convinced that the students are ready.

FIVE QUESTIONS TO BE ADDRESSED

With the teaching-cycle analysis approach, an upcoming teaching cycle (i.e., teaching unit or lesson) is designated for formative feedback. Then, as the teacher enters, controls, and concludes the cycle, the following five questions arc addressed:

1. Are the teacher's objectives appropriate? In other words: Are the objectives consistent with curriculum guidelines? Do they address student needs? Are they sufficiently, but not overly, ambitious?
2. Considering the aptitudes and prior achievements of the students and the time and resources available to the teacher, what pedagogical principles apply and what methods should be followed (according to research-based literature) in order to help students achieve the objectives? In other words, how should lessons be designed?
3. Are the lessons actually conducted in accordance with the pedagogical principles identified in the answer to question 2 above?
4. Is the teacher basing assessments of student achievement on cost-effective measurement results?

5. Are the lessons conducted not only in a manner that helps students achieve stated objectives, but also so that students are provided with positive experiences? (A teacher, for example, may conduct a lesson that helps students achieve stated objectives but the teacher's comments may be detrimental to a healthy, businesslike classroom atmosphere.)

INITIATING THE TEACHING-CYCLE ANALYSIS PROCESS

The five questions can be addressed by a process that is initiated as part of a formal system-wide program of formative evaluation. For example:

Terry Hives' school district uses staff development funds to support a formative evaluation program in which the teaching-cycle model is applied with each experienced teacher on one teaching unit per year and with each beginning teacher on three teaching units per year. The evaluations are scheduled throughout the school year, with each unit employing an evaluation team consisting of the teacher, a peer teacher from the same school, a peer teacher from another school, and a district-level teaching-area specialist.

Terry's unit on "selecting a domicile" is scheduled to be evaluated near the beginning of December.

The teaching-cycle analysis process may also be informally arranged simply because colleagues are inclined to help one another:

Kristine Scott and another primary grade teacher, Ebony Del Rio, talk in the faculty lounge:

KRISTINE: Do you have any ideas on dealing with a student who habitually interrupts classmates when they have the floor?

EBONY: The prescription has to fit the student and the situation. Why do you ask? Does one of your students have that problem?

KRISTINE: I don't really know. Tim Ziegler seems to be developing a pattern of interrupting classmates. I'm not sure if he needs me to teach him to break the habit or if it's only something I should deal with like an isolated disruption, instance by instance.

EBONY: Apparently it's bothering you enough that the problem merits some attention. Can we meet in your room at 3:45 to discuss how, if at all, you want to teach him to break this habit?

KRISTINE: Or if it's really a habit at all! I may just be overreacting to some isolated disruptions. I really appreciate your help! I'll be waiting for you at 3:45.

THE PLANNING CONFERENCE

The evaluation team meets to (1) determine the variables to be targeted by delimiting the model's five questions so that they fit the designated teaching cycle, (2) establish procedures, (3) determine data sources, and (4) schedule activities. Normally, the teacher will come to the initial planning meeting with a proposal. Here are two examples:

Besides Terry, his evaluation team consist of Vesna (another home economics teacher from Terry's school), Judith (a home economics teacher from another school), and Andrew (the district specialist for business and domestic education). At the initial meeting Terry distributes the following proposal for the team to consider and possibly amend:

• •

PROPOSAL FOR TEAM ACTIVITIES

Teaching cycle to be analyzed: Teaching unit, "Selecting a Domicile," that's scheduled for my fourth-period home economics class to begin on 11/25 and end on 12/6

Variables for the Team to Evaluate:

1. The appropriateness of the unit's goal and how well that goal is defined by the objectives
2. The appropriateness of the designs of the lessons (as described in the unit plan) for leading these particular students to achieve the objectives under the given circumstances
3. How closely I actually follow the agreed-upon lesson designs while conducting the class, and whether or not any deviations from those designs are based upon tenable formative feedback
4. The appropriateness of the procedures I use to assess student achievement of the unit's goal
5. Whether or not the lessons are conducted so that "side effects" on students are more positive than they are negative

Procedures by which the Team Evaluates the Five Variables:

1. *For variable 1*: By 10/11, I will send each of you a copy of the unit's goal statement and a list of objectives defining that goal. Attached will be one or two pages explaining my rationale for those objectives. The rationale will include pertinent information about the students, prior units, upcoming units, and any other factors I considered when formulating the objectives. By 10/18, each of you return the objectives with your notes indicating either that you agree to the objectives or how you think they should be modified. If I receive mixed feedback from you, I'll call a team meeting for 10/25. At the meeting we'll decide where to go from there. If all of you agree to the objectives or if we all seem to agree on how the objectives should be modified, I'll finalize them and then begin designing the lessons.
2. *For variable 2*: By 11/1, I'll supply you with three documents: (a) the agreed-upon objectives, (b) the lesson design plans, and (c) an approximately two-page rationale for the lesson designs. Among other factors, the rationale will include references to applicable teaching/learning principles. By 11/8, each of you return the lesson designs with your notes indicating either that you agree with them or how you think they should be modified. If I receive mixed feedback from you, I'll call a team meeting for 11/15. At the meeting we'll decide where to go from there. If all of you agree to the objectives or if we all seem to agree on how the designs should be modified, I'll finalize them and begin preparing to conduct the lessons.

3. *For variable 3*: Between 11/25 and 12/6 inclusive, you observe my fourth-period class according to whatever schedule you work out among yourselves. For each classroom observation, you will need to complete the district's lesson analysis form. By 8 A.M. on each of those days, I'll leave several copies of the day's lesson plans (including explanations of planned deviations from the unit design) for you to pick up from the main-office receptionist. On any day you observe, you will need to have that document beforehand in order to complete the district classroom observation form.

4. *For variable 4*: By 12/11, I will supply you with (a) the unit test I will have administered, (b) measurement results upon which my summative evaluations of their achievement of the unit's goal are based, (c) a statement summarizing my summative evaluations, and (d) a brief rationale for the evaluations, including data on the validity of the test. By 12/16, you complete and send to me the district's questionnaire relative to my procedures for assessing student achievement.

5. *For variable 5*: For each classroom observation you make, complete the column for "unanticipated outcomes" on the classroom observation form. By 12/11, you will get all of those completed classroom observation forms to me.

Idea-sharing meeting: On 12/20, we hold our idea-sharing meeting on what we learned and how we might do things to improve our teaching in the future.

• •

Copies of the district's instruments alluded to in Terry's plan are contained in Appendix Q.

The group agrees to Terry's proposal and works out details during the remainder of the meeting.

At 3:45, Kristine meets with Ebony as planned:

EBONY: Okay, so tell me about this problem you're having with Tim.

KRISTINE: I don't even know if it's a problem yet. But in the last three days, I'd bet he's interrupted someone speaking in class at least four times.

EBONY: What were the circumstances, group discussions, recitations, what?

KRISTINE: At least twice that I can remember, it was during a class meeting, when we have very strict rules governing who gets to speak. That's when I first began thinking he might be developing a habit. In the past, I hadn't really paid attention to it.

EBONY: Sounds like you need to collect some baseline data. That'll give us a better idea of whether it's habitual or not. Why don't you keep a chart indicating. . . .

The conversation continues with the two deciding to meet to analyze the baseline data Kristine collects. If they decide that Kristine should treat Tim's interruptions as a habit, Kristine will propose a plan of interaction that Ebony will critique.

EXPLANATION OF AND AGREEMENT TO LEARNING OBJECTIVES

The teacher is in the best position to determine what objectives are most appropriate for the students. Ideally, that teacher is the foremost expert regarding matters pertaining to his or her group of students, curriculum, and classroom. The teaching-cycle analysis does not depend on evaluators having greater pedagogical expertise than the teacher. However, to be in a position to provide the teacher with formative feedback, the evaluators need to understand the teacher's rationales for learning objectives, lesson designs, and assessment procedures. The burden of communicating those rationales to the evaluators lies with the teacher. Here is how Terry and Kristine attempted to communicate rationales for their objectives to the evaluators working with them:

As promised in the team meeting, Terry supplies Vesna, Judith, and Andrew with the following document:

• •

Goal and Objectives for Unit V: Selecting a Domicile

Goal: The unit is intended to help the students understand the relative advantages and disadvantages of different types of domestic housing and the factors that influence selections (e.g., budget, cost, personal preference, security, location, family situation, and available financing).

Objectives: Specifically, the student will:

1. Explain the similarities and differences between the rights, responsibilities, control, and flexibility of one who owns her/his domicile and those of one who rents her/his domicile (cognitive conceptual level)
2. Define the meanings of the following terms: "domicile," "real estate," "real estate agency," "home mortgage," "investment property," "property ownership," "renter," "renter's contract," "security deposit," "rent payment," "down payment," "house payment," "landlord," "home insurance," "renter's insurance," "apartment," "house," "duplex," "condominium," "housing," "housing project," "public housing," "homeless," "urban," "suburban," "rural," "hotel," and "motel" (cognitive simple-knowledge level)
3. Explain the general process by which a domicile is rented (cognitive knowledge-of-a-process level)
4. Explain the general process by which a domicile is financed and purchased (cognitive knowledge-of-a-process level)
5. Confronted with a particular set of circumstances (e.g., regarding income, family, job location, and personal preferences), select a type of housing to pursue and explain a rationale for the choice based upon a realization of the relative advantages and disadvantages of the choices (cognitive application level)

Rationale goal: The fifth unit of this home economics course should address the problem of selecting one's domicile because:

1. The *State Curriculum Standards Guide* (p. 314) stipulates that home economics programs are to help high school students prepare for "independent living." "Independent living" surely requires decision-making skills in selecting and acquiring one's place of living.
2. Unit IV, scheduled for completion on 11/22, deals with budgeting issues and skills. Since housing typically poses the single greatest drain on a domestic budget, the students should be ready to pursue Unit V's goal.
3. Unit VI, scheduled to begin on 12/9, deals with borrowing money. Examining the pros and cons of different types of housing in Unit V will involve them in the type of decision-making processes they'll need for Unit VI.
4. About half of the students are also taking an algebra course with Twila Stein. Twila and I have attempted to coordinate our units somewhat. About the time Unit V is scheduled, Twila plans to emphasize applications of algebra to problems involving interest.

Rationale for the objectives: Objective 5 is the culminating objective that's the most important relative to goal attainment. The other four are prerequisite to the fifth. Conceptualization of the relationships specified by Objective 1, the vocabulary from Objective 2, and the processes of Objectives 3 and 4 are needed before the students are ready to achieve Objective 5 at the application level. These objectives emphasize overall understanding rather than the technical aspects of real estate. The unit is supposed to provide an overview.

• •

The evaluators' responses to Terry's goal and objectives are extremely positive. They approve what he presents, with the following for him to consider:

- Vesna indicates that, besides the relationship specified by Objective 1, students also need to conceptualize relative advantages and disadvantages regarding other aspects of housing (e.g., urban versus suburban). She also questions why some of the terms in Objective 2's vocabulary list are included and others (e.g., "shelter") are not.
- Andrew expresses concern over "vocabulary overload." He worries that the vocabulary lessons will dominate the unit.
- Judith has no suggestions.

Terry reexamines Objective 2's vocabulary list and decides to leave it intact but notes that he needs to make it clear to the team that he plans to integrate the teaching of the vocabulary throughout the unit. Also, he decides to insert the following objective, calling it "Objective 5" and renaming the original Objective 5 as "Objective 6":

5. Based on personal preferences and goals, develop a list of the relative advantages of different types of domiciles for each of the following options: (a) location (urban, suburban, or rural), (b) ownership (rent or buy), and (c) structure (apartment/condominium, single-family house, multi-unit house, or hotel/motel) (cognitive conceptual level).

Three days of collecting baseline data on Tim's interruptions convinces Kristine that Tim has a persistent pattern that she needs to teach him to modify. Thus she already has an objective formulated when she meets with Ebony:

KRISTINE: Tim has definitely developed a habit. What do you think of this objective?

EBONY: Okay. (reading) "Tim will reduce the frequency of interrupting classmates who are speaking, from his baseline ratio of 35% of the time to a ratio of less than 10% within two weeks." Wow! Pretty ambitious.

KRISTINE: It's either that or I have to keep reacting to each incident one at a time, and he's just going to get deeper and deeper in trouble.

EBONY: We don't want that. But I have one question. This objective suggests you're going to focus on his breaking the habit. What have you got in mind for intervention?

KRISTINE: I haven't worked it out yet, but I guess I should apply the principle of extinction (Cangelosi, 1988a, pp. 218–20).

EBONY: But then you'd have to identify the positive reinforcers. For this type of behavior, that's going to be difficult to do and then to control.

KRISTINE: I agree. Do you have a suggestion?

EBONY: If you change your objective so that it focuses on teaching him an on-task behavior pattern that's incompatible with his pattern of interruptions, . . .

KRISTINE: Like quietly listening when others are speaking and raising his hand to speak.

EBONY: Exactly. Then a principle like shaping would apply and that would be a lot more efficient for this situation.

KRISTINE: So, I'll restate the objective. Give me a minute. . . . How docs this sound? "Tim will exhibit a pattern of quiet listening behaviors by waiting his turn to speak and raising his hand to be recognized at least 90% of the time that classmates are speaking. Two weeks after intervention begins, this pattern will have emerged." What do you think?

EBONY: I think you have a better chance of succeeding with that objective.

KRISTINE: Now, I have to design the intervention. I'll work on it tonight. May I pass it by you tomorrow?

EBONY: You bet; I'm anxious to see what you come up with.

EXPLANATION OF AND AGREEMENT TO LESSON DESIGNS

Because of its length, Terry's designs for the unit's lessons and his rationale for those designs are not included here. With the help of minor input from the evaluators, the designs are finalized. The design for Kristine's lesson is critiqued by Ebony during a brief conference:

EBONY: So what have you planned for your intervention?

KRISTINE: Well it's in no way finalized, but I'll continue to maintain a record of his behavior during relevant situations, just like for baseline. I'll try to anticipate the times when other students have the floor and be near Tim so I can use non-attention-getting body language to quickly intercept his interruptions. Now if that'll control his interruptions, then there's a chance shaping can work.

EBONY: How do you propose to use shaping?

KRISTINE: I'll really have to monitor him closely and then when he's displaying some patience and makes any kind of movement that even vaguely resembles raising his hand, I'll call on him to make a comment. Then I'd have to get on a gradually decreasing schedule of reinforcement for waiting to speak in turn.

EBONY: Do you think he finds attention rewarding?

KRISTINE: Not in general; I think it's more a desire to be heard.

EBONY: Okay, so you'll give him opportunities to talk as rewards for waiting.

KRISTINE: Right, but first I have to get him to begin raising his hand. That's the real key.

EBONY: I really think it'll work if you consistently stick to your reinforcement schedule.

KRISTINE: And I really have to know when to jump in and when to back off. It's not going to be easy. Will you spot-check me occasionally with a few observations?

EBONY: Yes, and you can also share what happens each day with me—we can discuss how closely you're sticking to the plan.

EVALUATION OF THE CONSISTENCY BETWEEN DESIGNS AND LESSONS

The variable "consistency between a lesson's design and the way the lesson is actually conducted," is evaluated in the next two examples:

Using Appendix Q's classroom observation instrument, Terry's evaluation team collects data relevant to variable 3 (as listed in the "Proposal for Team Activities") according to the following observation schedule:

Date	Fourth-Period Observers
11/25	Vesna, Judith, and Andrew
11/26	Andrew
11/27	Vesna
11/28	Judith
11/29	Judith and Andrew
12/2	Vesna and Andrew
12/3	Vesna and Andrew
12/4	
12/5	Vesna, Judith, and Andrew
12/6	

One of the reasons Terry's fourth-period class was targeted for the evaluation effort is that fifth period he does not have a class. Thus, post-observational conferences are held during fifth period. The conference of December 2 included the following conversation:

TERRY: I can see just from glancing at your descriptions on both the forms that my planned high-level questioning activity turned out to be a low-level questioning activity.

VESNA: Yeah, was that intentional?

TERRY: Not really. As you expected, we were supposed to be comparing renting to buying. But it quickly became obvious that they didn't remember the differences between the renting and buying processes; so I got frustrated.

ANDREW: And that's when you began quizzing them on the processes?

TERRY: Right.

VESNA: How many do you really think were unfamiliar with the processes?

TERRY: I hear what you're saying. I overacted to Ray's and Juaquin's lack of recall. I think I messed that session up.

ANDREW: But at least your adjustment was based on formative feedback.

TERRY: But misinterpreted formative feedback, I should have. . . .

After all of the observations are completed, Terry carefully analyzes the responses from the 15 completed observation forms. On the basis of that analysis, he draws some conclusions, which will be discussed with the team at the scheduled idea-sharing meeting.

Three times during the first week of Kristine's attempt to teach Tim to habitually raise his hand and patiently wait his turn to speak, she and Ebony discussed how the plan is progressing. Here is a portion of the second conference:

KRISTINE: This morning, just before I pulled the four reading groups together to share stories with one another, I moved right by Tim and then stayed with him for the whole discussion. Anytime he even looked as though he was going to interrupt, I'd be right between him and the rest of the class.

EBONY: Did he ever interrupt?

KRISTINE: Not once this morning. But here's the best part! Because I was blocking his view, he began to wiggle in his chair to look around me. That's when I pretended to think he was raising his hand and I called on him, thanking him for raising his hand.

EBONY: What did he say?

KRISTINE: What didn't he say? He talked on and on about the story his group read! I let him talk longer than I usually do to reinforce his waiting to be called on.

EBONY: But I bet it got boring for the others.

KRISTINE: They got really restless.

EBONY: So are the rest going to be encouraged not to wait their turn?

KRISTINE: Not only that, but. . .

The conversation continues along this vein. It ends with Ebony agreeing to observe twice the following week when Kristine has class meetings scheduled.

IDENTIFYING "SIDE EFFECTS"
OR UNANTICIPATED OUTCOMES

In the previous example, Ebony began raising the issue of side effects or unanticipated outcomes when she said, "But I bet it got boring for the others." Classroom
environments are so complex that it is virtually impossible for a teacher to pursue
one objective without having an impact on other teaching/learning variables. Terry's formative evaluation team is concerned with unanticipated outcome variables in
the following example:

When Vesna, Judith, and Andrew followed the classroom observation schedule (given
on page 154), they also filled out the third column of Appendix Q's instrument, intended
to identify unanticipated outcomes. Part of the post-observation conference on November 27 included this conversation:

TERRY: I see that you noted in the third column by my second learning activity that
I countered students' negative comments about urban housing projects
with positive comments. Why did you note that under "unanticipated
outcomes"?

VESNA: Consistently doing that may not further your stated objectives of the unit,
but it's going to further a far greater good.

TERRY: What are you talking about?

VESNA: These kids are always being bombarded by movies and television shows
putting down urban housing projects, as if you should be ashamed to live
there. You managed to present the positive side. That could be a long-
lasting side effect that encourages some healthy attitudes!

Unanticipated outcomes will also be a topic for discussion at the "idea-sharing"
meeting scheduled for December 20.

EVALUATION OF THE TEACHER'S ASSESSMENT
OF STUDENT ACHIEVEMENT

The variable of how well the teacher bases assessment of student achievement on
cost-effective measurements is evaluated in the next two examples:

By December 11, Terry has given Vesna, Judith and Andrew the following:

1. a copy of the Unit V test he administered on December 6
2. a list of the students' scores from that test
3. half-page descriptions of observations, other than the test, that he feels are
relevant to an assessment of student achievement
4. a brief report of the results of an informal validation of the unit test (i.e., a
table of specifications and a reliability coefficient)
5. an explanation of his evaluation of student achievement of Unit V's goal
(including a unit grade for each student)

During the December 20 idea-sharing meeting, issues related to how Terry assessed student achievement are discussed:

VESNA: Don't you think you could save a lot of your time by replacing a couple of these essay items on the unit test with 10 to 20 multiple-choice ones? I was playing around with some ways that could be accomplished without lowering the cognitive level of the test.

ANDREW: If you could do that, I bet you'd increase reliability also.

TERRY: I'd have trouble coming up with multiple-choice items relevant to either objectives 1 or 5. They're both conceptual level.

VESNA: Take a look at what I came up with and see what you think. . . .

The conversation continues.

In the middle of the second week of Kristine's intervention to shape Tim's behavior pattern, Kristine and Ebony have this conversation:

KRISTINE: The intervention isn't working. Tim's just not making progress.

EBONY: On what are you basing that judgment?

KRISTINE: Look at these data. It's been almost two weeks and he's exhibiting the hand-raising, patient pattern only 60 percent of the time!

EBONY: How are you counting these frequencies?

KRISTINE: Every time the pertinent situations occur, I count the number of times he raises his hand before speaking and divide that by the number of times he begins to speak.

EBONY: But when I observed today, there were instances when he spoke without raising his hand, but no one else was speaking either. How did you count those?

KRISTINE: If he didn't raise his hand, it was counted as a negative.

EBONY: Are we straying from our original intent, which was to get him to wait his turn to talk, not simply raise his hand?

KRISTINE: You may be right. But I was trying to be completely objective with. . . .

The conversation continues.

IDEA-SHARING CONFERENCES

Idea-sharing conferences provide opportunities for the formative evaluation team to discuss issues, raise questions, and make suggestions that typically provide in-service benefits to the evaluators as well as the teacher. In Terry's case, one idea-sharing conference was scheduled as the culmination of the formative evaluation effort. For Kristine, the conferences will continue informally as long as she and Ebony work in the same school.

THE LONG-RANGE BENEFITS OF ANALYZING TEACHING CYCLES

Formative evaluations based on analyses of teaching cycles are highly focused. Terry Hives' evaluation team concentrated on only one of the many units he teaches. Ebony's efforts working with Kristine addressed only modifying one behavior pattern exhibited by one student. However, the impact of such formative evaluations extends far beyond the teaching cycles upon which they are focused. Terry, as well as members of his evaluation team, will be better equipped to conduct subsequent teaching cycles as an outcome of the experience. Kristine and Ebony's thoughtful approach to solving the problem with Tim will serve them well in dealing with similar problems in the future.

The impact on the particular teaching cycle analyzed is not nearly as important as the impact the analysis process has on the subsequent performances of the teachers themselves.

SELF-ASSESSMENT EXERCISES FOR CHAPTER 6

I. Call to mind the same school situation that you reflected upon for self-assessment Exercise I of Chapter 5. Could the teaching cycle analysis approach work in that school? If "yes," then write a description of an efficient way of introducing the approach to the faculty. If "no," explain why in one or two paragraphs. Exchange your response with someone else who is completing this exercise. Discuss similarities and differences in what the two of you wrote.

II. Read the following scenario, and then respond to the items that follow it in light of what you read:

Byron Alley develops a teaching unit on applications of rational numbers for his sixth-grade mathematics students. The unit's goal is defined by 12 objectives. Three days are spent on a lesson for the fifth objective, which is for the students to be able to convert rational numbers in fraction form to percentages. The learning activities for the lesson include step-by-step explanations, drill and practice, error pattern analysis, and homework assignment and review. On the second day of the lesson, Byron becomes concerned with the number of students who did not complete the homework assignment. To convince them to be more diligent in completing homework, Byron on the third day administers a "pop quiz" that includes items that are nearly identical to the homework exercise. Byron notices that most of those who completed the assignment did better on the quiz than most who didn't. Because nearly everyone has their homework completed for the fourth day, he believes the pop-quiz strategy was successful.

On the basis of the results of the test he administers near the end of the unit, he judges that about 60 percent of the class understand rational numbers well enough to advance to the next unit.

Identify three teaching cycles implicit in the anecdote. For each one, describe what Byron did within each of the four stages of the learning cycle: (a) determining of a goal or objectives, (b) designing lessons, (c) conducting lessons and learning activities, and (d) assessing student achievement.

Compare your responses with the following:

Byron controlled a teaching cycle by developing and completing the teaching unit on applications of rational numbers. (a) The first phase of this cycle occurred when the determined the unit's goal and defined it by formulating 12 objectives. (b) Designing the lessons occurred when he did such things as decide to spend three days on objective 5 using step-by-step explanations, drill and practice, and so forth. (c) He conducted lessons by giving explanations, making assignments, reviewing homework, and the like. (d) Student achievement was assessed when he administered the test and evaluated that 60 percent of the students were ready to move on.

Byron also controlled lesson-level teaching cycles embedded within the unit. For example, his three-day lesson on converting fractions to decimals contained all four phases of a teaching cycle beginning with the determination of objective 5 and terminating with his judgments about who did better on the quiz.

Then Byron controlled a teaching cycle on the importance of completing homework. In this example he (a) determined that the students would become more diligent completing homework, (b) decided on the pop-quiz strategy, (c) gave the pop quiz, and (d) determined that the lesson was learned.

PART III
Summative Methods

Part III

Summary Sections

CHAPTER 7

Summative Evaluations for Beginning Teachers

Goal of Chapter 7

Chapter 7 suggests ways of resolving issues and problems related to summative evaluations for beginning teachers. Specifically, this chapter is designed to help you:

1. Describe factors unique to the beginning teacher experience that interfere with the success of beginning teachers' performances.
2. Explain the quality-control function of summative evaluations for beginning teachers.
3. Describe major ethical and legal issues related to summative evaluations of beginning teachers' instructional effectiveness and propose some realistic resolutions.
4. For a given situation, design and describe a practical program of summative evaluations of the instructional effectiveness of beginning teachers.

THE FIRST CRITICAL YEARS

The vast majority of teachers experience their most significant, career-threatening frustrations and challenges during the first two or three years of their professional careers (Lanier & Little, 1986. pp. 560–62). Beginning teachers are more likely than veteran teachers to leave the profession in favor of nonteaching occupations (Duke, Cangelosi, & Knight, 1988). Their situation is different from that of their experienced colleagues in many ways: They are adapting to a new career and working environment; they do not have a wealth of professional experiences on which to base decisions; they have not proven to themselves that they can survive in the classroom; they have yet to establish a reputation among students, parents, colleagues, and administrators; and they do not enjoy the security of having earned tenure (available in most states to experienced teachers).

While security with one's self and position is a virtual requisite to effective teaching performance, beginning teachers are generally occupied with feelings of doubt and fear of inadequacy (Glickman, 1985, pp. 157–59). There can be little wonder why beginning teachers, as a group, are less effective in the classroom than their experienced counterparts (Clark & Peterson, 1986, pp. 278–81). Particularly troublesome areas for beginning teachers are problems related to classroom management and discipline, acquiring needed instructional materials, assessing student work, interacting with parents, and organizing curricula (Arends, 1988, p. 530; Stallion, 1988).

It is during this most trying period of teachers' careers that they face summative evaluations of their instruction that influence whether or not they are allowed to continue as teachers. It should be noted, however, that *failure to perform organizational functions* and *to relate to school personnel* are more likely to lead to the dismissal of beginning teachers than is *teaching incompetence* (Arends, 1988, p. 22). Traditionally, teaching incompetence and poor teaching performance have been difficult to prove because of school administrators' failure to follow sound summative evaluation principles (Bridges, 1986, pp. 24–25).

SUMMATIVE EVALUATIONS FOR DECISIONS ABOUT RETENTION AND STATUS OF BEGINNING TEACHERS

Control of the quality of instruction depends on preservice preparation programs, in-service and staff development programs, instructional supervision, and screening individuals from the profession who are either unable or unwilling to teach effectively. Summative evaluations of the instruction of beginning teachers are the primary means of screening for teaching incompetence and ineffectiveness. Stated policies in virtually every public school district stipulate that decisions regarding extensions of beginning teachers' contracts and position statuses (e.g., a temporary probationary status versus tenured status) should be at least partially dependent on the outcomes of summative evaluations of their instruction.

Designing a summative evaluation program for beginning teachers that serves this critical quality-control function presents major dilemmas. Consider three types of beginning teachers.

- *Type I.* All beginning teachers struggle with difficulties endemic to the first few years of teaching, but some succeed in the classroom almost immediately. The instructional effectiveness of Type I beginning teachers will improve with experience, but it is already superior to that of most experienced teachers.

- *Type II*. Some beginning teachers need experience and instructional supervision before reaching satisfactory classroom performance levels. With reasonable support, these Type II teachers will overcome the difficulties of their first few years and blossom into highly competent instructors.
- *Type III*. Type III beginning teachers are those whose teaching performances will never be satisfactory without unreasonable and costly instructional supervision aimed at overhauling their whole approach to instruction (often requiring them to shed misconceptions and destructive attitudes).

Summative evaluations for beginning teachers need to be at least accurate enough to distinguish among these three types. A failure to identify a Type III beginning teacher unleashes instructional incompetence that is virtually impossible to stem once that teacher is no longer classified as "beginning" (Bridges, 1986, pp. 19–73). Allowing instructional ineffectiveness to continue not only disserves the students and community but also contaminates the profession and prevents Type III teachers from seeking more satisfying careers for themselves.

A failure to recognize a Type II beginning teacher may result in either the discarding of a potentially effective teacher, or retention of that teacher but without adequate instructional supervision. The former leads to the loss of a valuable resource and a ruined career. The latter perpetuates instructional ineffectiveness in the classroom. Distinguishing between types II and III poses a major challenge for summative evaluators. Both types struggle in their beginning years, but what key signals distinguish potential for success from potential for failure? That is a question to be addressed when summative evaluation variables are defined.

Summative evaluators generally have an easier (and more pleasant) time identifying Type I beginning teachers than attempting to distinguish between Types II and III. Moreover, Type Is, by comparison, do so well that their instructional supervision needs are often neglected in favor of helping the less competent. It should be noted that some Type I beginning teachers who are highly effective in the classroom are dismissed because they fail to meet noninstructional expectations (e.g., those involving personal relations with colleagues and administrators). Others change careers after becoming disenchanted with what they perceive as a lack of support for quality teaching and professional standards (Biddle, 1987; Duke, Cangelosi, & Knight, 1988).

RESPONSIBILITY FOR DIFFICULT DECISIONS

Who is responsible for decisions regarding retention and status of beginning teachers? Ultimately, decisions lie with school boards. However, school board members depend on recommendations from district office personnel who, in turn, depend on school principals. In most districts, the school principal's recommendation carries the greatest weight (Ryan & Cooper, 1988, pp. 399–402). To whatever degree teaching competence and effectiveness affect retention and status decisions about beginning teachers, summative evaluations of instruction influence these difficult decisions. Unfortunately, principals and others do not typically have access to tenable summative evaluation feedback upon which to base these judgments (Bridges, 1986, pp. 34–36; Medley, Coker, & Soar, 1984, pp. 29–51). Standards of ethics dictate that the most cost-effective available data sources be used to provide accurate summative evaluations. After all, both the welfare of students and the careers of professional teachers are at stake.

Ethical conflicts abound in summative evaluations of instruction in ways that do not occur in formative evaluations. Formative evaluators enjoy a oneness of purpose with the teacher: both of them are focused on how to do a better job for students. In contrast, a summative evaluator's agendas and that of the teacher may come into conflict. The summative evaluator's overall purpose of quality control is not always in perfect harmony with the teacher's purpose of protecting her or his position or advancing in status.

LEGAL CONCERNS

In an ideal world, responsible, ethical practice not only is protected from legal attacks, but is encouraged by legal statutes. However, in today's litigious society, there appears to be no course for summative evaluators to take that is free from legal challenges. However, prudence dictates adherence to the following principles:

1. Summative evaluations focus on variables that are appropriate according to research-based or rational-based arguments contained in the professional literature.
2. The (a) summative evaluation variables, (b) criteria by which teaching competence, teaching performance, or student outcomes are assessed, and (c) general process for conducting summative evaluations are public and made known to the beginning teacher as a precondition of employment in the school district.
3. The beginning teacher has a voice in procedural decisions in the summative evaluation process (e.g., how an evaluation team is formed and the scheduling of classroom observations).
4. Summative evaluations are based upon validated measurement results.
5. The school principal (or representatives) provides adequate support and reasonable opportunities for the beginning teacher to succeed in the classroom. Doing so requires the principal to see that competent instructional supervision (and thus formative evaluations) are available to help the teacher prepare for the summative evaluations. Note the conflict of roles faced by the principal. On one hand, principals are responsible for making recommendations affecting tenure and status, and on the other hand they are responsible for seeing that adequate formative evaluations and instructional supervision are provided. Suggestions on how the two roles can be separated were presented in Chapter 5.
6. Professional confidence is maintained throughout the process. Neither evaluation outcomes nor information gained from the process are shared with unauthorized persons (unless by the teacher her- or himself).

7. Evaluators report complete results to the teacher and to those (e.g., the principal) who are responsible for making the decision regarding retention or status.
8. In general, the evaluation process should be consistent with published professional standards such as those of the Joint Committee on Standards for Educational Evaluation (1988) that are listed in Appendix R.
9. Evidence of adherence to the above eight principles needs to be documented.

THE DESIGN OF ONE SUMMATIVE EVALUATION PROGRAM FOR BEGINNING TEACHERS

A summative evaluation program for the beginning teachers of Silver County School District is designed with the nine aforementioned principles in mind by a task force of teachers, supervisors, and administrators in consultation with evaluation specialists. The first challenge is to determine the evaluation variables. The availability of cost-effective measurements ultimately plays a role in the task force's decisions regarding such variables.

Initially, the task force plans a "comprehensive" program focusing on teaching competence, teaching performance, and student outcome variables.

The argument for including *teaching competence* variables is that beginning teachers typically struggle for a year or two adapting to new situations and gaining valuable experiences, and it is their *potential* for expert teaching that should be considered for decisions regarding tenure and status. Thus, teaching competence variables should be examined in summative evaluations. The evaluations need to *predict* what teaching performance levels will be after the teachers have had time to develop their methods and techniques. Otherwise, the process will fail to identify Type II beginning teachers.

The argument for including *teaching performance* variables is that what a beginning teacher actually does to develop curricula, conduct lessons, manage students, and assess student achievement can hardly be ignored. Furthermore, for purposes of evaluating instruction, measurements of teaching performance variables are more likely to produce valid results than measurements of either teaching competence or student outcome variables (Cangelosi, 1986; Harris, 1986, pp. 77–154; Medley, Coker, & Soar, 1984, pp. 1–51).

The argument for including *student outcome* variables is that since serving students is the primary function of schools, what beginning teachers accomplish with students needs to be considered in evaluations of their instruction.

For the three categories, the task force suggests that the following variables be targeted:

1. Teaching competence variables
   A. Understanding of generic principles of pedagogy and educational psychology
   B. Understanding of pedagogical and educational psychological principles specific to the beginning teacher's specialty area (e.g., primary grades or health science)
   C. Understanding of classroom management principles

    D. Ability to effectively use communications and language arts skills (including reading, writing, speaking, and listening)

    E. Level of mathematical literacy

    F. Level of scientific literacy

    G. Level of literacy regarding society (e.g., history and current events)

    H. Understanding of content subject areas specific to the beginning teacher's specialty area

    I. Willingness to learn from experiences and openness to instructional supervision

    J. Level of self-confidence and respect for students as individuals

    K. Degree to which the beginning teacher is free from ethnic, cultural, religious, sex, and age prejudices

2. Teaching performance variables

    A. Appropriateness of teaching units with respect to school curriculum guidelines and student needs

    B. Appropriateness of learning goals and objectives with respect to unit plans, student needs, pedagogical principles, and clarity

    C. Appropriateness of lesson designs with respect to targeted objectives, pedagogical principles, and characteristics of the students and the situations

    D. How well learning activities are conducted in accordance with lesson designs

    E. The conduciveness of the classroom environment to maximal student engagement in learning activities

    F. The efficacy with which the teacher deals with off-task student behaviors and motivates on-task behaviors

    G. The efficacy with which the teacher obtains and utilizes formative feedback data relative to student achievement

    H. The accuracy of summative assessments of student achievement and the appropriateness of the teacher's reports of those assessments (with respect to clarity of communications and maintenance of professional confidences)

    I. The teacher's demeanor and communication styles that are associated with affecting students in ways not subsumed by stated learning goals (e.g., whether or not racist attitudes are displayed)

3. Student outcome variables

    A. How well students achieve learning goals as compared with a prediction of how well those students would have achieved those goals in the given circumstances under the tutelage of a minimally competent teacher ("minimally competent" to be operationally defined for each specialty area)

    B. Effects on students that are not subsumed by learning goals but that are associated with the teacher's instructional activities

       Working with the evaluation consultants, the task force reviews relevant literature in an attempt to determine cost-effective methods of measuring their variables. The results of validation studies of existing teacher competency tests discourage pursuing ways to measure the teaching competence variables. One task-force meeting includes the following discussion over the issue of retaining or deleting the teaching competence variables:

    BOB: I don't think we could ever defend evaluations based on currently available teaching competency tests.

    QUINN: So we have to develop our own.

BOB: What makes you think we could do any better than the experts who have tried in the past?

QUINN: What other choices do we have?

EVA: We could just concentrate on the other two areas.

QUINN: But we agreed that evaluating potential is critical for these beginning teachers.

BOB: You're right, but I still agree with Eva. Our list of teaching competence variables contains things that should be evaluated before we hire a teacher. Knowledge, understanding, and attitudes about students and self—those are things that we should screen them for *before* we ever offer them a contract!

YOLANDO: I would hope that the colleges qualified them on those variables before they turned them loose on the job market! Now that I've thought it through again, it's their performances at the schools that should be the focus of the evaluations.

QUINN: You've got a point, but I promise you that unless we further examine potential, we're not going to distinguish between the Type IIs we want to keep and the Type IIIs we want to eliminate.

BOB: But if we can't find valid measures of teaching competence, the question is moot.

YOLANDO: I've got a compromise proposal that might satisfy both of you. Let's drop the list of teaching competence variables from our list and recommend that they be evaluated somehow at the hiring phase.

CABELL: There's already some attempt to do that.

YOLANDO: Okay, good, then we only have to emphasize that the problem of evaluating those variables be pursued more systematically when job candidates are screened. Anyway, what I'm trying to get at is this. We drop the teacher competence variables but then adjust the teaching performance variables so that they include indicators of potential.

QUINN: What?

YOLANDO: We should reword some of them so that they focus on beginning teachers' improvements over time. Shouldn't improvement reflect potential?

BOB: So reword one for me.

YOLANDO: Okay, I'll try C. Instead of "appropriateness of lesson designs," C could read: "Improvement the beginning teacher displays regarding designing lessons that are appropriate with respect to targeted objectives, pedagogical principles, and characteristics of the students and the situations." How's that?

CABELL: It's clear, but what about the Type I beginning teacher whose performances are super from the very beginning? You aren't going to require that teacher to improve in order to keep her or his job!

EVA: And what if a Type III starts off so terrible that anything would be an improvement?

YOLANDO: I hear you. So instead of rewording, let's just add one at the end of the list that deals with level of improvement relative to all of the other variables.

QUINN: Could we also add one similar to teaching competence variable I? It could be reworded so that it falls within the domain of teaching performance.

After further discussion and work, the task force eliminates the teaching competence category and adds the following to the list of *teaching performance variables:*

J. Response to instructional supervision in terms of impact on teaching performances
K. Degree to which the beginning teacher's performances improve with respect to variables A–J.

Because the task force's pursuit of measures to be used in predicting what student achievement would be if the beginning teacher were replaced by a "minimally competent" teacher proves futile, the student outcome variables are also eliminated for the summative evaluation program.

Having determined the variables, the task force turns its attention to the problems of *measuring the variables* and *designing the overall program:*

The task force decides that classroom observation, document examination, and interview measurements will be selected or developed and validated by a second task force, one working with measurement and evaluation consultants. The procedures and instruments are to be explained in a handbook for summative evaluators. After weeks of work, the taskforce settles on a program targeting teaching performance variables A through K and containing the following phases:

1. *Prior to hiring a new teacher:* Candidates for teaching positions are screened with respect to teaching competence variables. Before being offered a contract, a new teacher is informed in writing regarding the purposes, requirements, and procedures of the summative evaluation program for beginning teachers. The Silver County School District contract for a new teacher stipulates that by signing the contract the teacher agrees to abide by the program as a condition of employment.
2. *The first year of the probationary period:* Just prior to the start of the first school year, the beginning teacher, principal, and department head plan, arrange for, and schedule the year's summative evaluation activities. A summative evaluation team (SET) is organized consisting of three persons: two experienced teachers working in the beginning teacher's specialty area at other schools, and an outside consultant (e.g., from another school district or a college faculty) also in the specialty area. The SET meets with the beginning teacher, principal, and beginning teacher's formative evaluation team (FET) to clarify procedures, schedules, responsibilities, and ground rules. FET consists of an experienced peer teacher from the school, the department head, and a district office specialist in the teaching area.
Ground rules include the following:

A. The principal serves as liaison between FET and SET but never becomes involved in the evaluation activities of either team. The principal serves to facilitate the teams' work, but does not participate in it.
B. During the course of the school year, FET and SET work independently from one another, maintaining complete separation.
C. SET bases its summative evaluations of the beginning teacher's teaching solely on measurement results obtained during three two-week periods scheduled for November, February, and April.
D. FET provides the beginning teacher with instructional supervisory services throughout the school year except during the three two-week summative periods. FET's instructional supervision should include, but is not limited to, the same 11 teaching performance variables (A–K) that are targeted by SET.
E. During the three summative evaluation periods, SET obtains measurement results utilizing the classroom observation, document examination, and beginning teacher interview instruments contained in Silver County School District's *Summative Evaluator's Handbook*. These results may be supplemented by other measurements to which both the beginning teacher and SET agree. However, all such measurements must be administered within the designated time periods.
F. Within a week after each of the three summative evaluation periods, SET presents copies of a written report to the beginning teacher, the principal, and the superintendent. The report contains (1) documentation of SET's activities, (2) an evaluation of the beginning teacher's instructional effectiveness that addresses the 11 variables A–K, and (3) all measurement results gathered during the two-week period.
G. SET and the principal are restricted from sharing evaluation report results with anyone not authorized either in writing by the beginning teacher or by the school superintendent, or by action of the school board.
H. After each of SET's three reports, the principal, in consultation with the beginning teacher, writes a recommendation regarding the status of the beginning teacher's position. Regarding *instructional effectiveness*, only SET's evaluations and measurements may influence the recommendation. (Regarding noninstructional related factors that may influence retention and status decisions according to school board policy, this restriction does not apply.) The recommendation is sent to the superintendent with a copy to the beginning teacher. Consistent with standard policy on all such matters, the beginning teacher has the right to a formal hearing on recommendations and evaluations.
I. Although the principal is restricted from involvement in FET's work, he or she is allowed and encouraged to provide the beginning teacher with instructional supervisory services outside of that provided by FET.
J. The superintendent is responsible for apprising the beginning teacher by May 15 regarding the status of his or her position for the next year.
   Plans developed at the meeting are followed during the year.
3. *The second year of the probationary period:* The program for the second year follows the same lines as that for the first except that the composition of SET must change, at least one member being replaced. An end-of-the-year decision is made to either award tenure, extend the probationary period one more year, or not rehire.
4. *The extended probationary period:* If the decision is to extend the probationary period to a third and final year (either tenure must be awarded for the fourth year or the teacher cannot be rehired), then the summative evaluation program continues in a

similar fashion. However, the third-year probationary teacher, principal, and FET are required to work out a very specific prescription for addressing the concerns raised by the prior year's SET reports.

5. *Tenure:* The teacher receives tenure by the third or fourth year and the summative evaluation program is no longer applicable. The teacher is now eligible for summative evaluation programs for promotion and merit-pay increases (e.g., using the model presented in Chapter 8).

The Silver County School Board approves the program, and it becomes operational after measurements are selected, developed, and validated and training sessions for evaluators are initiated.

TWO NECESSARY CONDITIONS FOR SUCCESS

Silver County School District's summative evaluation program is designed with careful attention to the nine principles listed on pages 166–167. Two factors are critical to the success of such a carefully designed program. The first is *the cost-effectiveness of the measurements used to make the evaluations.* The teachers, supervisors, and consultants who select, develop, validate, administer, and interpret the classroom observations, document examinations, interviews, and other data sources must be willing and able to apply the principles from Chapters 2–4 of this text. Doing this requires not only literacy in the area of measurement and evaluation, but also a sophisticated grasp of teaching/learning principles and how they can be realistically applied in specific classroom situations (Hunter, 1988).

The second critical factor is *teachers', supervisors', and administrators' commitment to quality control for the benefit of students.* Even well-designed programs coupled with cost-effective measurements are readily subverted by personnel with priorities and agendas that are inconsistent with published school goals. Programs such as Silver County's should include protections from unscrupulous behaviors. However, goodwill is hardly a function of policy. The evaluation model for beginning teachers presented in this chapter, like those in other chapters, is based on the assumption that responsible professionals assert themselves.

SELF-ASSESSMENT EXERCISES FOR CHAPTER 7

I. Call to mind the same school situation that you reflected upon for self-assessment Exercise I in Chapter 5. Could Silver County's summative evaluation program for beginning teachers work in that school? Explain why or why not. Exchange your response with someone else who is completing this exercise. Discuss similarities and differences in what the two of you wrote.

II. Explain why you agree or disagree with the following statement:

Type II beginning teachers are far more likely to improve their instruction over the next two years than are veteran teachers whose teaching performances are equally ineffective.

Exchange your explanation with another and discuss similarities and differences. Did you consider the unique disadvantages with which beginning teachers must contend?

III. Select one of the 11 variables (A–K) focused upon by the Silver County summative evaluation program for beginning teachers. Design one measurement to be relevant to that variable for use by a beginning teacher's SET. Have someone who is familiar with the content of Chapters 2–4 critique your measurement for its cost-effective potential.

IV. Critique Silver County's summative evaluation program for beginning teachers with respect to how well it adheres to the nine principles raised under the chapter's section on "Legal Concerns." Identify aspects of the program that would be especially open to legal challenges, and propose remedies. Exchange your work on this item with someone else and discuss the similarities and differences between your two responses.

V. Appendix S contains documents used in the program for summative evaluations of instruction in the Davis County (Utah) School District (1988). Examine those documents along with another person who is completing this exercise. Together, discuss what from the documents you would want to incorporate into a summative evaluation program for beginning teachers that the two of you designed.

CHAPTER 8

Evaluations for Advancement of Expert Teachers

Goal of Chapter 8

Chapter 8 presents ideas for designing summative evaluations of instruction for use in an advancement program for expert teachers. Specifically, this chapter is designed to help you:

1. Identify teacher advancement programs (e.g., merit-pay, master-teacher, and career ladder plans) within which summative evaluations of the instruction of expert teachers are needed.
2. Describe the general process by which the *design–execution performance model* for evaluating expert instruction is followed.
3. Explain, relative to alternatives, the advantages and disadvantages of applying the design–execution performance model in a given situation.

THE NEED TO IDENTIFY EXEMPLARY INSTRUCTION

The Problem of Retaining Expert Teachers and Motivating Exemplary Instruction

Retaining adequate numbers of qualified, expert teachers continues to be a major concern of school administrators and professional educators (Ryan & Cooper, 1988, p. 510). Lack of opportunities for advancement, failure to be treated like professionals, failure to reward excellence, lack of involvement in decision making, and low salaries are among the more prominent reasons qualified, experienced teachers give for deciding to leave the profession (McGrath, 1986; Metropolitan Life Insurance Company, 1986). Even during periods in which the supply of teachers seemed to exceed the overall demand, the need for expert teachers and teachers qualified in certain critical areas (e.g., mathematics) remained in short supply (Cangelosi, 1988b).

In addition to shortages of qualified, expert teachers, there are also the problems of how to motivate teachers to strive to be more effective in the classroom, and how to extend the reach of expert teachers so their work is not limited to their own classrooms.

Merit-Pay Programs

A seemingly straightforward approach to rewarding and motivating teaching excellence is simply to pay teachers according to their levels of "productivity" (Bush, 1988; Cameron, 1985). "Give the raises to those who deserve them!" is a popular cry in political arenas. However, for the most part, merit-pay plans have failed to motivate improved instruction, for several reasons. Typically, summative evaluations of instruction have not been based on cost-effective measurements; in some cases, the variable *instructional effectiveness* was not even considered a factor in decisions regarding who receives raises, and poorly conceived and administered programs often discouraged collegiality among teachers and encouraged competitiveness (Harris, 1986, pp. 220–24; Silverman, 1983).

Career Ladder Programs

The term "career ladder programs" refers to a variety of schemes to enhance teachers' opportunities for promotions and receipt of monetary bonuses for exemplary work or for accepting additional responsibilities. Harris (1986, p. 225) states:

> Career ladders as they are now being promoted and mandated are curious mixtures of old staffing concepts and political concerns for fiscal restraint on salaries, control of educational policy, and the continuation of teacher shortages into a new century. With such diversity of forms, evaluation of quality for making individual promotion decisions will be very difficult.

The success of career ladder programs designed to motivate instructional effectiveness (e.g., Holdzkom, Stacey, Guard, Kuligowski, & LeGette, 1989; Tennessee Department of Education, 1985; Utah State Board of Education, 1985) depends on how well summative evaluations discriminate meritorious, exemplary instruction from instruction that is simply competent (Cangelosi, 1986).

Expert-Teacher or Differentiated Staffing Plans

In ideal differentiated staffing schemes, opportunities exist for the expert teacher to lead a teaching team and have instructional responsibilities that extend beyond the teacher's conventional complement of students. Differentiated staffing programs offer promise for involving teachers in professional decisions that extend beyond their own classroom, for rewarding and motivating expert teaching, and for extending the reach of exemplary teachers beyond conventional limits (Carnegie Forum on Education and the Economy, 1986; Harris, 1986, p. 230; Holmes Group, 1986; Ryan & Cooper, 1988, pp. 510–11; Tucker & Mandel, 1986). The success of differentiated staffing programs depends on identifying expert teachers.

LEGAL CONCERNS

Summative evaluations for beginning teachers, as well as for marginal teachers (treated in Chapter 9), affect whether or not individuals are allowed to continue in their positions. Firing an individual is usually perceived as an antagonistic act. Thus, summative evaluations for beginning and marginal teachers are especially open to legal attacks. Summative evaluations for expert teachers, on the other hand, do not cause individuals to lose their existing positions, but rather allow them to advance their positions. Thus the potential for antagonism is not as great.

Summative evaluations for advancement of expert teachers do affect individual professional satisfaction and income, however, and antagonism and perceptions of unfair treatment may arise from expert teachers who do not achieve advancement after a summative evaluation, or from teachers who believe others were unfairly promoted ahead of them. Consequently, adherence to principles similar to those listed in Chapter 7 under "Legal Concerns" (p. 166) is advisable. Particular attention should be given to the following questions:

1. How well does performance relative to the summative evaluation variables correlate with qualifications for meeting the responsibilities of the advanced position? For example, will an expert teacher whose instructional performance rates higher according to the summative evaluation be better qualified to serve as master teacher for a teaching team than one whose teaching receives lower ratings but whose interpersonal skills rate higher?
2. Does the evaluation discriminate only on relevant variables (i.e., ones subsumed by teaching performance) and not on irrelevant variables (e.g., ethnicity or sex)?
3. Are criteria, evaluation variables, and the process for making evaluations communicated to all affected parties?

SELECTION OF CANDIDATES

The competence of any teacher who merits consideration for a career ladder advancement, master or lead teacher status, or salary bonus should already be established. Summative evaluations for expert teachers are not designed to discriminate between competent and incompetent levels of instruction, but rather to identify exemplary, meritorious instruction. Thus, designers of the evaluations presuppose that candidates have been screened. For example, teachers might not be considered for candidacy until they have (1) accumulated high performance ratings on summative evaluations of their instruction over a two-year period, (2) received endorsements for the advancement from their peers, (3) fulfilled any certification or credential requirements for the advanced position (e.g., for some positions in some states, certification as an instructional supervisor may be required), and (4) volunteered as a candidate for advancement and agreed to accept the additional work and responsibilities required by the evaluation process.

Each teacher advancement program should publish detailed criteria directed at its particular goals. Whether requirements for candidacy are stringent or lenient depends on the philosophies within the school districts and the resources committed to the evaluation process. Where resources are limited, a choice must be made between two possibilities. In the first, the teaching performances of many candidates are evaluated, but the scope and depth of those evaluations are extremely limited. For example, only one lesson per candidate is examined. In the second approach, only one or two candidates are considered at a time, but evaluations encompass a wide range of teaching responsibilities (e.g., from long-range curriculum planning to assessing student achievement) or they provide in depth information.

The first option seems to have worked well in some situations (e.g., in the Lake Washington School District in Washington), while the second has succeeded in others (e.g., in the Toledo District in Ohio) (Wise, Darling-Hammond, McLaughlin, & Bernstein, 1984).

THE DESIGN–EXECUTION PERFORMANCE MODEL

Focusing on Aspects of Teaching

The *design–execution performance model* for summative evaluations of instruction operates in a vein similar to that of the analysis of teaching cycle model for formative evaluations. With this model, as with analyses of teaching cycles, teachers accept a leadership role working with a team of evaluators. Successfully implemented in a variety of school districts (Cangelosi, 1986; Charlotte-Mecklenburg Schools, 1983), the design–execution performance model focuses on how well the expert teacher designs and carries out selected aspects of instruction. The selection of the aspect of instruction should be a function of either the responsibilities associated with the expert teacher's advancement or published criteria for the merit raise. For example:

- The evaluation for an advancement to a position as the paid leader of a standing curricula-review committee focuses on how well the candidate *develops a particular curriculum.*
- The evaluation for a salary advance based on meritorious instruction focuses on how well the candidate *develops and implements a teaching unit.*

- The evaluation for an advancement to a position helping other teachers assess their students' achievements focuses on how well the candidate *develops and validates a sequence of tests.*
- The evaluation for an advancement to lead teacher of the Primary Grade Department in a school focuses on the quality of *the instructional supervision provided by the candidate in working with a colleague on a particular problem.* (Note that instructional supervision is a form of instruction.)

Availability of Qualified Evaluators

Identifying and training qualified individuals who are available to serve as evaluators pose problems for implementing almost any evaluation model. The design–execution performance model focuses on variables that require evaluators to be familiar with both the particular nuances of a given situation (e.g., needs of a specific group of students and social climate of a particular school) and the related professional literature. Because such persons are not readily available, the model assigns to the *candidate* the responsibility of providing evaluators with information needed to evaluate his or her teaching performance relative to the selected variables. Thus, evaluators are not required to possess greater expertise than the teacher for whom the evaluation is being conducted. The process by which the candidate "teaches" the evaluators is embedded in the 12 phases of the model.

Twelve Phases

Before the design–execution performance model can be applied, the criteria for the merit raise or the responsibilities of the advanced position must be spelled out. Application of the model involves 12 phases:

1. *Selecting the aspect of focus:* Those responsible for fitting the model to the particular case in question select the aspect of instruction upon which the evaluation is to focus. The selection, of course, depends on either the responsibilities of the advanced position or published criteria for the merit raise.

2. *Determining the evaluation variables:* The aspect is operationally defined in terms of a set of variables to be measured. If, for example, the evaluation is to focus on the *development and implementation of a teaching unit,* then the variables might be those shown in Table 8.1.

3. *Constituting the evaluation panel:* Several persons comprise the panel responsible for evaluating the teacher's performance relative to the variables. The selection of these evaluators should be influenced by (a) the availability of professionals capable of addressing the variables, (b) pertinent legal and ethical issues (Peterson, 1983), (c) concerns of teachers' professional organizations and unions (Ficklen, 1983), (d) concerns over administrative control (Thomas, 1979), (e) the concern for maintaining separation between formative and summative evaluation programs (Scriven, 1988), and (f) the availability of resources (e.g., funds to compensate evaluators and pay for substitutes for teachers who serve on the panel).

The panel should be selected and oriented to its task so that its members (a) have the open-mindedness to view designs from the candidate's perspective, (b)

TABLE 8.1. SAMPLE VARIABLES FOR A DESIGN–EXECUTION PERFORMANCE MODEL EVALUATION FOCUSING ON THE DEVELOPMENT AND IMPLEMENTATION OF A TEACHING UNIT

1. *The soundness of the teacher's rationale for the unit's learning goal and objectives*
   The rationale is defined to be *sound* if the goals and objectives are clearly justified in terms of:
   A. consistency with curriculum guidelines
   B. needs of the particular group of students
   C. applicable teaching/learning principles
   D. circumstantial factors (e.g., availability of learning materials)
2. *The soundness of the teacher's rationale for the way the unit is organized, lessons are sequenced, and activities are scheduled*
   The rationale is defined to be *sound* if the organization, sequences, and schedules are justified in terms of:
   A. concern for efficiency
   B. applicable teaching/learning and curriculum development principles
   C. circumstantial factors
3. *The soundness of the teacher's rationale for the unit's lesson designs*
   The rationale is defined to be *sound* if the lesson designs are clearly justified in terms of:
   A. motivational factors related to the particular group of students
   B. applicable teaching/learning principles
   C. circumstantial factors
4. *The consistency between the lesson designs and how lessons are managed and learning activities conducted*
5. *The soundness of the teacher's rationale for any deviations of the lessons from the lesson designs*
   The rationale is defined to be *sound* if the deviations are clearly justified in terms of:
   A. formative feedback
   B. applicable teaching/learning principles
   C. circumstantial factors
6. *The soundness of the teacher's rationale for the way student achievement is assessed*
   The rationale is defined to be *sound* if the assessment process is clearly justified in terms of:
   A. measurement cost-effectiveness
   B. circumstantial factors

have the professional expertise adequate for both understanding the candidate's rationale for designs and judging how well those designs are executed, and (c) represent a balance between the interests of teachers and administrators.

4. *Establishing procedures:* Ground rules, individual responsibilities, measurements, and schedules of the candidate's and panel's activities (including data collection) are cooperatively established and agreed to by the candidate and the panel.

5. *Communicating the purpose of the design:* The candidate explains the purpose of the design to be evaluated by the panel. If, for example, the design of a lesson is to evaluated, at this stage the candidate clarifies the objectives of the lesson. The explanation may be communicated in a variety of ways (e.g., in writing or during a discussion).

6. *Accepting the purpose of the design:* Panel members may not all agree with the candidate on the importance of the design's purpose. However, they all must

understand the purpose and agree to evaluate the design relative to its purpose (during the eighth phase).

7. *Communicating the design plan:* The candidate explains both the design plan and the rationale for it to the panel.

8. *Evaluating and accepting the design plan:* The panel judges the design plan. However, even if members do not agree with the candidate's rationale, they agree to base their evaluations in the ninth phase on the consistency between the candidate's execution and the design plan.

9. *Executing the plan and evaluating for consistency with the design:* The candidate implements the plan. The panel evaluates how well the candidate's execution adheres to the design. If, for example, the candidate conducts a learning activity that was designed to engage students in inductive reasoning, the panel judges whether or not the candidate actually does the things that according to the plan should get the students to reason inductively.

10. *Explaining deviations from the plans:* If the candidate knowingly deviated from the design during the ninth stage, he or she provides the panel with a rationale.

11. *Evaluating the execution of the plan:* In light of any rationales provided in the tenth stage and their evaluations during the ninth stage, panel members make a final evaluation on how well the plan was executed.

12. *Reporting findings:* For each variable, the panel reports its evaluation to both the candidate and those responsible for making the recommendation regarding advancement.

THE MODEL IN OPERATION

Here is an example of an application of the design–execution performance model:

Metro Consolidated School District has a career ladder program in which a review committee considers proposals offered by teachers for funding to support special projects. Javier Delacruz, a veteran mathematics teacher at Westside Middle School, proposes to develop and validate a sequence of tests designed to be relevant to the National Council of Teachers of Mathematics' (1989) *Standards* for seventh grade. Javier submits the proposal to his principal, Agnes Garvey, for her approval signature. Instead of signing the proposal after carefully reading it, Agnes engages Javier in the following conversation:

AGNES: I'm really impressed with what you've put together.

JAVIER: Do you think it has a chance of being approved by the career ladder committee?

AGNES: Yes. But before we send it, I have an alternative proposal for you to consider. Frankly, I'm persuaded by the case you made for the need to develop these tests. But I'm even more influenced by your argument that most teachers are unaware of state-of-the-art methods of testing their students, especially at the conceptual and application levels.

JAVIER: If I develop these tests, they would emphasize conceptual- and application-level learning.

AGNES: I don't doubt that. You apparently know a lot more about testing students at higher cognitive levels than any of the rest of us around here. And that point gets me to my alternative proposal for you to consider. If you don't go for it or it doesn't get accepted by the school board, then I'll still support your original proposal.

JAVIER: What do you have in mind?

AGNES: I want to use parts of your proposal to convince the superintendent that he should get the school board to approve a new position for you.

JAVIER: (laughing) Is this your ploy for getting rid of me?

AGNES: No, it's my ploy for making better use of your testing expertise. I want to ask for an addition to our salary budget to release you from one class and get you a one-step salary increase so that you work with a select group of our teachers, helping them develop better tests.

JAVIER: What *select* group?

AGNES: That's something we'd have to work out. We would identify enough teachers to justify the promotion but not so many that you can't reach them all. In the beginning, we'd include only volunteers who would welcome this kind of help; otherwise, it would never work.

JAVIER: I like the idea.

AGNES: Before you go for it, keep in mind the district's policy for promotions. If the position is approved, and you're nominated, you'll have go through a design–execution performance evaluation. That'll take some work on your part.

JAVIER: Not any more than I would do following up on this career ladder proposal. It would be worth a try, and if we get turned down, I can still submit the original proposal.

With the support of the superintendent, the school board approves the position on a one-year trial basis at Westside. If the experiment proves successful, the board plans to fund the position permanently and open up similar opportunities at other schools.

The first three phases of the evaluation process are completed after Javier, Agnes, and the district's associate superintendent determine the following:

1. The evaluation will focus on how Javier develops and validates one seventh-grade mathematics test targeting a set of objectives that range from knowledge-level through application-level achievement (Phase I).
2. The evaluation variables will be:
   A. The soundness of Javier's plan for developing and validating the test
   B. How well Javier follows his plan for developing the test
   C. How well Javier follows his plan for validating the test
   D. The cost-effectiveness of the test (Phase 2)
3. The evaluation panel will consist of three persons: a testing specialist from a neighboring school district, a mathematics teacher from Central Middle School, and a fifth-grade teacher from Washington Elementary School (Phase 3).

Agnes and the assistant superintendent meet with the panel members to make sure they understand the concept of the design–execution performance approach, their responsibilities, and the responsibilities of the candidate, Javier.

Procedures are established at the first meeting Javier has with the panel (Phase 4). They agree to the following schedule:

1. On March 1, Javier will meet with the panel to explain the purpose of developing and validating the test. As part of the explanation, Javier will provide a list of the learning objectives the test is intended to measure (Phase 5). The evaluation may not move to the next phase until all panel members clearly understand the learning objectives to be measured (Phase 6).

2. By March 8, Javier will provide each panel member with a written description of the step-by-step procedures by which he plans to develop and validate the test. Also to be included is a rationale for why Javier decided to follow these particular procedures. Attached to the rationale will be copies of references on test construction and validation that are relevant to Javier's argument (Phase 7).

3. Prior to March 15, each panel member will study Javier's materials and make a preliminary evaluation regarding the rationale for the choice of development and validation procedures (Phase 8).

4. On March 15, the panel will meet with Javier to raise questions about the procedures and clarify the rationale one final time before evaluating the soundness of the plan. Panel members are expected to accept the design for continuation to the next step in the evaluation. However, if some members find the plan so unacceptable that they feel it would be futile for Javier to pursue it in a subsequent phase of the evaluation, then those feelings must be brought out at this meeting. If this occurs, the matter is to be resolved either by (a) Javier convincing dissenting panel members of the worthiness of the design, (b) retreating to the seventh phase of the model, in which Javier presents a modified design, or (c) reconstituting the panel and beginning again with the fourth phase.

5. Prior to March 22, panel members will have reviewed the rationale for the design. On March 22, they will meet to formulate a report of their evaluations of the soundness of Javier's design (Phase 8).

6. Prior to March 29, Javier will have developed the test and documented adherence to the planned developmental procedures by noting on the blueprint for the test (Cangelosi, 1990b, pp. 45–49) how steps in the planned procedures were carried out (Phase 8).

7. On March 29, Javier will meet with the panel to present the test and explain the procedures by which it was developed. Javier will also present his rationale for any deviations from the original design (e.g., why one objective received more weight on the test than was originally planned). The meeting is to continue until all panel members are comfortable with their understanding of the procedures Javier used to develop the test and his rationale for any deviations from the planned procedures. If panel members are prepared, then they should formulate an evaluation on how well Javier followed his plan for developing the test. Otherwise, the report is to be developed at a panel meeting held prior to April 5 (Phase 8).

8. Prior to April 5, Javier will have administered the test to a group of students to assess effectiveness of test items and measurement reliability (Phase 9).

9. At an April 5 meeting, Javier will present the results of his validation efforts along with an explanation of the procedures he used (Phase 9/10).

10. By April 12, the panel will report its evaluations for the four variables at a meeting with Javier, Agnes, and the associate superintendent. At that meeting

the contents of the panel's written evaluation report are to be determined (Phase 11/12).
11. By April 19, the written report is to be sent to the superintendent, who will use it as the basis for a recommendation to the school board (Phase 12).

The schedule is met and the school board approves the advancement for Javier at its June meeting.

THE HUMAN ELEMENT

Completing the 12 phases of the design–execution performance model depends on having expert teachers who are willing and able to assert themselves as leaders in the process and having evaluators who are willing and able to judge the tenability of expert teachers' points of view even when those views are contrary to their own.

Implementation of such a model requires professional commitment and cooperation among teachers, supervisors, and administrators.

SELF-ASSESSMENT EXERCISES FOR CHAPTER 8

I. Call to mind the school situation that you reflected upon for self-assessment Exercise I in Chapter 5. Could the design–execution performance model work in that school? Explain why or why not. Exchange your response with someone else who is completing this exercise. Discuss similarities and differences in your two responses.

II. Critique the evaluation process as described in the scenario of Javier's consideration for promotion. What are the advantages and disadvantages of what was done relative to what could have been done. Discuss your ideas with another professional educator.

III. Investigate merit-pay, master-teacher, or career ladder programs in a school district in your area. Describe one of the models used for summative evaluations of instruction within one of those programs.

CHAPTER 9

Evaluations for Retention of Marginal Teachers

Goal of Chapter 9

Chapter 9 suggests ways of resolving issues and problems related to summative evaluations for marginal teachers. Specifically, this chapter is designed to help you:

1. Explain what is meant by "marginal teachers," how marginal teachers exist because of failed programs for summative and formative evaluations of instruction, and the consequences of retaining marginal teachers in the profession.
2. Describe major ethical and legal issues related to summative evaluations of marginal teachers' instructional effectiveness and propose some realistic solutions.
3. For a given situation, design and describe a practical program of summative evaluations of the instructional effectiveness of marginal teachers.

MARGINAL TEACHERS

Who Are They?

A *marginal teacher* is an experienced teacher (i.e., no longer a beginning teacher) whose instruction is deemed by an administrative supervisor to constitute malpractice and, consequently, whose dismissal from his or her position should be considered. Do not confuse marginal teachers with teachers whose positions are in jeopardy because of some alleged incidence of misconduct (e.g., unseemly behavior with a student outside of school) or failure in relations with colleagues or administrators (e.g., insubordination). A marginal teacher is one whose contract with a school system is jeopardized by concerns regarding *teaching* performance, not regarding noninstructional responsibilities.

How can an experienced teacher, usually with tenure, suddenly be labeled "marginal"? The labeling process may or may not have occurred suddenly. For example:

Six years ago Mike Musso completed the preservice secondary school science teacher preparation program at a major university. Concerns about Mike's student teaching performances were raised by both the cooperating teacher and university supervisor. However, they decided to "pass" him with a lukewarm recommendation because he seemed so likable and conscientious. They both lamented Mike's having been assigned to student teach with apparent weaknesses in his preparation, but they found it difficult either to eliminate him from the program or to require remedial work at such a late stage. Even without strong recommendations from the supervisor and cooperating teacher, Mike received several job offers from school districts in need of science teachers.

As a beginning teacher at Sunrise High School, Mike quickly earned a reputation as a friendly, helpful individual who could be counted on to volunteer for extra bus duty, serve as cafeteria monitor, and sell tickets for athletic events.

Sunrise's *formative evaluation* program for beginning teachers came from two sources. One was *Principal Ada Hopkins' "open-door" policy*. On a number of occasions, Ada told Mike, as she did all her teachers: "My door is always open. If you have the least problem, anything at all, you let me know and I'll work with you. My job is to help you be a better teacher. Just let me know." The second aspect of his formative evaluation was *the opening-of-the-year and end-of-the-year science department meetings*. At the beginning of each year the science faculty would meet to discuss ways of improving curricula; at the close of the year they would discuss problems teachers raised and suggest how they might be resolved for the following year. The closing meeting always included a promise that the teachers would visit one another's classes to provide each other with feedback. Mike, however, was never visited by other science teachers, nor did he observe other teachers during his first three years at Sunrise.

The *summative evaluation* program for beginning teachers also had two elements. First were *Principal Ada Hopkins' twice-a-year classroom visits*. In accordance with school district policy, Ada visited each beginning teacher's class at least two times per year and completed a rating form similar to the one in Appendix B for each visit. Mike received a copy of each completed form and another was added to his personnel file. According to the forms, his instruction was at least satisfactory. Second, there was a *once-a-year visit from the district science education specialist*. Using the same form as Ada, and obtaining similar results, the specialist would observe Mike's class and then engage him in a post-observational conference. Mike was told at these conferences that, other than some classroom management problems he needed to work on, his instruction was satisfactory.

After his third year, Mike signed a contract to continue teaching at Sunrise. By offering him this contract, the district, according to policy, had awarded Mike tenure. Ada recommended in favor of offering him the contract, although she held some reservations about Mike's abilities to manage student behavior and to excite students about science. These reservations arose from some informal measurements derived from overhearing students talk and from twice listening to parents complain that their children couldn't concentrate because of the noise in Mike's class. But she liked Mike and didn't feel she should recommend against tenure in light of the satisfactory ratings he had received.

Since that time, the frequency of complaints from parents has increased. Also, Ada has noticed that fewer of Mike's former students choose to take science courses than former students of any other Sunrise science teacher. Because of her concern, Ada, who has not formally observed one of Mike's classes since he was tenured, begins observing every other week. Mike finds this sudden attention disconcerting, and he becomes especially uncomfortable when he detects a change in Ada's attitude after a month of visits. More observations confirm Ada's worse fears about Mike's instruction. Finally, Mike and Ada meet to discuss the problem:

MIKE: Ada, what's going on? You've never shown this much interest in my classes before!

ADA: I'm sorry, Mike. I should have. But I have to be frank; you have some major classroom management problems.

MIKE: When did you decide this? I control the students as well as I ever have. I don't get any complaints!

ADA: But I do!

MIKE: Who complained? Can't they come to me?

ADA: This discussion is headed off in the wrong direction. I'm trying to be open with you.

MIKE: I would appreciate your being open. Anything else you're concerned about?

ADA: Well, yes. There's a problem with kids being turned off to science.

MIKE: Really? That's a surprise to me!

ADA: Look, you and I have been friends for a long time. There's no one I respect more than you, Mike. But . . .

The conversation continues, with Mike feeling hurt and Ada feeling guilty. Little is accomplished, but Ada decides to ask the district science specialist and another of Sunrise's science teachers to monitor Mike's classes and then recommend whether or not he should be assigned "marginal teacher" status. In the district, assignment of marginal teacher status triggers a formal evaluation process to determine if tenure should be revoked.

The science specialist honors Ada's request, but the science teacher says that she is too busy. Ada would have asked the science department head to participate, but two years ago she appointed Mike head of the department.

Up until two years ago, when Nancy Goldberg became principal, none of the current faculty could remember Froebel Elementary School ever having any systematic program for either formative or summative evaluations of instruction. Through Nancy's leadership, both formative and summative evaluation systems are in place. Consequently, Lynae Mason, a veteran of 18 years teaching fifth grade, who had never before received negative ratings, is placed on marginal status.

Actually, Lynae was a reasonably effective teacher for about ten years. However, differences between the fifth graders she first taught and those she teaches now, compounded by a lack of appropriate instructional supervision, have soured her attitude toward students and diminished her level of competence to the point that she is no longer effective.

For five years Andy Hancock has demonstrated his effectiveness as a junior high school industrial arts teacher. Last month two students got into a fight in his classroom resulting in one being hospitalized with a concussion. An ensuing investigation raised concerns about Andy's ability to maintain discipline in his class. Consequently, Andy is completing the remainder of the year as a marginal teacher.

For purposes of examining how summative evaluation programs for marginal teachers should be designed, consider three types of marginal teachers:

- *Type III*. Marginal teachers are considered Type III if their teaching performances are markedly ineffective and they are not responsive to instructional supervision. In other words, these are teachers who are beyond any reasonable level of help. In thinking about how to deal with Type III marginal teachers, it is convenient to differentiate between (1) those who are either nearing retirement or planning to leave the profession voluntarily in the near future and (2) those who are expected to pursue their teaching career for some years to come.
- *Type II*. Teaching performances of Type II marginal teachers are ineffective, but the teachers are responsive to instructional supervision and thus have the potential of succeeding in the classroom with reasonable levels of help.
- *Type I*. Some teachers have been designated marginal because unwarranted concerns about their instruction have been raised. Andy Hancock from the previous example may be a case of a Type I marginal teacher. Accurate summative evaluations of his instruction are needed to determine whether he is a Type III who should be dismissed, a Type II who should be retained but provided with special help, or a Type I who should be retained under ordinary status.

A Failure of Evaluations of Instruction

Evidence suggests that the number of malpracticing teachers far exceeds the number who are labeled "marginal" (Bridges, 1986, pp. 1–47; Cangelosi & Martinez, 1989; Jesunathadas, 1990). The existence of malpractitioners in the classrooms (either marginal or not) points to a history of failed summative evaluations for not maintaining quality control standards, and failed formative evaluations for not providing direction for instructional supervision.

Victims

Wherever evaluating instruction is either underpracticed or malpracticed, teaching malpractice continues to victimize *students* by wasting their opportunities to learn, *society* by failing to provide a service for which it paid, *teachers* by perpetuating their failures, and *the teaching profession* by diluting quality, contaminating its ranks, and tarnishing its image, thus causing it to lose political power.

SUMMATIVE EVALUATIONS FOR DECISIONS ABOUT RETENTION OF MARGINAL TEACHERS

Obviously, programs for accurately evaluating the instruction of marginal teachers are needed for decisions about retention. Although that need is unfulfilled in most school districts, there are an increasing number of districts either with exemplary programs in place (Wise, Darling-Hammond, McLaughlin, & Bernstein, 1984) or in the process of designing promising ones (Manatt, 1988).

RESPONSIBILITY FOR DIFFICULT DECISIONS

Even when a sound summative evaluation program provides irrefutable evidence of instructional ineffectiveness by a marginal teacher, firing an experienced colleague is at best distasteful. Only assertive, courageous administrators can properly resolve the problem of a Type III marginal teacher. Type III marginal teachers must be swiftly removed from the classroom. "Damage control" may be effected by reassigning those nearing retirement to positions with minimal instructional responsibilities, but it isn't tenable to retain a Type III marginal teacher as a salaried faculty member for more than a year.

As soon as a marginal teacher is identified as a Type II, she or he should be engaged in a concentrated instructional supervision program that is guided by formative feedback.

Historically, school principals are responsible for these difficult decisions. However, sometimes legal entanglements preclude principals and other professional educators from resolving marginal-teacher issues in the best interest of students, society, teachers, and the teaching profession (Bridges, 1986, pp. 19–24; Stanley & Popham, 1988a).

LEGAL CONCERNS

Although avoiding legal hassles or "winning" in court is problematic even for administrators and evaluators who have taken the most prudent course of action in regard to marginal teachers, rulings in past court cases indicate that the following should be kept in mind (Bridges & Gumport, 1984; Bridges, 1986, pp. 4–18):

1. School board approved provisions for dismissing or reassigning tenured teachers should be clearly articulated and made public. As a precondition to signing a teacher to a contract, the school district should obtain documented evidence that the teacher has been informed about the provisions. The provisions should spell out the variables (e.g., level of professional conduct, record of criminal convictions, and level of teaching performance) upon which retention/dismissal decisions may be based. Commonly, state-wide or district-wide policies list causes such as "unprofessional behavior," "criminal conviction," "subversive activity," and "teaching incompetence" as causes for revoking tenure. However, for purposes of summative evaluations of instruction, only *instructional effectiveness* variables and causes such as *teaching malpractice* or *teaching incompetence* are of concern. Other variables (e.g., criminal record) or causes (e.g., unprofessional conduct outside of the classroom) are not within the purview of the evaluation of instruction.

2. Evaluations regarding instructional effectiveness should be based solely on valid measurements. Of course, measurements cannot be shown to be relevant (and thus valid) unless the evaluation variables upon which decisions are based are clearly defined prior to the administration of the measurements.

3. Summative evaluations of instruction need to address performance of a marginal teacher over a continual span of time of reasonable length. Judgments of malpractice based on sporadic measurements or data collected over a brief period of time are considered dubious (Rosenberger & Plimpton, 1975).

4. Even irrefutable evaluations indicating continued instructional malpractice may not be sufficient to withstand legal challenges to the dismissal of a teacher unless factors that contributed to the malpractice can be identified. A court decision may, for example, depend on whether or not the school can refute claims against it for failing to provide support services to the marginal teacher. Instructional supervision, guided by formative feedback, is one of the services teachers need if they are expected to be successful.

5. Once a marginal teacher is identified as either a Type III or Type II, he or she should be provided with instructional supervision that, according to formative evaluation results, addresses the causes of instructional ineffectiveness. Because of legal concerns, this service needs to be made available to even Type III marginal teachers. The availability of instructional supervision must be documented in such a way that summative evaluations do not interfere with formative evaluations.

6. To avoid libelous conduct, evaluators should share information gained during the process only with authorized persons.

7. In general, the evaluation process should be consistent with published professional standards such as those of the Joint Committee on Standards for Educational Evaluation (1988), listed in Appendix R.

8. Evidence of adherences to the seven principles stated above needs to be documented.

THE DESIGN OF ONE SUMMATIVE EVALUATION PROGRAM FOR MARGINAL TEACHERS

The following example relates one school district's attempt to gain control over the quality of its own instruction:

Stung by a judge's decision overturning the dismissal of a Type III marginal teacher because of, in the judge's words, "simplistic and haphazard evaluations based on indefensible data," Claysburg School District Superintendent Charles Cocora initiates a top-priority project to develop a system-wide summative evaluation program for marginal teachers. Charles constitutes a task force consisting of three principals, an assistant superintendent, and six teachers (one of which is a former Type I marginal teacher and another a former Type II marginal teacher) to develop a detailed proposal to be submitted to the district's teachers, supervisors, and administrators for review. He also hires two evaluation-of-instruction consultants and retains one of the school district's lawyers to work with the task force.

Here is a portion of one of the discussions at the task force's first meeting:

VARNELL: We're supposed to design a summative evaluation program that discriminates among Type III, Type II, and Type I marginal teachers.

VEDA: That's right, but we can't lose sight of the fact that it's not going to do us any good to be able to have a summative program in place as long as we have no formative evaluation program for providing help to these people after they've been identified.

ANNA: So are you suggesting we design a formative program also?

VEDA: No, I just think we should recommend that one be developed that parallels the summative program. Then, for marginal teachers, the two will have to be coordinated.

CITO: But we're in no position even to begin to design a program for distinguishing between competent and incompetent instruction until "competent instruction" is defined.

VARNELL: Who should do that, Superintendent?

CHARLES: I'm hoping that will be the first thing accomplished by this task force.

CITO: I think this group has the expertise to propose a definition, but we shouldn't proceed any further until our definition is approved by your office and the teachers at large.

ANNA: Do we have to do that? That'll take forever!

CITO: If we don't, we could waste a lot of time designing something for a purpose that may not be agreeable to the majority.

VARNELL: I suggest we form a subcommittee to draft a definition for consideration at our next meeting. If we finalize a definition then, we can present a rationale for it and seek either input or approval from the teachers, supervisors, and administrators. The superintendent's office can take care of the logistics.

Varnell's motion is approved, and the subcommittee reports at the next meeting:

CITO: We did a rather extensive review of related literature and discovered that although most states list instructional incompetence as one reason tenured teachers may be dismissed, very few have even attempted to define incompetent instruction or malpractice. But we did locate a number of definitions in the professional literature as well as a few in court records. One of the more notable I'll quote from a 1979 ruling on Beebe versus Haslett Public Schools from the Michigan Court of Appeals (Bridges, 1986, p. 4):

> School boards and the Tenure Commission should in each case, make specific determinations concerning the challenged teacher's knowledge of his subject, his ability to impart it, the manner and efficacy of his discipline over his students, his rapport with parents and other teachers, and his physical and mental ability to withstand the strain of teaching. In each case, the effect on the school and its students of the acts alleged to require dismissal must be delineated.

You can see that their focus is on teaching competence. The evaluation literature convinced us to focus on teaching performance instead, but we thought this court opinion gave us something to begin working with.

FRED: Why performance rather than competence?

VEDA: Measurements addressing performance variables are more likely to be valid than ones trying to measure competence.

VARNELL: So what's the subcommittee's proposed definition?

CITO: Okay, I'll read it:

> *Satisfactory teaching performance* follows fundamental tenets derived from combinations of research-based teaching models (e.g., direct training, nondirective teaching, inductive approaches, drill and practice skill development, group investigation, assertiveness training, behavior modification, advance organizer models, and deductive teaching [Joyce & Weil, 1986]). Teachers *demonstrate* satisfactory teaching performance by basing their rationales for instructional plans on combinations of research-based models and then adhering to those plans. Instruction is not limited to delivering in-class lessons. Performance in all areas of curriculum development are included under teaching performance (e.g., establishing goals, classroom management, and assessment of student achievement).

What do you think?

JARVIS: Can't we come up with something simpler?

VEDA: I don't think so. The definition has to be limiting enough to be meaningful, and yet we don't want to violate academic freedom and say everyone has to teach the same way.

CITO: The idea is to require teachers to be thoughtful about how they teach.

ANNA: I'm with you on that, but why "combinations"? Wouldn't it be simpler to give them a choice of acceptable models and then see how well they follow the one they choose? *Combinations* complicate things.

CITO: But no one model is appropriate for all types of learning. Precision teaching, for example, is good only for skill acquisition, not for developing critical thinking.

VEDA: Before continuing to get your input on the definition, let me complicate things a little more. We don't feel that any definition will be workable unless the process by which marginal teachers are first identified specifies what aspects of instruction raise concerns. For example, if concerns are raised about John Doe's classroom management and how he organizes subject matter, then summative evaluations should focus on those two areas to determine if John is a Type I, II, or III. If he's a Type I, the marginal designation is dropped and no further action is taken. But if he's a Type II or III, then formative evaluations need to look even further into those areas to provide guidance for an instructional supervision program. In the meantime, . . .

The meeting continues. Three weeks later the task force has a proposal ready for review. Here is an outline of the main features of the proposed program:

I. *Development and validation of measurements to be used for data gathering in the summative evaluation program:*
   Prior to program implementation, the superintendent is responsible for developing and offering to all qualified agencies and individuals a request for a proposal (RFP) to develop and validate cost-effective measurements for use in the program as described herein. The school board will award the contract and the project will be completed within a year.

II. *Events that trigger the summative evaluation program for a marginal teacher:*
   A. Via summative evaluation and administrative procedures that occur prior to this program being evoked, a teacher is assigned marginal status.
   B. The assignment of marginal status is accompanied by a listing of the questions that have been raised about teaching performance. The questions are worded so that aspects of teaching performance in which the concerns have been raised are clearly identifiable within the following framework:
      1. establishing and defining learning goals that:
         a) are congruent with curriculum guidelines
         b) reflect the needs of students
         c) are ambitious, but also realistic
         d) provide clear directions for lesson designs
      2. Applying research-based classroom management and discipline principles (found in the professional literature) to:
         a) establish a purposeful, businesslike learning environment
         b) orchestrate smooth, efficient transition periods
         c) obtain student engagement for learning activities
         d) maintain student engagement during learning activities
         e) efficiently teach students to supplant off-task behaviors with on-task behaviors
      3. Applying research-based instructional design and teaching/learning principles (found in the professional literature) to:
         a) plan and prepare lessons that target stated learning objectives
         b) conduct learning activities in a manner that is consistent with lesson plans and/or formative feedback relevant to student progress

4. Applying research-based measurement and evaluation principles (found in the professional literature) to:
   a) obtain accurate formative feedback for guiding both the development of teaching units and the course of learning activities
   b) base summative evaluations of student achievement on cost-effective measurements
   c) communicate summative evaluations of student achievement to students, their parents, and other *authorized* professionals

III. *First phase of the summative evaluation program for marginal teachers:*

The *purpose* of the first phase is to determine if the marginal teacher is a Type III, II, or I. Thus a summative evaluation of the teacher's performance with respect to the areas of concern is undertaken via the following process:

A. The principal convenes the *planning committee*, which consists of the principal, the marginal teacher, a person (e.g., a teacher, teachers' union representative, or attorney) selected by the marginal teacher to serve as an advocate for her or his interests, a teacher selected by the principal, and a representative of the superintendent.

B. The planning committee selects a *summative evaluation team* (SET) consisting of three persons: two teachers within the marginal teacher's specialty area but from other schools, and a consultant who is not a regular employee of the district and who is qualified as a specialist in the evaluation of instruction or supervision of teaching.

C. Arrangements for recruiting and compensating persons to serve on SET are made through the district office. Alternate choices for SET may have to be made by the planning committee.

D. The planning committee meets with SET to clarify purposes and formulate procedures, schedules, and ground rules. The *measurements* developed and validated for the program that pertain to the areas of concern are reviewed. (If, for example, area 2 [applying research-based classroom management and discipline principles] is of concern, then the procedures for implementing a measurement such as the one appearing in Appendix E are clarified.)

E. SET follows the agreed-upon schedule and procedures to conduct summative evaluations relative to each of the identified areas of concern.

F. SET submits a written evaluation report to each member of the planning committee.

G. If the evaluation indicates that the marginal teacher is Type I, then the "marginal teacher" designation is dropped and no further action is taken. If the evaluation indicates that the marginal teacher is either Type II or III, then the program moves into the second phase.

IV. *Second phase of the summative evaluation program for marginal teachers:*

The purpose of the second phase is to evaluate the marginal teacher's performance in the areas of concern *after* he or she has been provided with an individualized program of instructional supervision.

The planning team meets to arrange for the instructional supervisory service. The service is to be provided for a limited time period (up to nine months) determined by the planning committee. Designing and providing instructional supervision fall outside the purview of this summative evaluation program. However, it should be noted that phase two of this program assumes that a specific program of instructional supervision tailored to the marginal teacher's needs will be provided that includes the following two features: (1) Formative evaluations will pinpoint problems within each area of concern that should be addressed by instructional supervision. (2) Formative evaluation outcomes and other information gained from the instructional supervision program may not be used to influence any subsequent summative evaluations.

Upon completion of this special, individualized instructional supervision program, SET reevaluates performance in the areas of concern. Unless modified by the planning committee, data collection and reporting procedures will be similar to those followed in phase one. The evaluation report will include a recommendation in favor of one of the following options:

A. The special instructional supervision program should continue for a designated period of time, after which there will be another reevaluation.

B. The marginal teacher label should be dropped and no further action should be taken.

C. The marginal teacher should be dismissed or reassigned to nonteaching duties on the grounds of continued malpractice.

A DIFFERENT AGE

Like most of the other approaches for evaluating instruction presented in this text, the model developed for Claysburg School District requires more time, professional commitment, and professional expertise than is common in most schools today. However, schools can no longer afford to depend on simplistic, untenable programs of evaluation for marginal teachers. On one hand, public and political pressures are mounting to rid our schools of malpracticing teachers. On the other hand, teachers rightfully expect to be granted due process whenever their instructional performances are called into question.

SELF-ASSESSMENT EXERCISES FOR CHAPTER 9

I. Call to mind the school situation that you reflected upon for self-assessment Exercise I of Chapter 5. Could the summative evaluation program for marginal teachers proposed for Claysburg School District work in that school? Explain why or why not. Exchange your response with someone else who is completing this exercise. Discuss similarities and differences in what the two of you wrote.

II. Think (this is not a writing exercise) about teachers with whom you have worked. Do you recall any whom, if they had been labeled marginal teachers, you would consider Type IIs? Would you consider any Type III marginal teachers? Now recall what you observed about their teaching performances that led you to make these judgments.

III. Design one measurement to be relevant to *teaching performance* within one of the four areas ("establishing and defining learning goals," "applying research-based classroom management and discipline principles," "applying research-based instructional design and teaching/learning principles," or "applying research-based measurement and evaluation principles") outlined in the

Claysburg proposal. Use the subcommittee's definition of *satisfactory teaching performance* that Cito proposed to the task force to clarify the variable for which your measurement should have relevance. Have someone who is familiar with the content of Chapters 2–4 critique your measurement for its cost-effective potential.

IV. Critique Claysburg School District's proposed summative evaluation program for marginal teachers with respect to its vulnerability to legal challenges. Take into account the eight ideas listed under this chapter's section on "Legal Concerns." Propose remedies for weaknesses you identify. Exchange your work on this item with someone else and discuss the similarities and differences between your two responses.

Evaluating Instruction
for Research Studies

Goal of Chapter 10

Chapter 10 adverts to evaluations of instruction for purposes of conducting research. Specifically, this chapter is designed to help you:

1. Explain how evaluations of instruction for research studies differ from those for quality control and for instructional supervision with respect to purpose, design, the role of teachers, and the reporting of results and conclusions.

2. For a given research project, explain the advantages and disadvantages of using a group approach in evaluating instruction as opposed to using a single-subject approach.

THE NATURE OF RESEARCH STUDIES
OF TEACHING

Research Questions and Research Variables

A *formative evaluation* of instruction attempts to answer questions relative to the guidance of instructional improvement efforts of a particular teacher or teachers at a particular school. A summative evaluation of instruction for purposes of *quality control* attempts to answer questions about the effectiveness of the instruction that a particular teacher delivers or is capable of delivering. On the other hand, an evaluation of instruction conducted as part of *research study* attempts to answer questions about the practice of teaching itself rather than the way it is practiced by any one teacher or by teachers at any particular school.

Research, as it is commonly defined, examines phenomena that extend beyond the confines of a particular individual or setting. The idea of *generalizability* of explanations or answers to heretofore unanswered questions is central to conventional definitions. For example: "Research is systematic inquiry aimed at obtaining generalizable knowledge by testing claims about the relationships among variables, or by describing generalizable phenomena" (Worthen & Sanders, 1987, p. 23). "Research is the manner in which we attempt to solve problems in a systematic effort to push back frontiers of human ignorance or to confirm the validity of the solutions to problems others have presumably resolved" (Leedy, 1985, p. 4). "Research is a detailed and systematic attempt, often prolonged, to discover or confirm through objective investigation the facts pertaining to a particular problem or problems and the laws and principles controlling it" (Wolman, 1989, p. 292).

Research studies on teaching contribute to the understanding of what constitutes effective instruction and how instruction can be more effective. Research questions such as the following lead to the need for evaluating classroom instruction variables:

- Is there a relationship between middle school teachers' use of assertive communications (Canter & Canter, 1976, pp. 155–78) in their classrooms and their students' levels of on-task behaviors?

  Addressing this question requires the researcher to evaluate two variables: (a) the degree to which teachers use assertive communications in their classrooms and (b) students' levels of on-task behaviors. The first is a *teaching performance* variable, the second a *student outcome* variable.
- Are ninth-grade students better able to apply experimental procedures to test hypotheses after those procedures have been introduced in a biology lesson utilizing the learning cycle approach (Saunders, 1988) than they are after a lesson using a more traditional "text-tell-teach" approach?

  Addressing this question requires the researcher to evaluate: (a) how well students apply certain experimental procedures (a *student outcome* variable) and (b) whether or not teachers are using the learning cycle approach in specified lessons (a *teaching performance* variable).
- Do teachers who have earned a Master's degree in education conduct lessons that are any more or less consistent with research-based teaching principles than teachers who do not have a Master's degree?

  Addressing this question requires evaluation of two variables: (a) whether teachers have earned a Master's degree or whether they have no Master's degree and (b) the consistency between how lessons are conducted and research-based teaching principles. You might consider the first a *teaching competence* variable if you believe that earning a Master's degree in education reflects a degree of competency to teach. The second is clearly a *teaching-performance* variable.

Many, but not all, educational research studies involve teaching competence, teaching performance, or student outcome variables. Those that do must include some process for measuring and evaluating instructional effectiveness.

Teachers and Students as Research Study Subjects

Research studies requiring instruction to be evaluated need teachers and their students for research subjects. Ethical standards for researchers require that research designs include steps to protect the reputations of both teachers and students in such studies. Thus the proposal for the research study should clearly indicate that (1) it is the research variables (e.g., method of instruction) that are to be investigated, not individual study subjects themselves; and (2) nothing from the study (e.g., results and conclusions) will be reported in a way that reflects upon any individual person, classroom, or school.

When permissions are obtained, ground rules for maintaining professional confidences are agreed to (from school administrators, teachers, and students' parents) and compensation (in the form of stipends or service) for study subjects are arranged.

GROUP RESEARCH APPROACH

Some research designs require the instruction of a fairly large sample of teachers (more than 30) to be evaluated. This *group research approach* does not ordinarily require the in-depth level of evaluation required for formative evaluations or summative evaluations for purposes of quality control. In the next three examples, the group research approach is used; the first focuses on teaching competence variables, the second on teaching performance variables, and the third on student outcome variables:

As principal investigator for a nationally funded project to develop and field-test video programs for the in-service education of junior high mathematics teachers, Jim conducts a research study that addresses the following question:

Will junior high school mathematics teachers exhibit greater gains in their abilities to apply pre-algebra content to the solution of "real-world" problems after viewing video program A or after viewing video program B?

A detailed definition of the study's dependent variable, *ability to apply pre-algebra content to the solution of real-life problems*, is explained in the research proposal. Video programs, A and B are each three hours long and contain essentially the same content, but their presentation formats differ dramatically. Jim wants to determine which, if either, of the two presentation formats works better.

Because of the rationally based and research-based association between ability to apply pre-algebra and competence to teach pre-algebra (Cangelosi, 1988b), Jim considers the *ability to apply pre-algebra to the solution of real-life problems* a *teaching competence* variable. Thus, evaluations of teaching are included in the study. The independent variable, of course, is *whether teachers view program A or B*. Solving for this latter variable does not require an evaluation of instruction.

From the following overview of the study's procedures, note the steps that require teaching competence to be measured:

1. After a search for preexisting test relevant to the dependent variable proved futile, Jim, working with a team of mathematics education and measurement specialists, develops and validates a test of ability to apply pre-algebra content in the real world.
2. Eighty teachers from the study population are recruited to serve as study subjects.
3. The sample of 80 teachers is administered the test (with tests being identified only by code numbers rather than names).
4. Based on the pretest results, 40 matched pairs from the sample are identified. By random selection, one member of each pair is assigned to be in the A sample, the other in the B sample.
5. Sample A views program A, while sample B views program B.
6. Both samples are readministered the test (again using code numbers).
7. The following null hypothesis is tested using a matched-pairs t-test statistical routine with the post-test scores (Marascuilo & Serlin, 1988, pp. 414–417):

   Ho: the $\mu(A) = \mu(B)$ where $\mu(A) =$ the theoretical post-test–score mean of the population represented by sample A and $\mu(B) =$ the theoretical post-test–score mean of the population represented by sample B

8. The aggregated results are reported.
9. Conclusions are drawn and reported regarding a comparison of the two programs' impact on teachers' ability to apply pre-algebra (a teaching competency).

The following research question is also addressed in Jim's study:

   Will junior high school mathematics teachers incorporate more real-life application examples within pre-algebra lessons they conduct after viewing program A or after viewing program B?

For this question, the dependent variable is *number of real-life examples incorporated in pre-algebra lessons*. This is a *teaching performance* variable that will have to be evaluated. The independent variable is the same as before, namely, *whether teachers view program A or B*.

To address this second question, the following complements the nine procedural steps listed for the first question:

1. A classroom observation measurement relevant to the number of "real-life" examples incorporated in pre-algebra lessons is developed and validated.
2. Half of the 40 matched pairs from the sample (see step 4 of the procedures for the first question) are randomly selected. (This is done to reduce the sample to a size for which classroom observations would be usable.)

3. After the respective programs are viewed by samples A and B, the classroom observation instrument is used for lessons conducted by the 20 teachers from group A and by the 20 teachers from group B that were chosen in step 2 of these procedures.

4. The following null hypothesis is tested using a matched-pairs t-test statistical routine with the post-test scores:

Ho: The $\mu(A) = \mu(B)$ where $\mu(A)$ = the theoretical classroom observation mean score from the population represented by sample A and $\mu(B)$ = the theoretical classroom observation mean score from the population represented by sample B

5. The aggregated results are reported.

6. Conclusions are drawn and reported regarding a comparison of the two programs' impact on the number of real-life examples teachers use in their pre-algebra lessons (a teaching performance variable).

Jim's study also addresses a third question:

Over a two-month period, will junior high school pre-algebra students display greater gains in application-level achievement of mathematics after their teachers have viewed program A or after viewing program B?

For this question, the dependent variable is *student achievement of mathematics at the application level*. This is a *student outcome* variable that will have to be evaluated. The independent variable is the same as before, namely, *whether teachers view program A or B*.

To address this third question, the following complements the nine procedural steps listed for the first question:

1. A preexisting test relevant to *application-level achievement of pre-algebra* is selected and validated.

2. Each of the 80 teachers in the sample has one of his or her pre-algebra classes randomly selected for the study.

3. Based upon demographic factors associated with mathematical achievement gains (according to literature review), each of the 40 classes of sample A's teachers is matched to a class from sample B, forming 40 matched pairs of classes.

4. Two months after the two groups of teachers have viewed the video programs, the students in the 80 classes are administered the application-level test.

5. The following null hypothesis is tested using a matched-pairs t-test statistical routine with the post-test scores:

Ho: the $\mu(A) = \mu(B)$ where $\mu(A)$ = the theoretical student-test–score mean of the population represented by sample A's classes and $\mu(B)$ = the theoretical student-test–score mean of the population represented by the sample B's students.

6. The aggregated results are reported.

7. Conclusions are drawn and reported regarding a comparison of the two programs' impact on application-level student achievement (a student outcome).

SINGLE-SUBJECT RESEARCH APPROACH

Single-subject research designs provide an alternative to the group approach; it requires fewer study subjects (less than 10) but evaluations of instruction that are more in-depth. In the following example, a single-subject approach is planned to address a research question that requires the researcher to evaluate teaching competence, teaching performance, and student outcome variables:

From reading classroom management reports, Eva hypothesizes that familiarity with certain reinforcement principles (e.g., shaping, negative reinforcement, and extinction (Cangelosi, 1988a, pp. 33–42, 215–30) is critical to teachers' abilities to elicit their students' cooperation. Thus she undertakes a Master's thesis project that addresses the following research question:

What are the relationships among the following three variables?

1. Teacher's conceptual-level and application-level understanding of fundamental reinforcement principles
2. The methods teachers use in their classrooms to encourage on-task student behaviors and deal with off-task behaviors
3. The level of cooperative, on-task behaviors that students exhibit in the classroom

Eva is quite pleased when she locates three preexisting measurement instruments that appear to be relevant to the research variables. She thinks of using:

1. a written-response test that purportedly measures teaching competence with respect to understanding of reinforcement principles
2. a classroom observation instrument for teaching performance relative to the second variable
3. BOCAS (see Appendix D) for the student outcome variable

Originally, she planned to use a sample of at least 30 teachers with which she would use the three instruments and use a multiple correlation statistic to test a null hypothesis of "no relation" ($\rho = 0$) (Marascuilo & Serlin, 1988, p. 328–36). However, she changes her mind after making four discoveries:

1. An item-by-item examination of the test of teachers' understanding reveals a heavy emphasis on the vocabulary associated with reinforcement principles. She believes teachers' conceptual and application levels of understanding won't be measured if they are unfamiliar with the technical words used in the items.
2. The classroom observation instrument is too time-consuming to administer for a large number of teachers.
3. The classroom management instrument does not yield the type of scores that can be used tenably in a correlation formula.
4. BOCAS is too time-consuming to be administered in a large number of classes.

Thus, she decides to:

1. do a single-subject research (Sharpley, 1988) with a sample of five teachers
2. delimit the study to upper-elementary grade teachers only
3. supplant the vocabulary-loaded test for teachers with one-to-one interviews in which principles can be explained rather than referred to by their technical labels
4. use the classroom observation instrument with each of the five teachers on ten different occasions
5. use BOCAS on ten different students in each of the five classrooms
6. compile results with descriptive graphs and narratives rather than using inferential statistics
7. report results and conclusions about the relationships among the three variables in a way that the identities of the study subjects remain confidential

FLEXIBILITY OF EVALUATIONS
FOR RESEARCH STUDIES

Evaluations of instruction for purposes of instructional supervision or for quality control have an impact on individuals personally. Ongoing programs for such evaluations are often meant for implementation on a school-wide or system-wide basis and thus their designs need to be influenced by broadly based input from those affected by the programs. By contrast, evaluations of instruction for research studies are intended to contribute to our general understanding of teaching/learning principles. Professionally designed and conducted evaluations of instruction pose no threat to teachers or students who serve as research study subjects. Furthermore, the evaluations do not extend beyond the duration of the research study. Thus, researchers like Jim and Eva enjoy greater flexibility in designing and conducting their evaluations than do teachers and supervisors making evaluations as part of an ongoing program in a school or district. After encountering measurement cost-effective obstacles with her planned group research approach, Eva modified her study and used a single-subject design without engaging in the kind of elaborate group decision-making processes witnessed for the ongoing system-wide programs (e.g., the work in Claysburg School District outlined in Chapter 9).

SELF-ASSESSMENT EXERCISES FOR CHAPTER 10

I. Contrast the role of teachers in summative evaluations of their instruction for research study purposes to their role in summative evaluations for purposes of quality control. Make sure to point out differences regarding (a) what teachers have to gain, (b) what teachers have to lose, (c) their level of control of evaluation procedures, and (d) their options regarding whether or not to participate. Exchange your response with someone else who completes this exercise and discuss similarities and differences in what the two of you wrote.

II. Repeat Exercise I, but this time contrast the roles of teachers in summative evaluations of their instruction for research study purposes to their role in formative evaluations for purposes of instructional supervision.

III. In the last example of this chapter, what did Eva gain and what did she lose by deciding to use a single-subject approach instead of her original idea of a group approach? Discuss your answer with someone else who is familiar with the contents of Chapters 1–4 and 10.

PART IV

Looking Ahead

A Reason to Be Optimistic

Goal of Chapter 11

Chapter 11 is intended to stimulate you to reflect on the:

1. Evolution of models for evaluating instruction from unsystematic, oppressive administrative ratings to the emergence of measurement-based feedback systems for instructional improvement, quality control, and research on teaching

2. Continued, but narrowing, gap between (a) how the art of evaluating instruction is typically practiced and (b) rationally based and research-based principles for evaluating instruction

3. Need for hastening the potential marriage of the ideas of instructional supervision specialists (e.g., ideas disseminated through the Association for Supervision and Curriculum Development [ASCD] and those of educational measurement and evaluation specialists (e.g., ideas disseminated through the National Council on Measurement in Education [NCME]

DISMAL HISTORY

The Joint Committee on Standards for Educational Evaluation (1988, pp. 160–61) states:

Apart from the accreditation of schools movement that was launched in the late 1800s, there have been three major movements regarding educational evaluation in the United States. The first, which began and gained momentum in the early

part of the twentieth century, was concerned with evaluation of student performance and was embodied primarily in the standardized testing movement. The
second involved the evaluation of projects, especially externally funded projects,
and was started in the middle 1960s. The third concerned evaluations of teachers
and other education personnel and has become a major movement only in recent
years. The establishment of standards for educational evaluation work has paral-
leled these three major developments in evaluation.

Standards in the area of student evaluation appeared first in the 1950s in the
form of *Standards for Educational and Psychological Tests*, with three subsequent editions of those standards (NEA, 1955; APA, 1966, 1974, 1985). The
Standards for Evaluation of Educational Programs, Projects and Materials were
published in 1981 (Joint Committee on Standards for Educational Evaluation,
1981). This book, *The Personal Evaluation Standards: How to Assess Systems for
Evaluating Educators*, provides the first set of standards for evaluation of educational personnel.

Of course, instruction had been continually evaluated long before the recent
movement examining how instruction should be evaluated and the establishment of
the Joint Committee's (1988) standards. In the past, typical evaluations of instruction (or what were often perceived as evaluations of *teachers*) failed at every level:

1. Formative evaluations of *student teaching* were subverted by the fact that
   the formative evaluators, usually cooperating teachers and college supervisors, also served as summative evaluators. Even the summative evaluations generally failed to screen incompetent teaching because of (Stones,
   1987, pp. 683–84) (a) a reluctance to be responsible for preventing
   individuals from completing a program after they have invested four years
   in it,(b) failure to identify tenable evaluation variables (e.g., mimicking
   the cooperating teacher appears to have been the safest route to receiving
   positive evaluations), and (c) failure to base evaluations on valid measurements.
2. Recommendations from previous supervisors (e.g., during student teaching), poise and appearance during interviews, and characteristics of the
   completed job application forms were the deciding factors in the *hiring* of
   most teachers (Bridges, 1986, pp. 124–25, 162).
3. In the critical first few years of their careers, only a minute portion of
   beginning teachers received formative feedback that provided clear guidance to their instruction (Stallion, 1988). Summative evaluations usually
   consisted of mandatory one to three classroom visits per beginning teacher
   by administrators with pseudo measuring instruments (e.g., Appendix B's
   rating scales) (Duke, Cangelosi, & Knight, 1988).
4. Evaluations, of the instruction of *mid-career teachers* other than unsystematic self-evaluations, were virtually nonexistent (Stiggins & Duke,
   1988, pp. 1–6).
5. *Marginal teachers* were among the many victims of the aforementioned
   failures. Without defensible evaluation programs of instruction in place,

only a minute proportion of marginal teachers were ever reassigned or dismissed for reasons of instructional malpractice (Bridges, 1986, pp. 1–46; Stanley & Popham, 1988a).

CONCERN AND CHANGE IN THE STATE OF THE ART

Out of such a dismal history came the education reform movements of the 1980s decrying, among other things, low student achievement and incompetent teaching practice (Ryan & Cooper, 1988, pp. 176–82). While preservice teacher preparation programs were one of the main targets of criticism (Darling-Hammond & Berry, 1988; Feistritzer, 1988), awareness of the critical need to provide in-service teachers with ongoing nonthreatening, cooperative programs of instructional supervision surfaced. After all, no legions of "super teachers" were available to supplant existing in-service teachers, even the malpracticing ones (Cangelosi, 1988b). In addition, the complexities and dynamics of classrooms dictate that teachers either continue to develop throughout their careers or be incompetent. The traditional model whereby preservice programs provide their graduates with "teaching tools" and the wish, "Good luck in learning how to use these tools on the job!" simply doesn't work for most. Quality on-the-job help is essential to effective practice (Stallion, 1988).

Such concerns motivated scholarship leading to vast improvements in the state of the art of instructional supervision (e.g., Acheson & Gall, 1987; Cooper, 1984a; Glickman, 1985; Harris, 1986; Oliva, 1989; Sergiovanni & Starratt, 1983; Zumwalt, 1986). Table 11.1 categorizes some of the examples from this text as being either in or out of line with the norm of research-based instructional supervision principles.

The state of the art in the evaluation of instruction has also benefited from recent scholarship (e.g., Harris, 1986; Joint Committee on Standards for Educational Evaluation, 1988; Medley, Coker, & Soar, 1984; Stanley & Popham, 1988b; Stiggins & Duke, 1988). Table 11.2 contrasts some of the examples from this text according to whether they adhere to what has historically been the traditional practice or research-based instructional principles for evaluating instruction.

LAGGING PRACTICE

However, most in-service teachers and school administrators are still under the impression that supervision, and consequently evaluations of instruction, are in the same state they were in prior to the current movement (Duke, Cangelosi, & Knight 1988; Stiggins & Duke, 1988, p. 1–6). Common practice is unlikely to fall in line with state-of-the-art theory until the following occurs:

1. *An amalgamation of the art and science of instructional supervision and the art and science of measurement and evaluation produces useful*

210

TABLE 11.1. EXAMPLES OF TWO KINDS OF INSTRUCTIONAL SUPERVISORY PRACTICE FROM CHAPTERS 1–10

Malpractice	Exemplary Practice
Principal Margaret Roth evaluating John Gonzales instead of his teaching (beginning on p. 5)	Science Department Chairperson Kent Kenfield's work in helping Oscar Gibbs examine his class lectures (beginning on p. 62)
The subversion of instructional supervision by Julie Hanks' fear of summative evaluations by her principal (beginning on p. 123)	Nora and Sheldon providing peer assistance for one another (beginning on p. 95 and continuing through p. 104)
Leinka Borachek being overloaded with information from Jacelyn Frank after a classroom observation (beginning on p. 128)	How Principal Allison Heinemann handled Edmond Krause's inappropriate teaching behavior (beginning on p. 116)
Tamaria Michaels' failure to focus on one aspect of instruction at a time in a post-observational conference with Ed Jones (beginning on p. 143)	Principal Ron O'Connell's efforts to help Lynn Smith focus on application-level learning in her mathematics classes (beginning on p. 122)
Principal Ada Hopkins' "open-door" policy and twice-a-year classroom visit program for supervising beginning teachers (beginning on p. 185)	Assistant Principal Wilmo Stockton helping Magdalene Leckner prepare for an upcoming summative evaluation of her teaching (beginning on p. 126)
	Upper Grade Department Chairperson Abbie Wagner's work in helping beginning teacher Mary Tinsely organize for teaching (beginning on p. 130)
	Principal Dewanna Johnson's work in helping two teachers make more efficient use of their aide (beginning on p. 132)
	Grant's effort to help Bill, his colleague, to manage his time better (beginning on p. 134)
	Principal Blair Eisenrich's post-observational conference with fifth-grade Teacher Faye Black (beginning on p. 140)

TABLE 11.2. EXAMPLES OF TWO KINDS OF EVALUATION PRACTICE FROM CHAPTERS 1–10

Malpractice	Exemplary Practice
Principal Carl DeVarona misinterpreting results of his informal classroom observations (beginning on p. 19)	Aaron and Betsy making norm-referenced interpretations of results from Appendix A's instrument (beginning on p. 23)
Pam Soldwedel's evaluation of Pruitt's teaching based on an irrelevant variable (beginning on p. 19)	Art and Zina making criterion-referenced interpretations of results from Appendix A's instrument (beginning on p. 24)
Drake School District supervisors using Appendix B's instrument for classroom observations (beginning on p. 23)	Principal Inez Martinez's method for designing a summative evaluation program for beginning teachers at Van Buren Junior High School (beginning on p. 31)

Malpractice	Exemplary Practice
Principal Lee Farmer's method for obtaining a summative evaluation of Vickie's teaching (beginning on p. 36)	Kent and Oscar's informal method for assessing measurement relevance of a classroom observation instrument (beginning on p. 62)
Associate Superintendent Blaine Swenson's use of Appendix J's interview instrument for screening applicants for teaching positions (beginning on p. 93)	Method for designing a summative evaluation program of the instruction of Knight State College's student teachers (beginning on p. 65 and continuing through p. 77)
Artie Kinyo's principal's misinterpretation of her lesson plans (beginning on p. 99)	How Jan, Adonis, Louise, and Ted go about designing a program for evaluating the performance of beginning teachers (beginning on p. 37 and continuing through p. 83)
Kohn Johnson's student teacher supervisor's confounding formative evaluations with summative evaluations (beginning on p. 100)	
Misuse of students' standardized tests to evaluate teaching in Oil County School District (beginning on p. 104)	Vinnie Mason's use of closed-structure interviews in an effort to determine if the Woodpine County Teachers Association should recommend assertiveness workshops for teachers (beginning on p. 86)
Use of an ambiguously worded questionnaire for an evaluation of teaching performance (beginning on p. 112)	
How a university committee went about developing a program for evaluating the teaching of its instructors (beginning on p. 113)	Julio's use of a structured interview to measure the teaching competence of candidates for student teaching at Knight State College (beginning on p. 91)
How Mike Musso's teaching was evaluated throughout his career from his student teaching days until he became a marginal teacher (beginning on p. 185)	Ann Given-Bell's use of Appendix P's questionnaire to obtain formative feedback relevant to her impact on first graders' attitudes toward school (beginning on p. 112)
Froebel Elementary School's program for evaluating teaching prior to Nancy Goldberg's becoming principal (beginning on p. 186)	How Terry Hives' evaluation committee formally used the analyses-of-teaching-cycles model to evaluate his teaching (throughout Chapter 6)
	How Kristine and Ebony informally used the analysis-of-teaching-cycles model to evaluate Kristine's handling of a behavior management problem (throughout Chapter 6)
	The process by which the Silver County School District's task force designed a summative evaluation program for beginning teachers (beginning on p. 167)
	Metro Consolidated School District's program for summamtive evaluations for expert teachers being considered for advancement (beginning on p. 181)
	The process by which the Claysburg School District's task force designed a summative evaluation program for marginal teachers (beginning on p. 190)

evaluation-of-instruction models for implementation in schools. Models such as those presented in Chapters 5–9 that incorporate cost-effective measurements (as defined in Chapters 2–4) become a reality in schools when supervision and evaluation principles are brought into concert. A partnership of ASCD and NCME could provide the leadership necessary for a coordinated effort of scholars from both fields.

2. *To implement models in schools, concentrated in-service programs for teachers, supervisors, and administrators are collaboratively sponsored by state and local school districts, colleges and universities, and funding agencies.*

3. *Somehow the widespread (but not universal) lack of application-level understanding of pedagogical principals among many (but probably not most) teachers, supervisors, and administrators must be overcome.* Look at examples of model practices from Tables 11.1 and 11.2. The success of each depends on the involvement of someone with a sophisticated under-standing of research-based pedagogical principles. Overcoming ignorance about teaching is a major challenge.

THE FUTURE

Even in the face of seemingly insurmountable challenges, the future for the evalua-tion of instruction appears, at the very least, brighter than its past. Recent well-funded initiatives to publicize problems and propose realistic solutions (e.g., the Carnegie Forum on Education and the Economy [1986], Holmes Group [1986], and Joint Committee on Standards for Educational Evaluation [1988]) appear to be making an impact (Ryan & Cooper, 1988, pp. 507–31). Significantly, an increasing number of model programs are proving successful even under some of the more trying school situations (Stiggins & Duke, 1988, pp. 25–92).

Ultimately, people like you will determine whether or not the failures of the past are replaced by accurate evaluations leading to improved classroom practice, quality control, and research on teaching. The ball is in your court.

Example of a Filled-In Observation Instrument for Communication Style

COMMUNICATION STYLE AND LEVEL OF QUESTIONS

Observer trained in the use of this instrument _____ *Betsy Yen* _____

Class observed *3rd hour pre-algebra* _____ Date of observation _____ *1/26* _____

Subject or grade level _____ *8Th* _____ Unit ID _____ *II (Probability* _____

Unit segment ID _____ *4Th (5Th day)* _____

Time observation began _____ *9:10 A.M.* _____ Time observation ended *10:10 A.M.* _____

Directions for Using the Accompanying Recording Form
(Note: Refer to the form as you read these directions.)

For Section I: Time Line

The observation can cover up to 60 minutes of class time. By completing Part I, you indicate how that time is partitioned into (T) transition time, (A) allocated time, (X) other types of time, and (?) time that you are unsure how to classify. As you observe, fill in the appropriate portion of each time bar.

For Section II: Teacher Talk

Remember to include only teacher talk that is intended for a group of students to hear (i.e., one-to-one conference talk with an individual is not recorded). For each instance of teacher talk write one of the following symbols under the appropriate time line Part II:

D for a descriptive comment (The teacher verbally portrays a situation, behavior, achievement, or feeling without labeling it.)

J for a judgmental comment (The teacher verbally characterizes a behavior, achievement, feeling, or person.)

S for a supportive reply to a student's comment (The teacher verbally responds to a student's expression of a feeling with a message indicating that the student's expression was understood and the feeling accepted.)

N for a nonsupportive reply to a student's comment (The teacher verbally responds to a student's expression of a feeling with a message contradicting that the student has that feeling or indicating unacceptability of the feeling.)

H for asking a high-level question (The teacher asks a question that requires the use of reasoning, as opposed to only memory, to answer.)

L for asking a low-level question (The teacher asks a question that only taxes students' memories for the answer.)

X for talk that does not apply to any of the above categories

? for talk that you are unsure how it should be classified

For Section III: Student Talk

Remember to include only student talk that is intended for the class to hear (i.e., when the student "has the floor"). For each instance of student talk write one of the following symbols under the appropriate time line Part III:

H for asking a high-level question (A student asks a question that requires the use of reasoning, as opposed to only memory, to answer.)

L for asking a low-level question (A student asks a question that only taxes memory for the answer.)

X for talk that does not apply to any of the above categories

? for talk that you are unsure how it should be classified

For Computing the Ratios

The Descriptive to Judgmental Ratio for Teacher Talk = (number of **D**s from Part II) ÷ (number of **J**s from Part II).

The Supportive to Nonsupportive Ratio for Teacher Replies = (number of **S**s from Part II) ÷ (number of **N**s from Part II).

The Ratio for Teacher to Student Talk = (number of entries in Part II) ÷ (number of entries from Part III).

The Ratio for Teacher-Asked to Student-Asked Questions = [(number of **H**s from Part II) + (number of **L**s from Part II)] ÷ [(number of **H**s from Part III) + (number of **L**s from Part III)].

The Ratio of High-Level to Low-Level Teacher-Asked Questions = (number of **H**s from Part II) ÷ (number of **L**s from Part II).

The Ratio of High-Level to Low-Level Student-Asked Questions = (number of **H**s from Part III) ÷ (number of **L**s from Part III).

(Instrument on the next page)

TRAINED OBSERVER'S RECORDING FORM

Minutes from the beginning of class

0 5 10 15 20 25 30 35 40 45 50 55 60

I Time line

T:
A:
X:
?:

II Teacher talk

XX   XDHD   LSJH   H??   DDXJ   SDHN   HDHD   S NJ   S   DS D
X   HSS?   NNH   SDSS   N??X   JSJ   S
LL?   NDJJ   XXDDD   XN
      J   JDDX
                                 DDLX
                                   ?

III Student talk

XL   LLXX   XHHX   X   XXX   XLXX   XX   XHX   HHX   XHXXX
      XXX   XXXX   X   X   XXX   XLXXX
LXXX L   X

Example of a Pseudo Measuring Instrument

Drake School District
Supervisor's Classroom Observational Rating Form

Teacher
observed _____

Date of
observation _____

School _____ Subject or grade level _____

Time observation began _____ Time observation ended _____

Scoring key: $+2$ = strongly agree, $+1$ = mildly agree, 0 = no opinion or does not apply, -1 = mildly disagree, -2 = strongly disagree.

The teacher: (circle one for each statement)

1.	displayed knowledge of subject matter.	$+2$	$+1$	0	-1	-2
2.	was well prepared for the lesson.	$+2$	$+1$	0	-1	-2
3.	used effective methods.	$+2$	$+1$	0	-1	-2
4.	had the classroom well organized.	$+2$	$+1$	0	-1	-2
5.	used effective and appropriate communications.	$+2$	$+1$	0	-1	-2
6.	maintained students on-task and engaged in the lesson.	$+2$	$+1$	0	-1	-2
7.	displayed a professional manner and attitude.	$+2$	$+1$	0	-1	-2
8.	projected an enthusiasm for learning.	$+2$	$+1$	0	-1	-2

Total score for the observation _____

Observer's comments:

Example of a Lesson Plan Analysis Form

Form completed by _____ on (date) _____

Teacher who wrote the lesson plan _____

Class designation _____

Subject _____ Unit _____

Lesson # _____ Scheduled dates for the lessons _____

ANALYSIS OF THE WRITTEN LESSON PLAN

Objective(s)

1. How many objectives are stated? _____
2. Identify each objective that is subsumed by the goal statement of the unit.

   _____
3. Which objectives are stated so that you clearly understand the behavioral constructs?

   _____
4. Which objectives are stated so that you clearly identify the subject matter contents?

   _____

Learning Activities

5. For each objective that you listed in both items 3 and 4, do you see a description of a learning activity that is appropriate for the objective's content and its behavioral con-

   struct? _____
   If, you answered "no," then list the ones from items 3 and 4 for which you can't identify

   appropriate learning activities. _____
6. Identify descriptions of learning activities that you are unable to relate to any of the objectives you listed in both items 3 and 4.

   _____

   _____

   _____

   _____

Classroom Management Strategies

7. Are plans included for obtaining and maintaining students engaged in this lesson?

   _____
8. Does the combination of (a) the teacher's classroom procedures and rules of conduct and (b) descriptions in this lesson plan address the question of how student off-task

   behaviors will be handled? _____

9. If you answered "no" to either items 7 or 8, list aspects of the planned lesson that may lead to classroom management problems.

_____

_____

_____

_____

Evaluation of Student Achievement

10. Is a sample measurement item included for each item? _____
11. List those objectives that you listed for both items 3 and 4 for which relevant sample measurement items are included.

_____

NOTES AND QUESTIONS FOR DISCUSSION WITH THE TEACHER

_____

Behavioral Observation for Citizenship Attitudes and Skills (BOCAS)

SPECIFIC DIRECTIONS FOR ADMINISTERING

The proper administration of BOCAS requires prior in-depth study of the definitions of the terms and their physical placement on the checklist. The terms must become so familiar to the observer that upon observation a determination of behavior category and item can be made instantaneously. The following steps lead to accurate administration:

1. Familiarize yourself with the BOCAS format. There are three categories of behavior:
   I   Respect for Authority
   II Respect for Peers
   III Respect for Classwork

   There are positive and negative behaviors:
   ⓐ Behaviors are positive
   ⓑ Behaviors are negative
2. Memorize the placement of the observable behaviors in each category.
3. Study very carefully the definitions of the observable behaviors in the glossary. All terms must be clearly understood to reduce subjective interpretation.
4. Secure a seating chart, photograph or other identifying information necessary to locate the child.
5. Remain as unobtrusive as possible. Enter the room before the student. Take a seat where you can easily view the student but where you are not obvious to him. View the student silently, marking and observing discreetly.
6. Observe subject. Observe the student for one minute and stop. Place a check in the appropriate space of each observable behavior which you observed during that minute as being exhibited by the subject. Repeat process until 15 one-minute observations have been recorded.
7. A minimum of one check mark per minute must be recorded in each of the three categories. A choice should be made between 1(1a) or 1(7b), 2(12a) or 2(13b), and 3(20a) or 3(22b, 23b, 24b), unless both a and b behaviors occur during the same minute. In that case, mark both, as numerous check marks may be recorded per minute. The checklist should be an accurate accounting of all behavior exhibited during each minute.
8. Score your observation. (1) Complete positive scores of each ⓐ line by totaling the count of every space which has a check. (2) Complete the positive scores of each ⓑ line by totaling the count of every space that does not have a check. (3) Add the line counts within the category to get the positive score for each of the three respective categories. (4) DO NOT total the three categories.
9. Record your results in the designated spaces.
10. Complete the identifying data at the top of the checklist.

"Behavioral Observation in Citizenship Attitudes and Skills (BOCAS)," Snyder, Messer, Cangelosi. *Bocas Manual*, 1977. Duval County School District, Jacksonville, Florida, publisher.

PROCEDURE FOR SCORING BOCAS

Behavior I section records 15 one minute observations (one session of 15 minutes) on each of four positive indicators of respect for authority and on each of four negative indicators of respect for authority. Therefore, a total of 120 markings is possible. This section is scored as follows: (1) each positive behavior cell (i.e., cells in rows 1a, 2a, 3a, and 4a) which the observer marked counts one point toward a pupil's total for Behavior I, and (2) each negative cell (i.e., cells in rows 5b, 6b, 7b, and 8b) which is left blank by the observer counts one point toward a pupil's score for Behavior I. Consequently, to the same degree that this section is valid the following relationship holds: the greater a pupil's score, out of a maximum of 120, the greater the indication that the pupil behaves in a desirable manner with regard to Behavior I.

Behavior II section also provides for 60 positive indicators of respect for peers (i.e., rows 9a, 10a, 11a, and 12a) and for 60 negative indicators (i.e., rows 13b, 14b, 15b, and 16b) of the behavior in question. The scoring procedure is identical to that described for the Behavior I section.

Behavior III section provides for 15 one minute observations of each of five positive indicators of respect for classwork (i.e., cells in rows 17a, 18a, 20a, and 21a) and on each of five negative indicators of respect for classwork (i.e., cells in rows 22b, 23b, 24b, 25b, and 26b). Therefore, a total of 150 check marks is possible. The plan for scoring is the same as described for the two preceding sections.

BOCAS Checklist

SUBJECT EXAMPLE OBSERVER _____ LOCATION _____ TIME _____ DATE _____

Positive Score 73
Positive Score 74
Positive Score 88

			Line Total
I	**RESPECT FOR AUTHORITY**		
1(1a)	Cooperating in activities involving total class	✓✓✓✓✓✓ ✓✓✓✓✓✓	14
1(2a)	Volunteering to help (answer questions)	✓	1
1(3a)	Indicating agreement with auth. fig. (nodding, smiling, eye cont.)	✓	1
1(4a)	Making supportive statements to or about the authority figure		0
1(5b)	Talking back to the authority figure		15
1(6b)	Making mocking facial expressions, gestures		15
1(7b)	Ignoring/disobeying instructions	✓✓✓	15
1(8b)	Failing to answer when called upon		12
II	**RESPECT FOR PEERS**		15
2(9a)	Making supportive remarks to or about peers	✓	1
2(10a)	Helping peers	✓	1
2(11a)	Sharing belongings with peers		
2(12a)	Cooperating with peers	✓✓✓✓✓ ✓✓✓✓✓✓	13
2(13b)	Making distracting remarks/actions to/about peers	✓✓✓	12
2(14b)	Arguing with peers		15
2(15b)	Threatening peers		15
2(16b)	Physically abusing peers		15
III	**RESPECT FOR CLASSWORK**		
3(17a)	Demonstrating attending behavior – (listening, asking questions)	✓✓ ✓ ✓	4
3(18a)	Beginning task promptly		0
3(19a)	Responding when called upon		15
3(20a)	Working on task	✓✓✓✓ ✓✓✓✓✓✓✓	12
3(21a)	Cooperating in small group, team activities		
3(22b)	Talking out/making interfering noises		0
3(23b)	Talking without permission to classmates	✓✓	15
3(24b)	Doodling, daydreaming or restlessness	✓	13
3(25b)	Resting head on the desk/slumping	✓	13
3(26b)	Playing with a foreign object	✓	15
IV	**CORRECTED BY THE AUTHORITY FIGURE**		14
4(27)	Any verbal or non-verbal interaction the authority figure has with the subject in an effort to inhibit behavior		

BOCAS GLOSSARY

The validity of this observation schedule relies heavily upon a uniform definition of terms enabling these behaviors to be interpreted unmistakably by various observers. For this instrument, the behaviors will be interpreted by the following definitions.

The observable behavior—

1(1a)	COOPERATING IN ACTIVITIES INVOLVING TOTAL CLASS	Any attempt to aid, participate, take part in total class activities.
1(2a)	VOLUNTEERING TO HELP (ANSWER QUESTIONS)	Offering to help the authority figure do a task; answer questions
1(3a)	INDICATING AGREEMENT WITH AUTHORITY FIGURE (NODDING HEAD, SMILING, EYE CONTACT)	Any nonverbal action, gesture, movement, hand signal, etc. demonstrating support of the authority figure
1(4a)	MAKING SUPPORTIVE STATEMENTS TO OR ABOUT THE AUTHORITY FIGURE	Any verbal comments to or about the authority figure of a constructive nature
1(5b)	TALKING BACK TO THE AUTHORITY FIGURE	Any verbal expression causing harm to, undermining the authority of, disrespectful of, the authority figure
1(6b)	MAKING MOCKING FACIAL EXPRESSIONS, GESTURES	Any response directed toward the authority figure that is nonsupportive, i.e., sticking out tongue, hand signals, etc.
1(7b)	IGNORING/DISOBEYING INSTRUCTIONS	Making no attempt to follow the prescribed activity or doing other than the directed action.
1(8b)	FAILING TO ANSWER WHEN CALLED UPON	Either answering inappropriately or not answering at all questions, requests directed to the student
2(9a)	MAKING SUPPORTIVE REMARKS TO OR ABOUT PEERS	Any statement made to or about a peer of a constructive nature
2(10a)	HELPING PEERS	Any attempt to aid any other person; offering explanation, helping with a task, etc.
2(11a)	SHARING BELONGINGS WITH PEERS	Any attempt to be cooperative by offering materials or possessions to another
2(12a)	COOPERATING WITH PEERS	Any attempt to get along with others, keeping to oneself, listening to peers
2(13b)	MAKING DISTRACTING REMARKS/ ACTIONS ABOUT/TO PEERS	Any action which disrupts a peer's attention from task
2(14b)	ARGUING WITH PEERS	Any verbal confrontations including yelling or shouting
2(15b)	THREATENING PEERS	Any promise/implication to do another harm or indicating force
2(16b)	PHYSICALLY ABUSING PEERS	Any physical act against a fellow student, including hitting, pushing, tripping, and/or shoving, pinching, etc.
3(17a)	DEMONSTRATING ATTENDING BEHAVIOR, i.e., PAYING ATTENTION, LISTENING, ASKING QUESTIONS	Any attempt to focus attention on the class activity by following the reading, listening, keeping up, etc.
3(18a)	BEGINNING TASK PROMPTLY	Any action taken immediately after being assigned a task to work toward completing that task

3(19a)	RESPONDING WHEN CALLED UPON	Answering questions or requests
3(20a)	WORKING ON TASK	Following instructions and proceeding in a manner to independently accomplish the assigned activity
3(21a)	COOPERATING IN SMALL GROUP/ TEAM ACTIVITIES	Participating, helping, encouraging, etc. small subgroup activities
3(22b)	TALKING OUT/MAKING INTERFERING NOISES THAT DISTURB THE CLASS	Any audible unsolicited remark, disturbance, screaming, yelling, hooting, laughing, whistling, toe tapping, humming, etc. that interferes with class attention.
3(23b)	TALKING WITHOUT PERMISSION TO CLASSMATES	Any talking to a peer not directly instructed by the authority figure
3(24b)	DOODLING, DAYDREAMING OR RESTLESSNESS	Any action indicating inattentiveness by drawing, staring into space, continuous changing of positions, tipping the seat, etc.
3(25b)	RESTING HEAD ON THE DESK/ SLUMPING	Any attempt to rest, sleep, doze, slide down or slouch in the seat
3(26b)	PLAYING WITH A FOREIGN OBJECT	Any fiddling, tapping, handling, spindling, etc. of an object
	CORRECTED BY THE AUTHORITY FIGURE	Any verbal or nonverbal interaction the authority figure has with the subject in an effort to inhibit behavior

Instrument Developed by Jan, Adonis, Ted, and Louise for Teaching Performance in the Area of Classroom Management and Discipline

CLASSROOM MANAGEMENT & DISCIPLINE

Observer trained in the use of this   Teacher conducting the

instrument _____   class _____

Class observed & videotaped _____ Date of observation _____

Subject or grade level _____ Unit ID _____

Unit segment ID _____

Time observation began _____ Time observation ended _____

NOTE: This instrument is designed to be relevant to the subvariables under area 2 (Classroom Management & Discipline) of the overall measurement of teaching performance. That is the degree to which the teacher:

A. establishes a purposeful, businesslike learning environment (10 points embedded in items 2 & 3 of Part I and items 4 & 5 of Part II)

B. orchestrates smooth, efficient transition periods (3 points embedded in items 1, 2, & 3 of Part II)

C. obtains student engagement for learning activities (7 points embedded in item 4 of Part I)

D. maintains student engagement during learning activities (5 points embedded in item 5 of Part I)

E. efficiently teaches students to supplant off-task behaviors with on-task behaviors (10 points embedded in items 4 & 5 of Part I)

This instrument produces a maximum of 35 of the 100 possible points for the overall measurements.

TRAINED OBSERVER'S RECORDING FORM FOR THE CLASSROOM
MANAGEMENT & DISCIPLINE AREA
Part I (on-site) & Part II (videotaped)

Part I
On-site

Minutes from the beginning of class

| 0 | 5 | 10 | 15 | 20 | 25 | 30 | 35 | 40 | 45 | 50 | 55 | 60 |

1. Time line

T:
A:
?:

2. Learning materials (Y, N, ?):

P:
V:
A:

3. Classroom rules of conduct_____ (Y, N, ?). If "Y," then (V1, V2, . . . & R1, R2, ...):

4. Obtaining student engagement for learning activities (Y, N, ?):

5. Maintaining student engagement during learning activities (Y, N, ?):

224

DIRECTIONS FOR USING THE ACCOMPANYING RECORDING FORM

(Note: Refer to the form as you read these directions.)

Arrange to have the class session you observe videotaped. The video camera operator should be instructed to maintain a wide shot of the classroom, but centered on the teacher.

As explained in your training meetings, you should mark Part I of the form as you observe during your on-site visit. Part II is marked as you view the videotape of the class session.

Compile the scores for items 2, 3, 4, & 5 of Part I and items 1, 2, 3, 4, & 5 of Part II and compute the total score (out of 35) for both parts combined *after* the observations are completed.

PART I DIRECTIONS

For Item 1 (Time Line):

- *TRANSITION TIME.* Use a pencil to shade in the **T** bar under the time scale for periods in which the class as a whole is in *transition* between the end of one learning activity and beginning another.
- *ALLOCATED TIME.* Shade in the **A** bar under the time scale for periods for nontransition times which the teacher has *allocated* for most students to be engaged in learning activities.
- *QUESTIONABLE TIME.* Theoretically, any time that is not allocated for learning activities is transition time. However, due to the complexity of the classroom environment, some class time may not be clearly identifiable to you as either transition or allocated. For such times shade in the **?** bar under the corresponding time scale.

For Item 2 (Learning Materials):

- Learning materials, for purposes of the observation, include hard copy (e.g., books, worksheets, displays, illustrations, recordings, or manipulatives) that are used in the observed learning activity and which must be prepared before it can be used in the learning activity.
- Using the **P** (for "prepared"), **V** (for "visual"), and **A** (for "audio") bars under the corresponding point under the time scale, code each example of learning material used as follows:
- Mark **Y** (for "yes") on the **P** bar if the example is prepared prior to when it is needed (i.e., its preparation did not delay the start of the activity or interfere with other class activities).
- Mark **N** (for "no") on the **P** bar if the preparation for the example clearly fails the criterion for a **Y**.
- Mark **?** (for "I don't know") on the **P** bar if either (a) prior preparation of the example is impossible (e.g., the need for the material became apparent only as a result of in-class formative feedback) or (b) it is unclear as to whether or not the preparation fails the criterion for a **Y**.
- Mark **Y** on the **V** bar if engagement in the learning activity is dependent on students' being able to clearly see the example and, in fact, the example is visually perceptible to all those students.
- Mark **N** on the **V** bar if engagement in the learning activity is dependent on students' being able to clearly see the example but it is not visually perceptible to all those students.
- Mark **?** on the **V** bar if neither the criterion for a **Y** nor the criterion for an **N** is clearly met.
- Mark **Y** on the **A** bar if engagement in the learning activity is dependent on students' being able to clearly hear the example and, in fact, the example's audio is clearly perceptible to all those students.
- Mark **N** on the **A** bar if engagement in the learning activity is dependent on students' being able to clearly hear the example but the audio is not clearly perceptible to all those students.
- Mark **?** on the **A** bar if neither the criterion for a **Y** nor the criterion for an **N** is clearly met.

Compiling and Computing Item 2's Score. After the observation period, the following numbers are tallied:

Y_P which is the number of **Y**s on the **P** bar,

N_P which is the number of **N**s on the **P** bar,

Y_V which is the number of **Y**s on the **V** bar,

N_V which is the number of **N**s on the **V** bar,

Y_A which is the number of **Y**s on the **A** bar, and

N_A which is the number of **N**s on the **A** bar.

Item 2's score, with a maximum of 2 points, is computed as follows:

Score for item 2 of Part I =

$$(.67) \times ([Y_P \div (Y_P + N_P)] + [Y_V \div (Y_V + N_V)] + [Y_A \div (Y_A + N_A)])$$

For Item 3 (Classroom Rules of Conduct): Prior to the observation obtain a copy of the classroom rules of conduct from the teacher. If the rules do exist and they are clearly designed to promote respect among the students, then mark a **Y** in the blank for item 3. If this criteria is clearly not met, then mark **N** in the blank. If it is unclear as to whether or not the criteria for a **Y** is met, then mark a **?** in the blank.

If either an **N** or **?** is marked in the blank, score this item **O** and do not include this item any further in your observation. On the other hand, if **Y** is marked then code each incident in which one or more students violate one of the classroom rules of conduct and the teacher's response to that violation in the following manner:

The first incident is marked **V1** under the corresponding time line. The second incident is marked **V2**, the third **V3**, and so forth. If and when the teacher clearly responds to the first violation, **R1** is marked under the appropriate time scale. Similarly, **R2** is marked if and when the teacher responds to the second violation, **R3** for the third, and so forth.

Compiling and Computing Item 3's Score. If **Y** is marked in the blank, then after the observation period, the following numbers are tallied:

V_i which is the number of **V**'s on the bar, and

R_i which is the number of **R**'s on the bar.

Item 3's score, with a maximum of 5 points, is computed as follows:

Score for item 3 of Part I =

$$5 \times (R_i \div V_i)$$

For Item 4 (Obtaining Student Engagement for Learning Activities): Unlike items 2 & 3, for which codes represented distinct incidents (e.g., a rule violation or an example of learning material being used), item 4 categorizes specific intervals of time. Each 5-minute time interval of the bar is partitioned into (a) the first two minutes, (b) the middle (i.e., third) minute, and (c) the last two minuets. Coding for each 5-minute internal should be as follows:

Only the first two and last two minutes of each 5-minute interval (according to the time scale) that includes (according to item 1) a *change from either (a) transition to allocated time* (i.e., the beginning of a learning activity occurs) or *(b) allocated to transition time* (i.e., the ending of a learning activity period occurs).

In the minute preceding such a two-minute period, you should focus on approximately 10 students for the upcoming observation. During the two-minute observation period, record whether or not at least 90% of the targeted students appear to be on-task (i.e., listening to directions and then promptly becoming engaged at the start of allocated time) for the entire two-minute period by:

Marking **Y** if the criterion for being on-task (as defined in your training session) is met,
Marking **N** if the criterion is not met, and
Marking **?** if it is unclear as to whether or not the criterion is met.

The **N**s, **B**s, and **?**s should be marked in the 5-minute interval spaces just before "[ ]" if the occurrence is in the first two minutes of the interval, and in the space just after the "[ ]" if the occurrence is in the last two minutes. The "[ ]" represents the one-minute nonobservational period which should be used for locating the 10 students for the next period. A different (but not necessarily disjoint) group of 10 students should be selected for each observational period. When it is impractical or impossible to select a different group, then the fact that the exact same group was used twice should be so noted in the margin by the item.

Compiling and Computing Item 4's Score. After the observation period, the following numbers are tallied:

Y$_o$ which is the number of **Y**s on the bar, and
N$_o$ which is the number of **N**s on the bar.

Item 4's score, with a maximum of 10 points, is computed as follows:

Score for item 4 of Part I =

$$10 \times [Y_o \div (Y_o + N_o)]$$

For Item 5 (Maintaining Student Engagement During Learning Activities): The procedure for coding item 5 is identical to that for item 4, with the following exception:
The observation periods occur *during allocated time,* and, thus, on-task behavior is always engagement in the learning activity.

Compiling and Computing Item 5's Score. After the observation period, the following numbers are tallied:

Y$_M$ which is the number of **Y**s on the bar, and
N$_M$ which is the number of **N**s on the bar.

Item 5's score, with a maximum of 9 points, is computed as follows:

Score for item 4 of Part I =

$$9 \times [Y_M \div (Y_M + N_M)]$$

Part II Directions

For Item 1 (Time Line): The **T, A,** and **?** bars should be shaded in following the same procedure as for the time line of Part I's item 1. Depending on the intra-observer consistency you achieve, the two time lines should be quite consistent. However, unlike Part I's time line, item 1 of Part II yields a score.

Compiling and Computing Item 1's Score. After the observation period, the following numbers are tallied:

M$_T$ which is the number of minutes estimated from the **T** bar, and
M$_A$ which is the number of minutes estimated from the **A** bar.

Item 1's score, with a maximum of 1 point, is computed as follows:

Score for item 1 of Part II =

$$M_A \div (M_A + M_T)$$

For Item 2 (Continuous Vs. Flip-Flop Transitions): Use item 2's bar to code each transition period indicated on the time line as follows:

C to indicate a *continuous transition* according to the definition from your training session (i.e., one learning activity was terminated and a second began without [a] a return to the first activity after the transition period began nor [b] an interruption after the second learning activity began in order to conduct transition business (e.g., change the directions for the activity).

F to indicate a *flip-flop transition* (i.e., the criterion for a continuous transition is not met).

? to indicate that it is unclear as to whether the transition is continuous or flip-flop.

Compiling and Computing Item 2's Score. After the observation period, the following numbers are tallied:

C_T which is the number of **C**s on the bar, and
F_T which is the number of **F**s on the bar.

Item 2's score, with a a maximum of 1 point, is computed as follows:

Score for item 2 of Part II =

$$C_T \div (C_T + F_T).$$

For Item 3 (Smooth Vs. Jerky Transitions): Use item 3's bar to code each transition period indicated on the time line as follows:

S to indicate a *smooth transition* according to the definition from your training session (i.e., all students disengaged in the first learning activity and engaged in the second at approximately the same time).

J to indicate a *jerky transition* (i.e., the criterion for a smooth transition is not met).

? to indicate that it is unclear as to whether the transition is smooth or jerky.

Compiling and Computing Item 3's Score. After the observation period, the following numbers are tallied:

S_T which is the number of **S**s on the bar, and
J_T which is the number of **J**s on the bar.

Item 3's score, with a maximum of 1 point, is computed as follows:

Score for item 3 of Part II =

$$S_T \div (S_T + J_T)$$

For Item 4 (Purposeful Vs. Nonpurposeful Teacher Talk): Use item 4's bar to code each instance of teacher talk as follows:

Whenever the teacher begins to speak following a pause in classroom talk, record **T** in the bar at the point corresponding to the appropriate part of the time scale. If that instance of teacher talk proves to be *purposeful* according to the definition from your training session (i.e., it is informative relative to the business of the transition period or learning activity), then *circle the T* (i.e., T). If the teacher talk proves to be *nonpurposeful,* leave the **T** alone. If during the observation period, it never becomes clear as to whether or not the teacher talk was purposeful, then place a slash across the **T** (i.e., $\not{T}$).

For any instance in which it is unclear as to whether or not a new sample of teacher talk occurred, mark **?**

Compiling and Computing Item 4's Score. After the observation period, the following numbers are tallied:

$$\text{T}_\text{T}$$ which is the number of Ts on the bar, and

$$\text{T}_\text{T}$$ which is the number of **T**s on the bar.

Item 4's score, with a maximum of 3 points, is computed as following:

Score for item 4 of Part II =

$$3 \times [\text{T}_\text{T} \div (\text{T}_\text{T} + \text{T}_\text{T})].$$

For Item 5 (Descriptive Vs. Judgmental Teacher Talk): For item 5, an instance of teacher talk is defined the same as for item 4. Use item 5's bar to code each instance of teacher talk as follows:
Mark **D** for the instance if it includes at least one descriptive comment and no judgmental comments as defined in your training session (i.e., [a] for a descriptive comment, the teacher verbally portrays a situation, behavior, achievement, or feeling without labeling it and [b] for a judgmental comment, the teacher verbally characterizes a behavior, achievement, feeling, or person).

Mark **J** for the instance which includes a judgmental comment.

Mark **?** if either (a) it is unclear as to whether or not the criterion for a **D** has been met or (b) the teacher talk is clearly neither descriptive nor judgmental.

Compiling and Computing Item 5's Score. After the observation period, the following numbers are tallied:

D which is the number of **D**s on the bar, and

J which is the number of **J**s on the bar.

Item 5's score, with a maximum of 3 points, is computed as follows:

Score for item 5 of Part II =

$$3 \times [\text{D}_\text{T} \div (\text{D}_\text{T} + \text{J}_\text{T})].$$

Directions for Computing the Total Score for Area 2 (Classroom Management & Discipline) Total score out of a possible 35 = sum of the 9 scores from items 2, 3, 4, & 5 of Part I and items 1, 2, 3, 4, & 5 of Part II.

Example of a Completed Narrative Description Item from a Structured Classroom Observation Instrument

OBJECTIVE/LESSON ANALYSIS SHEET RELATIVE TO OBJECTIVE _3_

Identify the content area and the level of learning (i.e. behavioral construct) targeted by the objective as listed on the attached sheet provided by the teacher:

Targeted Content: *The difference between facts and opinions*

Targeted Learning Level: *Conceptual*

Identify (with a brief description) those aspects of the observation period that related to Objective _3_ :

From approximately 11:15 am to 11:45 am, beginning when Ms. Formosan asked Amanda to tell the class something she knew, and ending with the assignment to cut out a newspaper advertisement.

Describe those activities and events from the period you identified above that would indicate that the lesson was appropriate for the content and learning level of Objective _3_ :

The learning activity began with students making statements that were then grouped into what eventually labeled as statements of facts and statements of opinions. The example/non-example pattern followed an inductive learning model associated with conceptual-level learning. The activity sequence went from a focus on specific examples & non-examples to categories to generalizations about the differences between facts and opinions.

Describe those activities and events from the period you identified above that
would indicate that the lesson was inappropriate for the content and learning
level of Objective _3_ :

> Virtually all appeared appropriate with one possible exception:
>
> The 3rd graders tended to dwell on details in their examples & it appeared that Ms. Formosan would stem this tendency by summing up with generalizations that needed (for purposes of conceptualization) to emanate from the students.

Describe student behaviors that you observed that would provide any evidence
of how well students progressed toward achievement of Objective _3_ :

> During the 30-minute span, 24 of the students had at least one opportunity to try a hand at clarifying an example as either fact or opinion. At the beginning, few did. Near the end, virtually all did it correctly. Also several students predicted the purpose of the assignment before Ms. Formosan made it explicit.

Specifications for Designing Appendix E's Measurement

**SPECIFICATIONS FOR DESIGNING
APPENDIX E's MEASUREMENT**

Teaching Performance Area:

Classroom management & discipline

Subvariables to Be Measured:

A, B, C, D, & E from Table 3.3.

Observable Indicators:

From Table 3.3: i–iv under A, i–iii under B,
i under C, i under D, &
i–iii under E.

Item Formats:

Structured classroom observations for the observable indicators of all subvariables. Both items that code specific events and those that categorize time intervals are satisfactory for this single-score instrument.

Usability Considerations:

1. It is anticipated that for any one teacher the instrument will be administered between three and nine times within two months.
2. Each administration requires only one on-site observational period.
3. The on-site observation period should take no more than 90 minutes (preferably less).
4. Videotape equipment and one camera operator can be available for each on-site observation.
5. The turnaround time between completion of the on-site observation and reporting of the score should be no more than 48 hours.
6. Each administration should require only one trained observer.
7. The trained observer should not in any way be associated with any formative evaluations or instructional supervision related to the observed teacher. Preferably, the trained observer is a professional educator, but *not* a member of the school faculty or staff.
8. The training of expert observers should take place within the equivalent of what the District Office defines as two full-day workshop sessions.
9. Reference materials for trained observers and documentation about the measurement and its validity should be available for production and distribution by the District Office.

Maximum Number of Points: 35

Distribution of the Maximum Number of Points by Subvariable & Observable Indicator

Sub-Var.	No. Pts	Obs. Ind.	No. Pts.	
A	10	_____	i	2
			ii	0
			iii	3
			iv	5
B	3	_____	i	1
			ii	1
			iii	1
C	7	_____	i	7
D	5	_____	i	5
E	10	_____	i	3
			ii	3
			iii	4

Method of Determining Cutoff Score:

The interpretation of the overall classroom management & discipline score (out of a possible 35) will be the following norm-referenced procedures:

1. A representative sample of the district's teachers will be identified for each of the following levels (the parenthetical number indicates the minimum size for the sample):
   A. *Kindergarten* (15)
   B. *Grades 1–2* (25)
   C. *Grades 3–5* (30)
   D. *Middle school* (50)
   E. *High school* (50)
2. The measurement will be administered with each member of the sample once.
3. The results of step 2 will be used to compute a mean and standard error of measurement (Cangelosi, 1982, pp. 255–306) for each of the five levels (A–E listed for step 1).
4. Criteria for cutoff scores are as follows:
   A. The score is labeled "significantly below the average" if it is two or more standard errors of measurement below the mean of the sample for its level.
   B. The score is labeled "marginally below the average" if it is within one and two standard errors of measurement below the mean of the sample for its level.
   C. The score is labeled "average" if it is within one standard error of measurement from the mean of the sample for its level.
   D. The score is labeled "marginally above the average" if it is within one and two standard errors of measurement above the mean of the sample for its level.
   E. The score is labeled "significantly above average" if it is more than two standard errors of measurement above the mean of the sample for its level.

Classroom Observation Measurement for Instructional Methods and Techniques

DIRECTIONS FOR THE TRAINED OBSERVER

(Please refer to the attached form (p. 236) as you read these directions.)

Preparing for the Observation

Review the operational definitions and procedures you learned in the training workshop. If it's been a while since you last observed with this instrument, you may want to practice with it in a colleague's class before using it for an actual evaluation of teaching.

The observation should be scheduled with the teacher at least a week in advance. Arrange for the teacher to supply you with a lesson plan that includes a list of the objectives to be targeted by the activities planned for the observation period.

Based on the lesson plan, complete Item 0 prior to the observation period. You will need to refer to it when completing Items 1–3.

For each objective you list for Item 0, label the implied learning level as either (a) memory cognitive, (b) higher cognitive, (c) psychomotor skill, or (d) affective. Use additional descriptors as needed. Separate the objectives by drawing a horizontal line across the page.

Completing the "Description of the Situation" on Page 1 of the Form

Take notes relevant to the "Description of the situation" prior to, during, and immediately after the observations. Compose the narrative from those notes after you have compiled the overall score.

Completing Items 1–3 During the Observation

ITEM 1: For each learning activity, describe what you see or hear that provides any indication as to which objective that activity targets. Clearly indicate which descriptions go with which objectives using horizontal lines across the page.
ITEM 2: Describe any teaching moves that can be classified as either "a" or "b" moves relative to student engagement.
ITEM 3: Describe each learning activity, pointing out those aspects that characterize it as direct teaching, drill and practice, etc. Use horizontal lines to make the associations between objectives and activities clear.

Scoring Items 1–3 Immediately After the Observation

ITEM 1: Based on the descriptive narrative you completed for Item 1 of the form, select the *one and only one true statement* from the following:

- **A.** There was no indication that any of the learning activities targeted any of stated objectives.
- **B.** There were indications that some, but not all, of the learning activities targeted stated objectives.
- **C.** There were indications that each learning activity targeted a stated objective.
- **D.** There was no evidence to suggest that any one of the above statements is more likely true than either of the other two.

Score Item 1:

+0 for selecting statement A, +1 for B, +2 for C, and +1 for D.

ITEM 2: Based on the descriptive narrative you completed for Item 2 of the form, select the *one and only true statement* from the following:

A. During the observation period, "b" teaching moves (i.e., moves that discourage student engagement) occurred with greater frequency than "a" teaching moves (i.e., moves that encourage student engagement).

B. There was virtually no difference in the frequency of "a" teaching moves and the frequency of "b" teaching moves during the observation period.

C. During the observation period, "a" teaching moves occurred with greater frequency than "b" teaching moves.

D. There was no evidence to suggest that any one of the above statements is more likely true than either of the other two.

Score Item 2:

+0 for selecting statment A, +1 for B, +2 for C, and +1 for D.

ITEM 3: The total score for Item 3 should be 0 if the score for Item 1 is 0. Otherwise, based on the descriptive narrative you completed for Item 1 of the form score,

+2 for each of the following statments that is true,

+0 for each of the following statements that is false, and

+1 for each statement on which there is no basis for judging it as true or false:

A. Either direct teaching or drill and practice methods were used within at least one learning activity that (according to Item 1) targeted either a memory-cognitive or psychomotor-skill level objective.

B. Systematic inquiry was incorporated in at least one learning activity that (according to Item 1) targeted a higher-level cognitive objective.

C. Either reinforcement theory or strategies for examining alternatives were used within at least one learning activity that (according to Item 1) targeted an affective learning objective.

Compiling the Overall Score

The overall score is the sum of the three item scores. Thus, the maximum possible overall score is 10 (2 + 2 + 6).

Classroom Observation Recording Form for Instructional Methods and Techniques

Teacher's name _____ Observation # _____

Observation date _____ Beginning time _____ Ending time _____

Trained observer's name _____

Description of the situation (identify the class and lesson and explain any special circumstances and factors that should be considered in the interpretation of the observation results):

0. OBJECTIVES FROM THE LESSON PLAN

Obj. ID #	Objective as Stated in the Lesson Plan	Implied Learning Level

1. ASSOCIATING OBSERVED ACTIVITIES WITH STATED OBJECTIVES (from "0")

Obj. ID #	Description of what was observed in the learning activity that made the objective being targeted apparent

2. TEACHING MOVES FOR OBTAINING AND MAINTAINING STUDENT ENGAGEMENT

Description of (a) moves the teacher used to lead students to engage in the learning activity (e.g., proximity to students, eye contact, incorporating students' names in presentations, advanced organizers, wait time for questions) and (b) teacher's moves that discouraged students from being engaged in the learning activity (e.g., judgmental, inane, hostile, or passive comments, flip-flop transitions)

3. TEACHING STRATEGIES AND TECHNIQUES ASSOCIATED WITH OBJECTIVES

Obj. ID #	Description of those aspects of the learning activity that are relevant to the type of teaching model applied

Interviewer's Instrument Used for the Woodpine County Needs Assessment Regarding Teachers' Assertiveness with Parents (TAP)

TAP Interviewer's Form

Note: The questions and directives to which the teacher is to respond appear inside quotes. Reminders for you, the interviewer, appear inside brackets.

1. "Within the last six weeks, about how many individual conferences with parents of your students have you had?"

   [Record number _____ and any other notable comments]

   [If number is less than 2, then clarify the question and rerecord. If the number is still less than 2, conclude the interview.]
2. "Without revealing the identity of any of the parties involved, recall two of those conferences. First, the one that in your judgment was the least successful. Second, the one that was the most successful. When you have both cases in mind, just say, 'okay.' "

   [Clarify as needed, without leading.]

   [After "okay":]

   "First, let's talk about the conference that did not go as well as the other. As you began this conference, what did you hope to gain from it? Please explain without revealing identities."

   [Summarize response:]

   [If no statement of purpose is included, mark +1 on the **P** (passive) scale. If a statement of purpose is implied that includes concern for enhancement of the teacher's effectiveness, mark +1 on the **A** (assertive) scale. If a statement of purpose is implied that includes defensiveness, mark +1 on the **H** (hostile) scale.]

   [**P** _____ **A** _____ **H** _____]
3. "Describe what happened during the conference that prevented it from going as well as it could have gone."

[Summarize response:]

[Score +1 on the **A** scale for *each* of the following about the response:

- For basing the judgment regarding the failure or success of the conference on how well the stated purpose was achieved.
- For including at least one description implying that the teacher displayed assertiveness.
- For identifying either a hostile or passive teacher behavior as possibly impeding the success of the conference.

[Score +1 on the **P** scale for *each* of the following about the response:

- For basing the judgment regarding the failure or success of the conference on the impact the conference had on the teacher's image.
- For including at least one description implying that the teacher displayed passiveness.

[Score + 1 on the **H** scale for *each* of the following about the response:

- For basing the judgment regarding the failure or success of the conference on how well the teacher fared in a competition with the parent(s) or the student.
- For including at least one description implying that the teacher displayed hostility.

[**P** _____ **A** _____ **H** _____]

4. "Now, let's talk about the conference that went better. As you began this conference, what did you hope to gain from it? Please explain without revealing identities."

[Summarize response:]

[If no statement of purpose is included, mark +1 on the **P** (passive) scale. If a statement of purpose is implied that includes concern for enhancement of the teacher's effectiveness, mark +1 on the **A** (assertive) scale. If a statement of purpose is implied that includes defensiveness, mark +1 on the **H** (hostile) scale.]

[**P** _____ **A** _____ **H** _____]

5. "Describe what happened during the conference that made it go better than the conference we first discussed."

[Summarize response:]

[Score +1 on the **A** scale for *each* of the following about the response:

- For basing the judgment regarding the failure or success of the conference on how well the stated purpose was achieved.
- For including at least one description implying that the teacher displayed assertiveness.
- For identifying a teacher behavior that you classify as assertive as possibly contributing to the success of the conference.

[Score +1 on the **P** scale for *each* of the following about the response:

- For basing the judgment regarding the failure or success of the conference on the impact the conference had on the teacher's image.
- For including at least one description implying that the teacher displayed passiveness.

[Score +1 on the **H** scale for *each* of the following about the response:

- For basing the judgment regarding the failure or success of the conference on how well the teacher fared in a competition with the parent(s) or the student.
- For including at least one description implying that the teacher displayed hostility.

[P _____   A _____   H _____]

TOTAL SCORES FOR:

P _____

A _____

H _____

Rating Form Blaine Completed after Interviewing Joyce

Personnel Form 3/I13-J
Applicant Interview

Cliffside School District
Interviewer's Rating Form

Teacher interviewed _Joyce Blueor_ Date of interview _3/21_
Teaching specialty _Elem._ Interviewer _Blaine Sivenson_

Scoring key: +2 = well above average, +1 = just above average, 0 = average,
−1 = just below average, −2 = well below average.

		(circle one for each statement)				
1.	enthusiasm for teaching	(+2)	+1	0	−1	−2
2.	knowledge of instructional methods	+2	(+1)	0	−1	−2
3.	knowledge of subject matter	+2	(+1)	0	−1	−2
4.	classroom management skill	+2	(+1)	0	−1	−2
5.	human relations skill	(+2)	+1	0	−1	−2
6.	professional manner & attitude	(+2)	+1	0	−1	−2

Total Score ___9___

Overall recommendation (check one and then comment on the back side):

Should the applicant be considered for a position?

Definitely ☑   Probably ☐   Unlikely ☐   No ☐

APPENDIX K

Instrument for Analysis of Unit Plan and Lesson Plan

ANALYSIS OF UNIT PLAN AND LESSON PLAN EXHIBIT A

TEACHER'S NAME _____ S. S. NO. _____ GRADE/SUBJECT _____

EVALUATOR _____ SCHOOL _____

EVALUATOR'S POSITION _____ DATE OF CONFERENCE _____

CHECK YES OR NO AS IT APPLIES   COMMENTS

UNIT PLAN

YES   NO

____ ____ At least one unit goal is stated.
____ ____ The unit goal(s) is/are consistent with the curriculum
____ ____ The goal(s) is/are appropriate for the students.
____ ____ Procedures for introducing the unit goal(s) to the students are given.
____ ____ Materials/media are listed for the unit.
____ ____ Learner understanding is assessed for the unit.
____ ____ The assessment of learner understanding relates to the stated goal(s) of the unit.

LESSON PLAN

____ ____ The lesson plan contains at least one objective.
____ ____ The objective(s) is/are stated in terms of student learning and behavior.
____ ____ The objective(s) is/are appropriate for students.
____ ____ The plan explains how student achievement of the objective(s) will be measured.
____ ____ The lesson plan contains some introductory statement or procedures related to the objective(s).
____ ____ The introductory procedures are motivational.
____ ____ The instructional procedures are related to the objective(s).
____ ____ The instructional procedures are complete.
____ ____ The instructional procedures are properly sequenced.
____ ____ The instructional procedures use more than one teaching strategy.
____ ____ The instructional procedures provide for student practice/review.
____ ____ The planned practice/review is related to the objective(s).
____ ____ The practice is planned for a specific purpose (feedback, independent study, grading).
____ ____ Alternative and/or supplemental activities for additional practice are included in the plan.
____ ____ The plan contains statements related to how the the learner will be involved.
____ ____ The material and media for the lesson are listed.

"State Model for Local Evaluation," The Tennessee Department of Education. Tennessee Career Ladder Better Schools Program, 1985. Published by The Tennessee Department of Education.

CHECK YES OR NO AS IT APPLIES | COMMENTS

YES   NO

___ ___   The material and media are appropriate for the
           students.
___ ___   An explanation is provided for how the material
           and media will be used.
___ ___   The plan contains specific procedures for
           reteaching, if necessary.

_____

EVALUATION TEAM MEMBER / DATE

_____

EVALUATION TEAM MEMBER (SUPERORDINATE) / DATE

_____

TEACHER'S SIGNATURE / DATE

TEACHER'S SIGNATURE ACKNOWLEDGES AN
OPPORTUNITY TO REVIEW THE ANALYSIS OF
UNIT PLAN AND LESSON PLAN. IT DOES NOT
NECESSARILY INDICATE AGREEMENT WITH
THE COMMENTS.

242

Examiner-Opinion Questionnaire Used in Hillyard School District's Summative Evaluation Process of Beginning Teachers' Performances

Hillyard School District
Peer Teacher/Examiner Questionnaire

1. What is your name? _____
2. Please identify the following with respect to the beginning teacher to whose performance this evaluation pertains:

   Name _____ School _____

   Teaching assignment _____

   _____

3. Explain any special or unusual circumstances or factors that should be taken into consideration as your responses to this questionnaire are being interpreted (e.g., extraordinary events that might have made the observation period particularly stressful for the beginning teacher or personal biases you hold that might influence your responses to these questionnaire items).

4. Please attach the instruments you completed as a result of your (a) classroom observations, (b) interviews, and (c) document examinations.
5. *Regarding organizing and planning for teaching:*
   A. Was the organization of the classroom conducive to learning? Explain.

   B. Was there a systematic and logical connection among (a) the curricula, (b) unit plans, and (c) lesson plans? Explain.

6. *Regarding learning goals and objectives:*
   A. Were the learning goals and objectives made explicit? Explain how.

B. How consistent were the learning goals with the prescribed curriculum guide? Explain.

C. Was there a systematic, logical connection between the learning goals and the learning objectives?

D. Did the learning objectives address students' needs (with respect to both content and learning levels)? Explain.

7. *Regarding subject-matter content:*
   A. Was the presentation of content to students organized in a manner consistent with the current thinking of recognized authorities? Identify areas of strength and weakness in how content was organized.

   B. Were students likely to be left with accurate or inaccurate conceptions regarding subject-matter content? Specify areas where inaccurate impressions may have resulted. Specify areas where especially accurate and insightful impressions may have resulted.

8. *Regarding instructional methods and techniques:*
   A. Were lesson *designs* appropriate to learning objectives? Specify types of objectives (e.g., knowledge level or application level) for which appropriate lessons were designed and types of objectives for which they were not.

   B. Were lessons *conducted* as they were designed? Include examples in your explanation.

C. What student outcomes, other than those related to stated objectives, may likely be attributed to the teacher's classroom activities? Explain using examples.

9. *Regarding classroom management:*
   A. How efficient were transition periods? Explain.

   B. Did students tend to be engaged at the beginning of learning activities? Explain.

   C. Did students tend to be engaged throughout learning activities? Explain.

   D. How well did the teacher deal with nondisruptive off-task behaviors? Explain.

   E. How well did the teacher deal with disruptive off-task behaviors? Explain.

10. *Regarding assessment of student achievement:*
    A. Overall, did the teacher generally make accurate summative evaluations of student achievement of learning goals? Explain.

    B. Overall, did the teacher make accurate formative evaluations of student achievement? Explain.

C. How relevant were the teacher's measurements to student achievement of learning goals? Identify types of objectives (e.g., comprehension level or affective) that were measured particularly well and types that were not.

D. How reliable were the achievement tests?

11. Please add any other comments that you think would be helpful to those who will be making a summative evaluation of this teacher's instructional performance.

Student-Opinion Questionnaire Used at Utah State University and Weber State College

 WEBER STATE COLLEGE
UTAH STATE UNIVERSITY

COMBINED MASTER OF EDUCATION PROGRAM
INSTRUCTIONAL EVALUATION

Instructor: _____

Course Number: _____

Quarter: _____

Leave items blank for which you cannot make a judgment.

	Negative				Positive

1. The instructor adequately outlined the objectives and requirements of this course.   1   2   3   4   5

Comments: _____

_____

_____

2. The instructor was well prepared for class.   1   2   3   4   5

Comments: _____

_____

_____

3. The instructor presented material in a well-organized manner.   1   2   3   4   5

Comments: _____

_____

_____

4. The instructor seemed interested in the subject matter.   1   2   3   4   5

Comments: _____

_____

_____

5. The instructor made students feel free to ask questions, disagree and express their ideas.   1   2   3   4   5

Comments: _____

_____

_____

6. The instructor was helpful when students had difficulty.   1   2   3   4   5

Comments: _____

_____

_____

Courtesy of Weber State College, Ogden, UT, Dr. Dick Jones, Dean, College of Education. Used with permission.

7. The method of evaluation in the class was   1   2   3   4   5
    appropriate.

    Comments: _____

    _____

    _____

8. The instructor was fair and impartial in his/her   1   2   3   4   5
    dealings with students.

    Comments: _____

    _____

    _____

9. The instructor was accessible to students outside   1   2   3   4   5
    of class.

    Comments: _____

    _____

    _____

10. The textbook/reading materials made a valuable con-   1   2   3   4   5
    tribution to the course.

    Comments: _____

    _____

    _____

11. The amount of work required for the course reflec-   1   2   3   4   5
    ted the credit hours received.

    Comments: _____

    _____

    _____

12. In comparison to other instructors you have had,   1   2   3   4   5
    how would you rate this instructor?

    Comments: _____

    _____

    _____

13. Your instructor would like to know if there is something you believe he/she has
    done especially well in teaching this course.

    _____

    _____

    _____

14. Your instructor would like to know what specific things you believe might be done
    to improve his/her teaching of this course.

    _____

    _____

    _____

Student-Opinion Questionnaire
from the Center for Faculty Evaluation,
Kansas State University

iDEA SURVEY FORM -- STUDENT REACTIONS TO INSTRUCTION AND COURSES

Your thoughtful answers to these questions will provide helpful information to your instructor.

> • Describe the frequency of your instructor's teaching procedures, using the following code:
> 1—Hardly Ever   3—Sometimes
> 2—Occasionally   4—Frequently   5—Almost Always

The Instructor:

1. Promoted teacher-student discussion (as opposed to mere responses to questions).
2. Found ways to help students answer their own questions.
3. Encouraged students to express themselves freely and openly.
4. Seemed enthusiastic about the subject matter.
5. Changed approaches to meet new situations.
6. Gave examinations which stressed unnecessary memorization.
7. Spoke with expressiveness and variety in tone of voice.
8. Demonstrated the importance and significance of the subject matter.
9. Made presentations which were dry and dull.
10. Made it clear how each topic fit into the course.
11. Explained the reasons for criticisms of students' academic performance.
12. Gave examination questions which were unclear.
13. Encouraged student comments even when they turned out to be incorrect or irrelevant.
14. Summarized material in a manner which aided retention.
15. Stimulated students to intellectual effort beyond that required by most courses.
16. Clearly stated the objectives of the course.
17. Explained course material clearly, and explanations were to the point.
18. Related course material to real life situations.
19. Gave examination questions which were unreasonably detailed (picky).
20. Introduced stimulating ideas about the subject.

> • On each of the objectives listed below, rate the progress you have made in this course compared with other courses you have taken at this college or university. In this course my progress was:
> 1—Low (lowest 10 percent of courses I have taken here)
> 2—Low Average (next 20 percent of courses)
> 3—Average (middle 40 percent of courses)
> 4—High Average (next 20 percent of courses)
> 5—High (highest 10 percent of courses)

Progress on:

21. Gaining factual knowledge (terminology, classifications, methods, trends).
22. Learning fundamental principles, generalizations, or theories.
23. Learning to apply course material to improve rational thinking, problem-solving and decision-making.
24. Developing specific skills, competencies and points of view needed by professionals in the field most closely related to this course.
25. Learning how professionals in this field go about the process of gaining new knowledge.
26. Developing creative capacities.
27. Developing a sense of personal responsibility (self-reliance, self-discipline).
28. Gaining a broader understanding and appreciation of intellectual-cultural activity (music, science, literature, etc.).
29. Developing skill in expressing myself orally or in writing.
30. Discovering the implications of the course material for understanding myself (interests, talents, values, etc.).

> • On the next four questions, compare this course with others you have taken at this institution, using the following code:
> 1—Much Less than Most Courses
> 2—Less than Most
> 3—About Average
> 4—More than Most
> 5—Much More than Most

The Course:

31. Amount of reading.
32. Amount of work in other (non-reading) assignments.
33. Difficulty of subject matter.
34. Degree to which the course hung together (various topics and class activities were related to each other).

> • Describe your attitudes toward and behavior in this course, using the following code:
> 1—Definitely False
> 2—More False than True   4—More True than False
> 3—In Between   5—Definitely True

Self-rating:

35. I worked harder on this course than on most courses I have taken.
36. I had a strong desire to take this course.
37. I would like to take another course from this instructor.
38. As a result of taking this course, I have more positive feelings toward this field of study.
39. Leave this space blank. Continue with question A.

A. Blacken space number 4 on the Response Card.

> • For the following six questions, B-G, describe your attitudes, feelings, and behaviors by filling in the appropriate space:
> 1—Definitely False
> 2—More False than True   4—More True than False
> 3—In Between   5—Definitely True

B. In general, I like my instructors.
C. I try very hard to learn in all my courses.
D. I really wanted to take this course regardless of who taught it.
E. I really wanted to take a course from this instructor.
F. In general, I am a good student.
G. In general, I enjoy my courses.

If your instructor has extra questions, answer them in the space designated on the Response Card.

Your comments are invited on how the instructor might improve this course or teaching procedures. Use the back of the Response Card (unless otherwise directed).

Courtesy of Kansas State University, Manhattan, KS. William E. Cashen, Center for Faculty Evaluation and Development. Used with permission.

Descriptive Questionnaire Byron
Administered to His Civics Class

Please don't put your name on this questionnaire.

For the past four days, we have been looking at both sides of the gun-control issue. Please answer the following about what you did during this time:

1. Over the past four days, about how much time did you spend outside of class:
    A. trying to find magazines, newspapers, pamphlets, books, or other types of print materials on gun control _____
    B. locating, listening to, or recording television or radio programs on gun control _____
    C. discussing gun control with people other than people in our class and me _____
    D. doing other things related to what we were doing in class on gun control _____
2. Explain how the last four days have influenced your thinking about:
    A. gun control

    B. how people make up their minds

    C. politics

    D. the news media

    E. how people try to change one another's minds

    F. how people should try to change one another's minds

G. how to obtain information

H. anything else you want to include that is not listed above

3. Would you like us to look at another controversial issue the same way we looked at gun control? Why or why not?

4. If we did look at another issue, what topics would you be interested in?

Thank you for your help.

Descriptive Questionnaire Ann Used with Her First Graders

ANSWER SHEET

1.

2.

3.

4.

Artwork by Amanda Cangelosi.

5.

6.

7.

8.

DIRECTIONS FOR ANN TO READ ALOUD

1. Row one has two pictures. One is of a boy who is feeling sick. The other one is of that same boy playing a video game. Circle the picture of the boy doing what you would rather be doing. Don't circle the one you would rather not be doing.
2. Row two also has two pictures. One is of a boy doing work, cleaning up his room. The other is of that boy working at school in his classroom. Circle the picture of the boy doing what you would rather be doing.
3. Row three has two pictures. One is of a girl jumping rope at school. The other is of the girl jumping rope at the park. Circle the picture of the girl doing what you would rather do.
4. Row four has two pictures. One is of a girl talking to her neighbor. The other is the girl talking to her teacher. Circle the picture of the girl doing what you would rather do.
5. Row five has two pictures. One is of a girl coloring a picture in her classroom. The other is of the girl coloring a picture while riding in a car. Circle the picture of the girl doing what you would rather do.
6. Row six has two pictures. One is of a boy going to school. The other is the boy leaving school. Circle the picture of the boy doing what you would rather do.
7. Row seven has two pictures. One is a boy who is washing dishes at home. The other is of the boy clearning up at school. Circle the picture of the boy doing what you would rather do.
8. Row eight has two pictures. One is a girl laughing with her friends. The other is the girl who is looking for a book she lost.

SCORING KEY

First check to see that the student has circled the second picture for item 1 and first for item 8. If not, then do not score the answer sheet, since this would indicate that the student either didn't understand the directions or didn't follow them seriously. If items 1 and 8 are completed as expected, then score one point for each of the following:

Item	Picture Circled	Item	Picture Circled
2	second	5	first
3	first	6	first
4	second	7	second

Classroom Observation Instrument and Questionnaire Used by Terry Hives' Formative Evaluation Team

---

CLASSROOM OBSERVATION FORM—DISTRICT FORMATIVE EVALUATION TEAM

Observation ID _____ Date _____
Beginning time _____ Ending Time _____

In this first column, attach:	*In this second column, write a description of the activities and events that actually took place during the times corresponding to the scheduled planned learning activities listed in the first column.*	*In this third column, note any events or activities that would appear to have an impact on "unanticipated outcomes."*
The learning activity sequence for the observational period that the teacher provided as part of the day's lesson plan.		

255

**FORMATIVE EVALUATION TEAM'S QUESTIONNAIRE
REGARDING THE TEACHER'S PROCEDURES FOR ASSESSING
STUDENT ACHIEVEMENT OF THE UNIT'S LEARNING GOAL**

Unit ID _____ Date of analysis _____ Teacher _____

1. List the measurements that the teacher indicated were used to influence the assessment of student achievement.

2. For each of the measurements you just listed, what is your judgment of its validity?

3. For each of the measurements you listed for item 1, present the evidence you used to judge its relevance.

4. For each of the measurements you listed for item 1, present the evidence you used to judge its reliability.

5. What, if any suggestions, do you have for improving the cost-effectiveness of the measurements used by the teacher.

6. Do you agree with the teacher's assessment of student achievement of the unit's goal? Explain your answer.

The Personnel Evaluation Standards of the Joint Committee on Standards for Educational Evaluation

SUMMARY OF THE STANDARDS

P PROPRIETY STANDARDS

The Propriety Standards require that evaluations be conducted legally, ethically, and with due regard for the welfare of the evaluatees and clients of the evaluations.

- P1—SERVICE ORIENTATION: Evaluations of educators should promote sound education principles, fulfillment of institutional missions, and effective performance of job responsibilities, so that the educational needs of students, community, and society are met.
- P2—FORMAL EVALUATION GUIDELINES: Guidelines for personnel evaluations should be recorded in statement of policy, negotiated agreements, and/or personnel evaluation manuals, so that evaluations are consistent, equitable, and in accordance with pertinent laws and ethical codes.
- P3—CONFLICT OF INTEREST: Conflicts of interest should be identified and dealt with openly and honestly, so that they do not compromise the evaluation process and results.
- P4—ACCESS TO PERSONNEL EVALUATION REPORTS: Access to reports of personnel evaluation should be limited to those individuals with a legitimate need to review and use the reports, so that appropriate use of the information is assured.
- P5—INTERACTIONS WITH EVALUATEES: The evaluation should address evaluatees in a professional, considerate, and courteous manner, so that their self-esteem, motivation, professional reputations, performance, and attitude toward personnel evaluation are enhanced, or, at least, not needlessly damaged.

U UTILITY STANDARDS

The Utility Standards are intended to guide evaluations so that they will be informative, timely, and influential.

- U1—CONSTRUCTIVE ORIENTATION: Evaluations should be constructive, so that they help institutions to develop human resources and encourage and assist those evaluated to provide excellent service.
- U2—DEFINED USES: The users and the intended uses of a personnel evaluation should be identified so that the evaluations can address appropriate questions.
- U3—EVALUATOR CREDIBILITY: The evaluation system should be managed and executed by persons with the necessary qualifications, skills, and authority, and evaluators should conduct themselves professionally, so that evaluation reports are respected and used.
- U4—FUNCTIONAL REPORTING: Reports should be clear, timely, accurate, and germane, so that they are of practical value to the evaluatee and other appropriate audiences.
- U5—FOLLOW-UP AND IMPACT: Evaluations should be followed up, so that users and evaluatees are aided to understand the results and take appropriate actions.

Daniel Stufflebeam, The Personnel Evaluation Standards of the Joint Committee on Standards for Educational Evaluation. Excerpted from *The Personnel Evaluation Standards: How to Assess Systems for Evaluating Educators*. Copyright 1988 by Sage Publications, Inc. and the author.

F FEASIBILITY STANDARDS

The Feasibility Standards call for evaluation systems that are as easy to implement as possible, efficient in their use of time and resources, adequately funded, and viable from a number of other standpoints.

- F1—PRACTICAL PROCEDURES: Personnel evaluation procedures should be planned and conducted so that they produce needed information while minimizing disruption and cost.
- F2—POLITICAL VIABILITY: The personnel evaluation system should be developed and monitored collaboratively, so that all concerned parties are constructively involved in making the system work.
- F3—FISCAL VIABILITY: Adequate time and resources should be provided for personnel evaluation activities, so that evaluation plans can be effectively and efficiently implemented.

A ACCURACY STANDARDS

The Accuracy Standards require that the obtained information be technically accurate and that conclusions be linked logically to the data.

- A1—DEFINED ROLE: The role, responsibilities, performance objectives, and needed qualifications of the evaluatee should be clearly defined, so that the evaluator can determine valid assessment data.
- A2—WORK ENVIRONMENT: The context in which the evaluatee works should be identified, described, and recorded, so that environmental influences and constraints on performance can be considered in the evaluation.
- A3—DOCUMENTATION OF PROCEDURE: The evaluation procedures actually followed should be documented, so that the evaluatees and other users can assess the actual, in relation to intended, procedures.
- A4—VALID MEASUREMENT: The measurement procedures should be chosen or developed and implemented on the basis of the described role and the intended use, so that inferences concerning the evaluatee are valid and accurate.
- A5—RELIABLE MEASUREMENT: Measurement procedures should be chosen or developed to assure reliability, so that the information obtained will provide consistent indications of the performance of the evaluatee.
- A6—SYSTEMATIC DATA CONTROL: The information used in the evaluation should be kept secure, and should be carefully processed and maintained, so as to ensure that the data maintained and analyzed are the same as the data collected.
- A7—BIAS CONTROL: The evaluation process should provide safeguards against bias, so that the evaluatee's qualifications or performance is assessed fairly.
- A8—MONITORING EVALUATION SYSTEMS: The personnel evaluation system should be reviewed periodically and systematically, so that appropriate revisions can be made.

Sample Set of Documents Used for Summative Evaluations of Teaching in Davis County School District, Farmington, Utah, August 1988

EDUCATOR EVALUATION

Administrator Time Sequence

1. *Orientation.* The Principal shall orient every member of the instructional staff to the purposes, system, instruments, educator roles, and schedule of the Davis Educator Evaluation Program during the first month of each school year (Sept. 1–30).*
2. *Goal Setting.* The Principal shall conduct a goal-setting interview with each educator during the first term of each school year (Aug. 29–Nov. 3). One or more instructional improvement goals and one or more organizational support goals are required. Personal goals are encouraged but remain optional. Goals are to be cooperatively determined by the teacher and the principal. Goals should be entered on the district form prepared for this purpose.
3. *First Formal Observations.* The first formal classroom observation of all provisional and/or probationary educators and new performance pay applicants shall be completed between Oct. 19 and Nov. 30.
4. *Final Classroom Observations.* All formal classroom observations must be completed sixty calendar days prior to the end of the contract year (Apr. 3, 1989). (Ninety calendar days in cases likely to involve orderly termination of an educator [Mar. 3, 1989]). PERFORMANCE BONUS APPLICANT EVALUATIONS SHOULD BE COMPLETED AND SUBMITTED TO THE DISTRICT BY MARCH 31.

Number of Observations Required

Provisional and Probationary Educators	2
New Performance Pay Applicants†	2
Second & Third Year Performance Pay Participants†	1
All Other Educators	1

5. *Final Interviews.* Final interviews (goals and observation summaries) shall be completed thirty calendar days prior to the close of school (May 3, 1989).
6. *Summary Evaluation Reports.* Summary Evaluation Reports shall be sent to the Area Directors by May 15 of each year.

---

* Dates shown are target dates for 1988–89 school year.
†Classroom educators qualify for performance pay for periods of three years. Two classroom observations are required the first year and one classroom observation for each of the following two years. When they start into a second three-year period, two classroom observations will once again be required the first year.

Criteria for Davis Educator Evaluation Program & Time Sequence Form. Courtesy of Davis County School District, Farmington, UT. Richard E. Kendell, Superintendent. Reprinted with permission.

Davis Educator Evaluation Program (DEEP)* CRITERIA (Revised August 1988)

*Educators are encouraged to become thoroughly familiar with all eleven categories of the DEEP. They should understand the five evaluation criteria as well as the rationale statement in each category. All recent modifications are in parentheses.

Category 1: Learning Objectives

5. *Communicates** (at the most appropriate point in the lesson sequence) measurable learning objectives†; *checks* to make certain that students understand expectations; *responds* to student feedback and develops the objective.
4. *Communicates** (at the most appropriate point in the lesson sequence) measureable learning objectives†; *checks* to make certain that students understand expectations.
3. *Communicates** measurable learning objectives†.
2. *Prepares* learning objectives but does not communicate* them.
1. Directs classroom activities *without preparing* learning objectives.

*Communicates verbally and (where appropriate) in writing.
†Measurable ((behavioral)) learning objectives state what the learner is expected to do, the conditions under which the learning is to take place, and the standard used to measure mastery.

Rationale

Learning objectives are the center of daily instruction and are always directly observable and measurable in terms of student performance. (Objectives must be drawn from the established district curriculum.)

The value of developing specific objectives for the class session is to identify clearly the purpose for that session and to provide a definitive basis for assessing accomplishments.

The competent teacher will state and clarify the objectives of each lesson at the outset. This is based on the premise that all students will be more receptive for learning if they have a clear explanation of what they are expected to learn. (An exception might be a lesson in which the teacher purposefully uses questions to lead the class through a process of discovery with the intention of having the objective revealed, thoroughly discussed, and fully clarified at the end of the lesson.)

The expectations of the tasks to be performed should be explained carefully. The use of visual or other sensory aids serves to guarantee clarity of the learning objectives.

Inasmuch as the goals and objectives may apply to more than one class session, it may be necessary for the observer to ask the teacher for clarification on development of the objectives. This could be done in the post-observation session.

Category 2: Selection and Use of Instructional Materials

5. Demonstrates *exemplary* skill in the use and *improvement* of a variety of instructional materials used to develop learning activities (derived from the district curriculum).
4. Demonstrates *skill* in the use of a *variety* of *appropriate* materials* to develop learning objectives (derived from the district curriculum).
3. Demonstrates *skill* in the use of *appropriate* materials* to develop learning objectives.
2. Demonstrates *limited skill* in the use of *readily available* materials.
1. Uses *few or no* instructional materials.

*Appropriate materials (commercial or teacher-made) are those which meet the needs of the students in accomplishing both daily and long-range goals and objectives.

Rationale

The use of instructional materials in education requires not only the ability of the teacher to follow published instructions, but also the ability to modify the use of materials based on student needs. In addition, effective teachers should be able to create materials as needed to fill gaps which exist with commercial materials.

The observer should look for the following indications of skill in the effective use of instructional materials:

1. correlation of materials to goals and objectives;
2. consistent requests for feedback from students regarding materials used;
3. justification for any modification in the use of commercial materials; and
4. use of materials to implement multisensory approaches (i.e., tactile, visual, auditory).

Category 3: Instructional Techniques

5. Provides *varied* instructional techniques which meet the individual needs of *virtually all* students (80%).
4. Provides *varied* instructional techniques which meet the individual needs of *most* students (51–80%).
3. Provides a *limited* variety of instructional techniques which meet the individual needs of *most* students (51–80%).
2. Provides predominantly *one type* of instructional technique which meets the needs of *some* students (50%).
1. Provides *inappropriate* instructional techniques.

Rationale

Instructional techniques should be developed which are consistent with the learning objectives of the students. Because of the differences in student learning styles and learning rates, teaching techniques need to be varied to include some of the following: lecturing, modeling, demonstrating, questioning, experimentation, self-teaching, role playing, peer teaching.

The use of varied techniques permits far greater student involvement in the learning process. Some students learn better in selected ways; all students profit from experiencing a rich variety of appropriate experiences.

Category 4: (Student/Teacher Interaction)

5. Provides *abundant* opportunity for individual and group participation in activities related to learning objectives. Reacts positively to student responses and questions utilizing a *wide variety* of communication skills.
4. Establishes *student involvement* in the learning task and uses responses and questions from students to *clarify* directions and explanations when students misunderstand.
3. Encourages *limited* student participation and reacts *positively* to student responses.
2. *Dictates* classroom activities allowing students to interact only when called upon; reacts *inconsistently* to student responses.
1. *Discourages* student participation; *criticizes* incorrect responses and *ignores* student questions.

Rationale

Student participation is a vital part of any learning situation. Effective learning situations should provide for maximum student involvement. Dynamics of the learning environment are greatly enhanced by effective student involvement and active participation in the learning activities.

An effective technique for eliciting student responses is the consistent use of positive teacher reaction. Teacher reaction to student behavior is a crucial element in (1) setting the tone and climate of the classroom, (2) correction procedures, (3) eliciting behavior and attitudes, and (5) extending learning. Extending learning is accomplished when the teacher accepts and uses student responses to enhance the lesson plan.

The teacher who uses consequences effectively and responds appropriately to undesirable student behavior provides varied and postive feedback for constructive adaptive behavior. The effective teacher encourages students to ask questions, express their opinions, and make corrections. This creates a learning environment where students will not be afraid to respond for fear of failure or embarrassment.

The effective teacher develops the learning situation to accommodate productive interaction—student/teacher and student/student. Therefore, the observer should note (1) the opportunities for students to participate in discussions, and (2) the way in which student questions and responses are used by the teacher for clarification of the subject.

Category 5: Behavior Management

> 5. *Consistently* demonstrates the ability to *adjust* management techniques to control *virtually all* observed classroom activities.
> 4. Demonstrates *effective management* of *virtually all* observed classroom activities.
> 3. Demonstrates *adequate* management of *most* observed classroom activities.
> 2. Demonstrates *inconsistent* management of observed classroom activities.
> 1. Demonstrates *inadequate* management of observed classroom activities.

Rationale

The effective teacher is constantly monitoring student activities in all academic and social situations. The teacher must be able to direct classroom activities in a fair and just manner, to maximize learning opportunities. The effective teacher encourages positive behavior and controls negative behavior to insure a high level of on-task behavior. The effective teacher charts progress toward improvement on a daily basis and uses this information to adjust management techniques* which will benefit students. The effective teacher will develop and implement methods to get students to cooperate with one another and to assume responsibility for their work and behavior.

---

*Management techniques may include, but not be limited to, such actions as praise, contracting, punishment, and proximity control.

Category 6: Climate for Learning

> 5. Demonstrates *uniquely* own personal approach to learning by maintaining a productive, and pleasant atmosphere while providing a functional, orderly, and educationally stimulating environment.
> 4. Maintains a productive and pleasant atmosphere while providing a functional, orderly, and educationally stimulating environment.
> 3. Maintains a *productive and pleasant* atmosphere while providing a functional, orderly, and educational environment.
> 2. Maintains the classroom with *little* regard for pleasantness, order, or learning appeal.
> 1. Classroom feeling is *devoid* of positive atmosphere; classroom lacks a sense of function, order, and learning appeal.

Rationale

In any educational experience offered to students, the classroom environment is critical and can either enhance or repress the learning which is designed to take place.

Observers should look for the following indicators:

1. A pleasant environment includes a teacher who is encouraging, friendly, and accepting.
2. Functional and orderly classroom: a desirable seating arrangement permits easy teacher/student access as well as student movement which does not disrupt others. Work space should be arranged for convenience, with materials easily obtained, used, and returned. Special areas, where appropriate, such as for reading, science, and art, must be convenient, nondistracting, and easily managed.
3. Educationally stimulating environment: Orderly and functional classrooms are desirable at all levels. In elementary school classrooms and in most secondary school classrooms the use of interesting instructional displays can enhance learning.

Category 7: *Monitoring of Student Progress*

5. Makes regular use of *(appropriate) measurement procedures* to monitor each student's progress based on learning objectives; *adjusts* program as needed according to monitoring data.
4. Monitors individual progress *regularly* based on learning objectives; makes *adjustments* in the program based on monitoring data.
3. Monitors individual progress *periodically*; makes *some* adjustment in the program based on monitoring.
2. Makes a *general* evaluation of achievement of the individual student only at the *end* of a unit of study.
1. Makes *no attempt* to monitor individual data.

Rationale

The competent teacher carefully develops direct procedures to monitor and record individual student progress toward the achievement of the predetermined instructional objectives. The competent teacher will use these procedures on a regular basis to modify the instructional program. Direct measurement procedures are those which measure student progress by having the student provide a sample of the skill specified in a learning objective.

Frequent sampling of student performance using these procedures provides the teacher with data to make ongoing as well as end-of-unit modifications. Use of other measures, such as achievement tests and social rating scales, provides more limited information which may not be directly related to a student's progress in a specific unit of study.

To provide more complete data for this category, the principal may ask the teacher to provide some samples of related monitoring instruments or techniques following the observation (if the teacher's plan does not incorporate them during that observation session).

Teacher observation of students should be recognized as an effective means of assessing on-task behavior and monitoring involvement in learning activity. *Direct measurement procedures* (to include but not be limited to, quizzes, tests, performance demonstrations, interviews) are to be considered more reliable assessments of understanding and mastery. Appropriate use of both teacher observation of students and direct measurement procedures should be considered in assessing teacher effectiveness.

Category 8: *Preparation and Organization*

5. Demonstrated *thoroughness* and *resourcefulness* in the preparation of learning objectives and activities (clearly derived from the district curriculum) in the selection and organization of instructional materials, and in ongoing evaluation.
4. Demonstrates *effectiveness* in the preparation of learning objectives and activities (clearly derived from the district curriculum), in the selection and organization of instructional materials, and in ongoing evaluation.
3. Demonstrates *adequate* preparation of clear learning objectives and activities, selection and organization of instructional materials, and ongoing evaluation.

2. Demonstrates *limited* preparation of clear learning objectives and activities, selection and organization of instructional materials, and ongoing evaluation.
1. Demonstrates *inadequate* preparation of clear learning objectives and activities, selection and organization of instructional materials, and ongoing evaluation.

Rationale

Resourceful and thorough planning is vital to the success of each instructional session. Five elements of planning are essential for effective individualized instruction. These are: (1) developing goals and objectives, (2) developing learning activities, (3) selecting and using instructional resources, (4) organizing and scheduling instructional programs, and (5) developing ongoing evaluation procedure (all clearly related to the district curriculum).

The teacher develops specific and definitive learning objectives with carefully thought-out weekly lesson plans which can be flexible and adjusted as needed. After the goals and objectives are developed, materials are implemented to accomplish the objectives. In addition, each teacher will have on display an annual class or course disclosure statement which states class or course objectives, classroom rules, and grading procedures.

Ongoing evaluation provides information about each student's progress. Evaluation data should be used to make necesssary modification and adjustments in the instructional program.

Observers should secure information about the goals and objectives in the pre-observation conference and should note the use of learning activities, instructional resources, organizational strategies, and evaluation procedures during the observation. In the post-observation conference, further information can be obtained concerning the ongoing evaluation procedures and use of evaluation procedures.

Category 9: Organizational Support

5. Works *cooperatively* with the school administration and staff to implement and accomplish goals, policies, contractual obligations, and directives of the district and school; makes *suggestions for improvements* through appropriate channels.
4. *Supports and makes an effort* to accomplish the goals, policies, contractual obligations, and directives of the district and the school.
3. Makes *some effort* to implement the goals, policies, contractual obligations, and directives of the district and school.
2. Demonstrates a *lack of follow-through and dedication* in accomplishing the goals, policies, contractual obligations, and directives of the district and school.
1. Demonstrates a *lack of support* verbally or by action for goals, policies, contractual obligations, and directives of the district and/or school.

Rationale

To make an organization function effectively, established goals must be supported by the members of that organization. This includes positive response to reasonable administrative requests. The competent, supportive teacher shows support by developing teaching strategies and organizational procedures which are consistent with district and school policies and directives. Based on individual experience, the competent teacher works continually to refine and make suggestions for the improvement of district and school goals, policies, contractual obligations, and procedures.

Category 10: Interpersonal Relationships

5. Maintains and *consistently tries to improve* harmony between self and parents, students, staff, and the community.
4. Maintains and makes *some attempts to improve* constructive relationships between self and parents, students, staff, and the community.

3. *Maintains* constructive relationships between self and parents, students, staff, and the community.

2. *Occasionally* causes *disharmony* between self and parents, students, staff, and the community as a result of actions or statements.

1. *Often* causes disharmony between self and parents, students, staff, and the community as a result of actions or statements.

Rationale

The attitudes and feelings of people working together in the educational setting has an impact on student achievement.

The effective teacher works to establish and improve harmonious relationships and a cooperative attitude with parents, students, staff, and the community.

Category 11: Professional Support of the Staff

5. *Assists, offers suggestions, and shares* expertise with other staff members.

4. *Encourages* other staff members in achieving professional growth and in accomplishing programs.

3. *Allows* other staff members to accomplish their programs but offers or gives *little or no support.*

2. Accomplishes one's own program with *lack of concern* for the impact on other staff members.

1. Has *conflicts* with other staff members, downgrading their efforts and making cooperation difficult.

Rationale

Support of staff members and their goals is beneficial to the entire school. The competent teacher reaches out to other staff members to assist them in accomplishing their professional goals and programs.

Staff means all personnel employed by the school district within each school.

EDUCATOR EVALUATION CHECK SHEET

Name: _____   School Year: _____

This sheet is provided for the management of Educator Evaluation System records. Please check off each of the items listed below and attach them to this sheet before filing.

( ) **1.** Observation and Interview Scoring Form
( ) **2.** Observation and Interview Forms
( ) **3.** Goal-Directed Activity Plan
( ) **4.** Summary Evaluation Report

PRE-OBSERVATION INFORMATION

Teacher _____ Observer _____

1. Date of observation _____ Time _____

2. Subject(s) being taught _____

3. Objective(s) to be reached and at what point in the lesson _____

_____

_____

4. Planned learning activities (lecture, questioning, worksheets, seatwork, audiovisual aids, etc. _____

_____

_____

_____

_____

5. Learning will be measured by _____

_____

_____

6. Please describe any anticipated unusual student behavior; identify student(s) on the simplified seating chart below. _____

_____

_____

7. Please indicate (X) on the chart where you would like the observer to sit.

8. Other comments desired:

DAVIS COUNTY SCHOOL DISTRICT INSTRUCTIONAL OBSERVATION AND INTERVIEW FORM

1. LEARNING OBJECTIVES	2. SELECTION & USE OF MATERIALS	3. INSTRUCTIONAL STRATEGIES	4. STUDENT/TEACHER INTERACTION
Communicated & clarified, directly observable & measureable, expectations clearly explained, feedback encouraged.	Correlation to goals & objectives, justification for modification of commercial materials, effective teacher-made materials as appropriate.	Variety; modeling, peer teaching, demonstrating, questioning, experimentation, self-teaching role playing, etc.	Active participation; setting tone & climate, correcting, academic responses, molding appropriate behavior & attitudes, encouraging student responses, clarification, etc.
5. BEHAVIOR MANAGEMENT	6. CLIMATE FOR LEARNING	7. MONITORING OF STUDENT PROGRESS	8. PREPARATION & ORGANIZATION
On-task level, proximity control, praise, contracting, punishment, fairness, encouraging positive & controlling negative behavior, system for behavior management, etc.	Stimulating, productive, pleasant; teacher enthusiastic, encouraging, friendly, accepting; functional & orderly seating arrangement, student movement; work space convenient, easily managed, nondistracting; attractive classroom.	Frequent sampling, monitoring, recording of student progress by direct measurement techniques, adjustment of program as necessary, feedback to students, parents.	Developing, selecting, & organizing clear & sequential goals & objectives, learning activities, equipment & materials, evaluation; daily planning; pacing; knowledge of subject.

Teacher _____   Observer _____   Subject _____   Class Size _____   Date _____   Time _____

Teacher's Signature _____ Principal's Signature _____ Date _____

CATEGORY 9

Organizational Support

• How do you show support for goals, policies and directives of the district and school?

CATEGORY 10

Interpersonal Relationships

• What efforts do you make to ensure constructive relationships among parents, students, staff and the community?

Parents—

Students—

Staff—

Community—

CATEGORY 11

Professional Staff Support

• How do you show support for other staff members?

268

PROFESSIONAL EDUCATOR EVALUATION
GOAL-DIRECTED EDUCATOR ACTIVITY

Goals have become increasingly important in the Davis County School District. The Board of Education recently involved many educators and community members in the process of identifying major goals upon which the district will now focus. Local school administrators have been assigned the task of involving educators and the community in the determination of immediate and long-range goals for their individual schools.

These developments are consistent with the recommendations of authorities in the area of educator evaluation, who maintain that the identification of mutually acceptable goals and the empirical appraisal of the educator's resourcefulness in achieving them, constitute an especially meaningful approach to evaluation.

The program outlined here is intended to encourage teachers and administrators to engage in effective goal-directed activity which serves their own needs, local school needs, and, at the same time, contributes to the attainment of goals to which the entire school system is committed.

Guidelines

1. The Goal-Directed Activity Plan requires the participation of all educator personnel. Implementation and coordination of the plan is the responsibility of the school principal. It is to be a free-standing system related only indirectly to other segments of the Davis County Evaluation Program.
2. The identification of the goals is to be accomplished by the teacher in consultation with the principal. Goals are to be of the following types:
   Instructional. Goals in this area should enhance instructional skill or otherwise strengthen the instructional program of the teachers.
   Organizational. Goals in this area will in many instances be managerial in nature. They will frequently involve curriculum development and other forms of background work related to adjustments and changes in organizational systems of the school and district. Instructional goals and organizational goals are not mutually exclusive and may often be intertwined.
   Personal. Goals in this area are optional and may be selected at random by the teacher.
3. Assessment of goal attainment should be done empirically rather than through elaborate attempts at precise measurement. Goals should be set up in ways that permit results to be readily observable. Numerical scores and ratings are not consistent with the intent of this plan.
4. Principals should implement this plan early in each school year but not before they have defined for the faculty and the community the goals of the school district and goals that may have been identified at the local school level. With an understanding of district and local school goals and objectives teachers will be better prepared to set down goals of their own which support their programs as well as those of the school and istrict.
5. The Goal-Directed Educator Activity Program should culminate in a teacher–principal conference during the final term of the school year.
6. Educators—teachers and principals—are encouraged to view this plan as a positive approach to mutual support and cooperative effort.
7. Goals and related information should be recorded on the attached district form and kept on file in the local school.

DEEP EVALUATION CATEGORIES

1. *Learning Objectives*
   a. Communicates measurable objectives
   b. Checks students' understanding of expectations
   c. Responds to student feedback
2. *Selection/Use of Instructional Materials*
   Exhibits skill in use of instructional materials
3. *Instruction Techniques*
   Provides varied instructional techniques
4. *Student/Teacher Interaction*
   a. Provides opportunity for individual/group participation
   b. Reacts positively to students
5. *Behavior Management*
   Adjusts management techniques to control classroom activities
6. *Climate for Learning*
   a. Maintains a stimulating productive and pleasant atmosphere
   b. Provides functional, orderly, and attractive environment
7. *Monitoring Student Progress*
   a. Uses direct measurement procedures
   b. Monitors student progress based on learning objectives
   c. Adjusts program as needed
8. *Preparation and Organization*
   a. Setting clear learning objectives and activities
   b. Selection/organization of instructional materials
   c. Ongoing evaluation
9. *Organizational Support*
   a. Cooperates with administration/staff
   b. Accomplishes school district goals/policies
   c. Fulfills contractual obligations
10. *Interpersonal Relationships*
    a. Students
    b. Parents
    c. Staff
    d. Community
11. *Professional Support of Staff*
    a. Support of colleagues
       (assists, shares, offers, suggests)

GOAL-DIRECTED ACTIVITY PLAN

School: _____   Teacher _____

- INSTRUCTIONAL GOAL(S) (Suggested Reference: DEEP Evaluation Criteria)—

- ORGANIZATION GOAL(S) (To be determined after district and local school goals have been defined with the faculty by the principal):

- PERSONAL GOAL(S) (optional):

- *Teacher's End-of-Year Review Statement:*

White copy: Local school copy
Yellow copy: Teacher's personal copy

ARTIFACTS*

1. Briefly describe how this specific lesson relates to the district/core curriculum.

2. How do you plan to evaluate student achievement in this learning activity?

---

*Artifacts: Plans, procedures and materials used to teach this lesson.

OBSERVATION AND INTERVIEW SCORING FORM

Date _____

Teacher _____

Observer/
Interviewer _____
(Signature)

TEACHER COMPETENCE PROFILE

CATEGORY	5	4	3	2	1
1. Learning Objectives					
2. Selection and Use of Instructional Materials					
3. Instructional Techniques					
4. Student/Teacher Interaction					
5. Classroom Discipline					
6. Climate for Learning					
7. Monitoring of Student Progress					
8. Preparation and Organization					
9. Organizational Support					
10. Interpersonal Relationships					
11. Professional Support of the Staff					

Scales 1–8 *Observation* / Scales 9–11 *Interview*

Teacher's Comments (Optional) _____
_____
_____
_____
_____

_____
Teacher's Signature

Revised 8/88

Form Distribution:
Yellow—Teacher
White—Principal

DAVIS COUNTY SCHOOL DISTRICT
SUMMARY EVALUATION REPORT
Classroom Teacher

Teacher	Observer	Teaching Assignment	School

The Davis County School District Evaluation System is based upon the philosophy that the purpose of teacher evaluation is the upgrading of professional competence and hence the improvement of instruction.

This report represents a summation of teacher performance determined through teacher self-evaluation, principal and/or peer observation, and teacher–principal conferences. After the principal has completed this report, it will be submitted to the Superintendent of Schools and will be included in the teacher's personnel file.

CATEGORY (Refer to list of evaluation criteria and descriptors)	RATING	COMMENTS
1. Learning Objectives		
2. Selection and Use of Materials		
3. Instructional Techniques		
4. Student/Teacher Interaction		
5. Classroom Discipline		
6. Climate for Learning		
7. Monitoring of Student Progress		
8. Preparation and Organization		
9. Organizational Support		
10. Interpersonal Relationships		
11. Professional Support of the Staff		

I recommend that the status of this teacher for the next school year be as follows:

_____	Regular contract
_____	Regular contract with remediation
_____	Contract, NO increment
_____	NO contract

_____   _____
       Principal's Signature   Date

My signature below indicates that I have received a copy of this report and have held a conference with the principal and discussed all aspects of my evaluation.

_____   _____
       Teacher's Signature   Date

Teacher's comments: _____
_____
_____
_____

Reviewed by _____
            Superintendent   Date

Form Distribution:
Pink—Teacher
Yellow—Principal
White—District

Revised 8/88

References

Acheson, K. A., & M. D. Gall. (1987). *Techniques in the clinical supervision of teachers: Preservice and inservice applications.* (2nd ed.) New York: Longman.

Allen, J. E. (1986). *Beyond time management: Organizing the organization.* Reading, MA: Addison-Wesley.

Allen, R., T. Davidson, W. Hering, & J. Jesunathadas. (1984). *A study of the conditions of secondary mathematics teacher education.* San Francisco: Far West Laboratory.

American Psychological Association. (1966). *Standards for educational and psychological tests and manuals.* Washington, DC: APA.

American Psychological Association. (1974). *Standards for educational and psychological tests* (rev. ed.). Washington, DC: APA.

American Psychological Association. (1985). *Standards for educational and psychological testing* (5th ed.). Washington, DC: APA.

Arends, R. I. (1988). *Learning to teach.* New York: Random House.

Aubrecht, J. D. (1981). *Reliability, validity and generalizability of student ratings of instruction: Idea paper No. 6.* Manhattan, KS: Center for Faculty Evaluation and Development.

Ayers, J. B. (1988). Another look at the concurrent and predictive validity of the National Teacher Examinations. *Journal of Educational Research, 81,* 133–37.

Bang-Jensen, V. (1986). The view from next door: A look at peer "supervision." In K. K. Zumwalt (Ed.), *Improving teaching* (pp. 51–62). Alexandria, VA: Association for Supervision and Curriculum Development.

Berdie, D. R. (1986). *Questionnaire: Design and use.* Metuchen, NJ: Scarecrow Press.

Berk, R. A. (1984a). Conducting the item analysis. In R. A. Berk (Ed.), *A guide to criterion-referenced test construction* (pp. 97–142). Baltimore: Johns Hopkins University Press.

Berk, R. A. (Ed.). (1984b). *A guide to criterion-referenced test construction.* Baltimore: Johns Hopkins University Press.

Berk, R. A. (1984c). Selecting the index of reliability. In R. A. Berk (Ed.), *A guide to criterion-referenced test construction* (pp. 231–65). Baltimore: Johns Hopkins University Press.

Beyer, B. K. (1987). *Practical strategies for the teaching of thinking.* Boston: Allyn and Bacon.

Biddle, B. J. (1987). Teacher roles. In M. J. Dunkin (Ed.), *The international encyclopedia of teaching and teacher education* (pp. 625–34). Oxford, England: Pergamon Press.

Bloom, B. S. (Ed.). (1984). *Taxonomy of educational objectives: The classification of educational goals, Book I: Cognitive domain.* New York: Longman.

Brandt, R. (1989). A changed professional culture. *Educational Leadership, 46,* 2.

Brennan, R. L. (1984). Estimating the dependability of scores. In R. A. Berk (Ed.), *A guide to criterion-referenced test construction* (pp. 292–334). Baltimore: Johns Hopkins University Press.

Bridges, E. M. (1986). *The incompetent teacher.* Philadelphia: The Falmer.

Bridges, E. M., & P. Gumport. (1984). *The dismissal of tenured teachers for incompetence* (Technical report). Stanford, CA: Institute for Research on Educational Finance and Governance.

Brubacker, D. L. (1982). *Curriculum planning: The dynamics of theory and practice.* Glenview, IL: Scott, Foresman.

Bunting, C. E. (1981). The development and validation of the educational attitudes inventory. *Educational and Psychological Measurement, 41,* 559–65.

Bush, G. (1988). The Bush strategy for excellence in education. *Phi Delta Kappan, 70,* 112ff.

Cameron, D. (1985). An idea that merits consideration. *Phi Delta Kappan, 67,* 110–12.

Cangelosi, J. S. (1974). Measurement and evaluation: A broader perspective. *NCME Measurement News, 18,* 18–23.

Cangelosi, J. S. (1982). *Measurement and evaluation: An inductive approach for teachers.* Dubuque, IA: W. C. Brown.

Cangelosi, J. S. (1984). Evaluating teaching: A suggestion for school principals. *NASSP Bulletin, 68,* 19–23.

Cangelosi, J. S. (1986). Evaluating teaching within a teacher advancement plan. *The Clearing House, 59,* 405–9.

Cangelosi, J. S. (1988a). *Classroom management strategies: Gaining and maintaining students' cooperation.* New York: Longman.

Cangelosi, J. S. (1988b). Development and validation of the underprepared mathematics teacher assessment. *Journal for Research in Mathematics Education, 19,* 233–45.

Cangelosi, J. S. (1989, April). *A video inservice program for underprepared mathematics teachers.* A presentation at the annual meeting of the National Council of Teachers of Mathematics, Orlando, FL.

Cangelosi, J. S. (1990a). *Cooperation in the classroom: Students and teachers working together* (2nd ed.). Washington, DC: National Education Association.

Cangelosi, J. S. (1990b). *Designing tests for evaluating student achievement.* New York: Longman.

Cangelosi, J. S. (in press). Behavior management for reading lessons. In B. L. Hayes (Ed.), *Reading instruction and the effective teacher.* Boston: Allyn and Bacon.

Cangelosi, J. S., & A. Forsyth. (1985). *Case study of the ARTE II Utah math teacher academy.* San Francisco: Far West Laboratory.

Cangelosi, J. S., & I. A. Martinez. (1989, March). *Research, development, and service projects for improving the teaching of mathematics: A collaborative effort in Utah.* A paper presented at the annual meeting of the American Association of Colleges for Teacher Education, Anaheim, CA.

Cangelosi, J. S., L. R. Struyk, M. L. Grimes, C. R. Duke. (1988, April). *Classroom management needs of beginning teachers.* A paper presented at the American Educational Research Association annual meeting, New Orleans.

Canter, L., & M. Canter. (1976). *Assertive discipline: A take-charge approach for today's educator.* Seal Beach, CA: Canter and Associates.

Carlson, R. E., R. L. Pecheone, S. J. Stanley, & W. J. Popham. (1989, March). *Advances in teacher assessment technology.* A symposium presentation at the annual meeting of the American Educational Research Association, San Francisco.

Carnegie Forum on Education and the Economy. (1986). *A nation prepared: Teachers for the 21st century: The report of the Task Force on Teaching as a Profession.* Washington, DC: The Forum.

Cashin, W. E., & A. Noma. (1983). *IDEA technical report no. 5: Description of IDEA short (evaluation) form data base.* Manhattan, KS: Center for Faculty Evaluation and Development.

Castle, S. S. (1988). Using computers in the classroom. In R. I. Arends (Ed.), *Learning to teach* (pp. 520–26). New York: Random House.

Charles, C. M. (1989). *Building classroom discipline: From models to practice* (3rd ed.). New York: Longman.

Charlotte-Mecklenburg Schools. (1983). *Charlotte-Mecklenburg schools career development plan: Fact sheet*. Charlotte, NC: Charlotte-Mecklenburg Schools.

Chrisco, I. M. (1989). Peer assistance works. *Educational Leadership, 46*, 31–32.

Clark, C. M., & P. L. Peterson. (1986). Teachers' thought processes. In M. C. Wittrock (Ed.), *Handbook of research on teaching* (3rd ed.) (pp. 255–96). New York: Macmillan.

Coker, H., D. M. Medley, R. S. Soar. (1980). How valid are expert opinions about effective teaching. *Phi Delta Kappan, 62*, 131–34ff.

Cole, N. S. (1987). Holmes Group initiative to create standards of entry to the teaching profession. *Educational Measurement: Issues and Practice, 6*, 25.

Collins, E. (1940). Teacher selection by examination. *Harvard Educational Review, 10*, 4.

Conoley, J. C., J. J. Kramer, & J. V. Mitchell (Eds.). (1988). *The supplement to the ninth mental measurement yearbook*. Lincoln, NE: The Buros Institute of Mental Measurement & The University of Nebraska Press.

Converse, J. M. (1986). *Survey questions: Handcrafting the standardized questionnaire*. Beverly Hills, CA: Sage.

Cook, W. W., C. H. Leeds, & R. Callis. (1951). *The Minnesota Teacher Attitude Inventory*. New York: The Psychological Corporation.

Cooney, T. J., E. J. Davis, & K. B. Henderson. *Dynamics of teaching secondary school mathematics*. Prospect Heights, IL: Waveland Press.

Cooper, J. M. (1984a). Introduction and overview. In J. M. Cooper (Ed.), *Developing skills for instructional supervision* (pp. 1–9). New York: Longman.

Cooper, J. M. (1984b). Observation skills. In J. M. Cooper (Ed.), *Developing skills for instructional supervision* (pp. 79–111). New York: Longman.

Cross, L. H. (1985). Validation of the NTE tests for certification decisions. *Educational Measurement: Issues and Practice, 4*, 7–9.

Cubberly, E. (1906). *The certification of teachers: The fifth yearbook of the National Society for the Scientific Study of Education*. Chicago: University of Chicago Press.

Cunningham, G. K. (1986). *Educational and psychological measurement*. New York: Macmillan.

Darling-Hammond, L., B. Berry. (1988). Rand study raises questions about reforms regarding teachers. *Teacher Education Reports, 10*(9), 7–8.

David, J. L. (1989). Synthesis of research on school-based management. *Educational Leadership, 46*, 45–53.

Davis County School District. (1988). *Davis Educator Evaluation Program (DEEP)*. Farmington, UT: the District.

Denham, C., & A. Lieberman (Eds.). (1980). *Time to learn*. Washington, DC: U. S. Department of Education and the National Institute of Education.

Dick, W., & L. Carey. (1985). *The systematic design of instruction* (2nd ed.). Glenview, IL: Scott, Foresman.

Dick, W., & R. A. Reiser. (1989). *Planning effective instruction*. Englewood-Cliffs, NJ: Prentice-Hall.

Dillon, R. F., & R. J. Sternberg. (Eds.). (1986). *Cognition and Instruction*. San Diego, CA: Academic Press.

Dimock, E. M. (1985). *Teacher competency tests: Complete preparation for the California Basic Educational Skills Tests (CBEST)*. New York: Arco Publishing.

Douglas, G. (1988). Latent trait measurement models. In J. P. Keeves (Ed.), *Educational research, methodology, and measurement: An international handbook* (pp. 282–86). Oxford, England: Pergamon Press.

Dowdy, S., & S. Wearden. (1983). *Statistics for research*. New York: John Wiley.

Doyle, W. (1986). Classroom organization and management. In M. C. Wittrock (Ed.), *Handbook of research on teaching* (3rd ed.) (pp. 392–431). New York: Macmillan.

Dubelle, S. T. (1986). *Effective teaching: Critical skills*. Lancaster, PA: Technomic Publishing.

Dubelle, S. T., & C. M. Hoffman. (1986). *Misbehavin' II*. Lancaster, PA: Technomic Publishing.

Duke, C. R., J. S. Cangelosi, & R. S. Knight. (1988, February). *The Mellon Project: A collaborative effort*. Colloquium presentation at the annual meeting of the American Association of Colleges for Teacher Education, New Orleans.

Ebel, R. L. (1965). *Measuring educational achievement*. Englewood Cliffs, NJ: Prentice-Hall.

Ebel, R. L., & D. A. Frisbie. (1986). *Essentials of educational measurement* (4th ed.). Englewood Cliffs, NJ: Prentice-Hall.

Educational Testing Service (1986). *The ETS collection catalog: Volume 1: Achievement tests and measuring devices*. Phoenix, AZ: Oryx Press.

Ellington, H. (1985). *Producing teaching materials: A handbook for teachers and trainers*. London: Kagan Page.

Ellis, H. C., R. R. Hunt. (1983). *Fundamentals of human memory and cognition* (3rd ed.). Dubuque, IA: W. C. Brown.

Emmer, E. T., C. M. Evertson, & L. M. Anderson. (1980). Effective classroom management at the beginning of the school year. *Elementary School Journal, 80*, 219–31.

Emmer, E. T., C. M. Evertson, J. P. Sanford, B. S. Clements & M. E. Worsham. (1984). *Classroom management for secondary teachers*. Englewood Cliffs, NJ: Prentice-Hall.

Epstein, J. L. (1985). A question of merit: Principals' and parents' evaluations of teachers. *Educational Researcher, 14*, 3–10.

Evans, R. (1989). The faculty in midcareer: Implications for school improvement. *Educational Leadership, 46*, 10–15.

Everitt, B. S. (1988). Cluster analysis. In J. P. Keeves (Ed.), *Educational research, methodology, and measurement: An international handbook* (pp. 601–5). Oxford, England: Pergamon Press.

Evertson, C. M. (1989). Classroom organization and management. In M. C. Reynolds (Ed.), *Knowledge base for the beginning teacher* (pp. 59–70). Oxford, England: Pergamon Press.

Evertson, C. M., E. T. Emmer, B. S. Clements, J. P. Sanford, & M. E. Worsham. (1984). *Classroom management for elementary teachers*. Englewood Cliffs, NJ: Prentice-Hall.

Feistritzer, E. (1988). Exclusive interview. *Teacher Education Reports, 10*(12), 3–5.

Ficklen, E. (1983). At N.E.A., leaders erect a wall of words around opposition to merit pay. *The American School Board Journal, 170*, 39, 49.

Firth, G. R., & J. W. Newfield. (1984). Curriculum development and selection. In J. M. Cooper (Ed.), *Developing skills for instructional supervision* (pp. 207–47). New York: Longman.

Fisher, C. W., & D. C. Berlinger. (Eds). (1985). *Perspectives on instructional time*. New York: Longman.

Fisher, T. H., B. V. Fry, K. L. Loewe, & G. W. Wilson. (1985). Testing teachers for merit pay purposes in Florida. *Educational Measurement: Issues and Practice, 4*, 10–12.

Flanders, N. A. (1970). *Analyzing teaching behavior*. Reading, MA: Addison-Wesley.

Flippo, R. F., & C. R. Foster. (1984). Teacher competency testing and its impact on education. *Journal of Teacher Education, 35*, 10–13.

Fox, R. B., & R. F. Peck. (1978, March). *Personal characteristics of teachers that affect student learning*. Paper presented at the annual meeting of the American Educational Research Association, Toronto, Canada. (ERIC Document Reproduction Service No. ED 156 644).

Franklin, J. (1989, March). *Two different worlds: Research and practice in faculty evaluation*. Symposium presentation at the annual meeting of the American Educational Research Association, San Francisco.

Frick, T., & M. I. Semmel. (1978). Observer agreement and reliabilities of classroom observational measures. *Review of Educational Research, 48*, 157–84.

Frisbie, D. A. (1988). Reliability of scores from teacher-made tests. *Educational Measurement Issues and Practices, 7*, 25–35.

Garry, M., & J. Pear. (1983). *Behavior modification: What it is and how to do it* (2nd ed.). Englewood Cliffs, NJ: Prentice-Hall.

Ginott, H. G. (1972). *Teacher and child*. New York: Avon Books.

Glickman, C. D. (1985). *Supervision of instruction: A developmental approach*. Boston: Allyn and Bacon.

Glickman, C. D. (1989). Has Sam and Samantha's time come at last? *Educational Leadership, 46*, 4–9.

Goetz, J. P., & M. D. LeCompte. (1984). *Ethnography and qualitative design in educational research*. San Diego, CA: Academic Press.

Gronlund, N. E. (1982). *Constructing achievement tests* (3rd ed.). Englewood Cliffs, NJ: Prentice-Hall.

Gronlund, N. E. (1985). *Measurement and evaluation in teaching* (5th ed.). New York: Macmillan.

Guilford, J. P. (1959). *Personality*. New York: McGraw-Hill.

Guthrie, J. (1970). Survey of school effectiveness studies. In A. Mood (Ed.), *Do teachers make a difference?* Washington, DC: U.S. Government Printing Office.

Haefele, D. L. (1980). How to evaluate thee, teacher—let me count the ways. *Phi Delta Kappan, 61*, 349–52.

Haertel, E. H. (1987). Toward a national board of teaching standards: The Stanford Teacher Assessment Project. *Educational Measurement: Issues and Practice, 6,* 23–24.

Halasz, I., & S. R. Raftery. (1985). *Managing learning time: A professional development guide.* Columbus, OH: Center for Research in Vocational Education.

Hambleton, R. K. (1984). Validating the test scores. In R. A. Berk (Ed.), *A guide to criterion-referenced test construction* (pp. 199–230). Baltimore: Johns Hopkins University Press.

Hambleton, R. K., & H. Swaminathan. (1985). *Item response theory.* Boston: Kluwer-Nijhoff Publishing.

Harris, B. M. (1985). *Supervisory behavior in education* (3rd ed.). Englewood Cliffs, NJ: Prentice-Hall.

Harris, B. M. (1986). *Developmental teacher evaluation.* Newton, MA: Allyn and Bacon.

Harris, B. M. (1989). *Inservice education for staff development.* Boston: Allyn and Bacon.

Harrow, A. J. (1972). *A taxonomy of the psychomotor domain: A guide for developing behavioral objectives.* New York: McKay.

Hass, G. (Ed.). (1987). *Curriculum planning: A new approach* (5th ed.). Boston: Allyn & Bacon.

Healy, M. K. (1983). Learning logs: A rediscovery and an application. *The National Writing Project Network Newsletter, 6,* 1–4.

Help! Teachers can't teach! (1980, June 16). *Time.* 54–63.

Hills, J. R. (1986). *All of Hills' handy hints.* Washington, DC: National Council on Measurement in Education.

Hoffmann, R. I. (1975). Concept of item efficiency in item analysis. *Educational and Psychological Measurement, 35,* 621–40.

Holdzcom, D., D. Stacey, J. Guard, B. Kuligowski, & H. LeGette. (1989, March). *State and local perspectives on the development of a career development plan for educators in North Carolina.* A symposium presentation at the annual meeting of the American Educational Research Association, New Orleans.

Holmes Group. (1986). *Tomorrow's teachers: A report of the Holmes Group.* East Lansing, MI: Holmes Group.

Hunter, M. (1988). Create rather than wait your fate in teacher evaluation. In S. J. Stanley & W. James Popham (Eds.), *Teacher evaluation: Six prescriptions for success* (pp. 32–54). Alexandria, VA: Association for Supervision and Curriculum Development.

Jackson, P. W. (1966). *The way teaching is.* Washington, DC: National Education Association.

Jacob, E. (1987). Qualitative research traditions: A review. *Review of educational research, 57,* 1–50.

Jacobsen, D., P. Eggen, & D. Kauchak. (1989). *Methods for teaching: A skills approach* (3rd ed.). Columbus, OH: Merrill.

Jesunathadas, J. (1990). *Mathematics teachers' instructional activities as a function of academic preparation.* Unpublished doctoral dissertation, Utah State University, Logan.

Johnson, R. (1976). *Elementary statistics* (2nd ed.). North Scituate, MA: Duxbury.

Joint Committee on Standards for Educational Evaluation. (1981). *Standards for evaluations of educational programs, projects, and materials.* New York: McGraw-Hill.

Joint Committee on Standards for Educational Evaluation. (1988). *The personnel evaluation standards: How to assess systems for evaluating educators.* Newbury Park, CA: Sage.

Jones, S. (1985). Depth interviewing. In R. Walker (Ed.), *Applied qualitative research.* Brookfield, VT: Gower.

Jones, V. F., & L. S. Jones. (1986). *Comprehensive classroom management: Creating positive learning environments* (2nd ed.). Boston: Allyn and Bacon.

Joyce, B., & M. Weil. (1986). *Models of teaching* (3rd ed.). Englewood Cliffs, NJ: Prentice-Hall.

Kachigan, S. K. (1986). *Statistical analysis: An interdisciplinary introduction to univariate and multivariate methods.* New York: Radius Press.

Kaplan, S. (1987). The teacher as learner. In G. L. Bissex & R. H. Bullock (Eds.), *Seeing for ourselves: Case-study research by teachers of writing* (pp. 41–58). Portsmouth, NJ: Heinemann.

Kauchak, D. P., & P. D. Eggen. (1989). *Learning and teaching: Research-based methods.* Boston: Allyn and Bacon.

Keeves, J. P. (Ed.). (1988). *Educational research, methodology, and measurement: An international handbook.* Oxford, England: Pergamon Press.

Kim, E. C., & R. D. Kellough. (1987). *A resource guide for secondary school teaching: Planning for competence* (4th ed.). New York: Macmillan.

Krathwhohl, D., B. S. Bloom, & B., Masia. (1964). *Taxonomy of educational objectives, the classification of educational goals, handbook 2: Affective domain*. New York: Longman.

Kubiszyn, T., & G. Borich. (1987). *Educational testing and measurement: Classroom application and practice* (2nd ed.). Glenview, IL: Scott, Foresman.

Kuder, G. F., & M. W. Richardson. (1937). The theory of estimation of test reliability. *Psychometrika*, 2, 151–60.

Lamb, R. W., & M. D. Thomas. (1981). The art and science of teacher evaluation. *Principal*, *61*, 44–47.

Lanier, J. E., & J. W. Little. (1986). Research on teacher education. In M. C. Wittrock (Ed.), *Handbook of research on teaching* (3rd ed.) (pp. 527–69). New York: Macmillan.

Leedy, P. D., (1985). *Practical research: Planning and design* (3rd ed.). New York: Macmillan.

Lehman, I. J., & S. E. Phillips. (1987). A survey of state teacher-competency examination programs. *Educational measurement: Issues and Practice*, 6, 14–18.

Levine, J. M. (1989). *Secondary instruction: A manual for classroom teaching*. Boston: Allyn and Bacon.

Levis, D. S. (1987). Teachers' characteristics. In M. J. Dunkin (Ed.), *The international encyclopedia of teaching and teacher education* (pp. 585–89). Oxford, England: Pergamon Press.

Lewis, A. (1982). *Evaluating educational personnel*. Arlington, VA: American Association of School Administrators.

Likert, R. (1932). A technique for the measurement of attitudes. *Archives of Psychology, 140*, 52.

Long, J. D., & V. H. Frye. (1989). *Making it till Friday; A guide to successful classroom management* (4th ed.). Princeton, NJ: Princeton Book Company.

Lord, F. M., & M. L. Stocking. (1988). Item response theory. In J. P. Keeves (Ed.), *Educational research, methodology, and measurement: An international handbook* (pp. 269–72). Oxford, England: Pergamon Press.

Macleod, G. R. (1987). Microteaching: Effectiveness. In M. J. Dunkin (Ed.), *The international encyclopedia of teaching and teacher education* (pp. 726–9). Oxford, England: Pergamon Press.

Manatt, R. P. (1988). Teacher performance evaluation: A total systems approach. In S. J. Stanley & W. J. Popham (Eds.), *Teacher evaluation: Six prescriptions for success* (pp. 79–108). Alexandria, VA: Association for Curriculum and Supervision.

Marascuilo, L. A., & R. C. Serlin. (1988). *Statistical methods for the social and behavioral sciences*. New York: W. H. Freeman.

Marques, T. E., D. M. Lane, & P. W. Dorfman. (1979). Toward the development of a system for instructional evaluation: Is there consensus regarding what constitutes effective teaching? *Journal of Educational Psychology, 71*, 840–9.

Marsh, H. W. (1989, March). *Students' evaluations of university teaching: Research findings, methodological issues, and directions for future research*. Invited address at the annual meeting of the American Educational Research Association, San Francisco.

Marsh, H. W., & J. U. Overall. (1980). Validity of students' evaluations of teaching effectiveness: Cognitive and affective criteria. *Journal of Educational Psychology, 72*, 468–75.

McDiarmid, G. W., D. L. Ball, & C. W. Anderson. (1989). Why staying one chapter ahead doesn't really work: Subject-specific pedagogy. In M. C. Reynolds (Ed.), *Knowledge base for the beginning teacher*. Oxford, England: Pergamon Press.

McGrath, E. (1986). *The exodus syndrome: Factors affecting teacher career changing*. Unpublished doctoral dissertation, Boston University.

McGreal, T. L. (1988). Evaluation for enhancing instruction: Linking teacher evaluation and staff development. In S. J. Stanley & W. James Popham (Eds.), *Teacher evaluation: Six prescriptions for success* (pp. 1–29). Alexandria, VA: Association for Supervision and Curriculum Department.

McLaren, P. (1989). *Life in schools: An introduction to critical pedagogy in the foundations of education*. New York: Longman.

McNergney, R. (1988). Planning. In R. McNergney (Ed.) *Guide to classroom teaching* (pp. 23–42). Boston: Allyn and Bacon.

Medley, D. M., H. Coker, & R. S. Soar. (1984). *Measurement-based evaluation of teacher performance: An empirical approach*. New York: Longman.

Merrill, M. D. (1983). Component display theory. In C. M. Reigeluth (Ed.), *Instructional design theories and models: An overview of their current status* (pp. 279–333). Hillsdale, NJ: Lawrence Erlbaum Associates.

Metropolitan Life Insurance Company. (1986). *The American teacher survey, 1985*. New York: Metropolitan Life Insurance Company.

Mitchell, J. V. (Ed.). (1985). *The ninth mental measurement yearbook*, Lincoln, NE: The Buros Institute of Mental Measurements & The University of Nebraska Press.

Morine-Dershimer, G., & J. Pfeifer. (1986). In J. M. Cooper (Ed.), *Classroom teaching skills* (3rd ed.) (pp. 19–66). Lexington, MA: D. C. Heath.

National Council of Teachers of Mathematics. (1989). *Curriculum and evaluation standards for school mathematics*. Reston, VA: the Council.

National Education Association. (1955). *Standards for educational and psychological tests*. Washington, DC: NEA.

Nelsen, E. A. (1985). Review of NTE programs. In J. V. Mitchell (Ed.), *The ninth mental measurement yearbook* (pp. 1063–66). Lincoln, NE: The Buros Institute of Mental Measurements & The University of Nebraska Press.

Norusius, M. J. (1988). *SPSS/PC+ advanced statistics V2.0: For the IBM PC/XT/AT and PS/2*. Chicago: SPSS Incorporated.

Nunnally, J. C. (1978). *Psychometric theory* (2nd ed.). New York: McGraw-Hill.

Oliva, P. F. (1989). *Supervision for today's schools* (3rd ed.). New York: Longman.

Patton, M. Q. (1987). *How to use qualitative methods in evaluation*. Newbury Park, CA: Sage.

Perlberg, A. (1987). Microteaching: Conceptual and theoretical bases. In M. J. Dunkin (Ed.), *The international encyclopedia of teaching and teacher education* (pp. 715–20). Oxford, England: Pergamon Press.

Peterson, D. (1983). Legal and ethical issues of teacher evaluation: A research-based approach. *Educational Research Quarterly*, 7, 6–16.

Peterson, K. D. (1984). Methodological problems in teacher evaluation. *Journal of Research and Development in Education*, 17, 62–70.

Peterson, K. D. (1987). Use of standardized tests in teacher evaluation for career ladder systems. *Educational Measurement: Issues and Practice*, 6, 19–22.

Peterson, K. E., & A. Mitchell. (1985). Teacher-controlled evaluation in a career ladder program. *Educational Leadership*, 43, 44–47.

Phye, G. D. (1986). Practice and skilled classroom performance. In G. D. Phye & T. Andre (Eds.), *Cognitive classroom learning* (pp. 141–168). San Diego, CA: Academic Press.

Phye, G. D., & Andre, T. (Eds.). (1986). *Cognitive classroom learning*. San Diego, CA: Academic Press.

Popham, W. J. (1982). Catch-22 for teachers: The penalty for doing well. *Principal*, 61, 34–36.

Popham, W. J. (1988). *Educational evaluation* (2nd ed.). Englewood Cliffs, NJ: Prentice-Hall.

Quirk, T. J., B. J. Witten, & S. F. Weinberg. (1973). Review of studies of the concurrent and predictive validity of the National Teacher Examination. *Review of Educational Research*, 43, 89–114.

Raney, P., & P. Robbins. (1989). Professional growth and support through peer coaching. *Educational Leadership*, 46, 35–38.

Render, G. F., J. N. Padilla, & H. M. Krank. (1989). What research shows about assertive discipline. *Educational Leadership*, 46, 72–75.

Richardson-Koehler, V. (1988). Allocating time and space resources. In R. I. Arends (Ed.), *Learning to teach* (pp. 123–49). New York: Random House.

Rosenberger, D. S., & R. A. Plimpton. (1975). Teacher competence and the courts. *Journal of Law and Education*, 4, 468–86.

Rudner, L. M. (1988). Teacher testing—an update. *Educational Measurement: Issues and Practice*, 7, 16–19.

Ryan, K., & J. M. Cooper. (1988). *Those who can teach* (5th ed.). Boston: Houghton-Mifflin.

Saunders, W. L. (Ed.). (1988). *Learning cycle modules for secondary school science*. Logan, UT: National Science Foundation and Utah State University.

Scannell, D. P. (1985). Review of NTE programs. In J. V. Mitchell (Ed.), *The ninth mental measurement yearbook* (pp. 1067–68). Lincoln, NE: The Buros Institute of Mental Measurements & The University of Nebraska Press.

Scriven, M. (1988). Evaluating teachers as professionals: The duties-based approach. In S. J. Stanley &

W. J. Popham (Eds.), *Teacher evaluation: Six prescriptions for success* (pp. 110–42). Alexandria, VA: Association for Supervision and Curriculum Development.

Sergiovanni, T. J., & R. J. Starratt. (1983). *Supervision: Human perspective* (3rd ed.). New York: McGraw-Hill.

Sharpley, C. F. (1988). Single-subject research. In J. P. Keeves (Ed.), *Educational research, methodology, and measurement: An international handbook* (pp. 580–86). Oxford, England: Pergamon Press.

Shavelson, R., & N. A. Russo. (1977). Generalizability of measures of teacher effectiveness. *Educational Research, 19*, 171–83.

Shavelson, R. J., N. M. Webb, & L. Burstein. (1986). Measurement of teaching. In M. C. Wittrock (Ed.), *Handbook of research on teaching* (3rd ed.) (pp. 50–91). New York: Macmillan.

Shepard, L. A., & A. E. Kreitzer. (1987). The Texas test. *Educational Researcher, 16*, 22–31.

Shine, W. A., & N. Goldman. (1980). Reply to Fred G. Burke. *Educational Leadership, 38*, 201.

Short, J., & T. Lough. (1986). Using microcomputers in the classroom. In J. M. Cooper (Ed.), *Classroom teaching skills* (3rd ed.) (pp. 401–57). Lexington, MA: D. C. Heath.

Silverman, B. R. S. (1983). Why their merit pay system failed in the federal government. *Personnel Journal, 62*, 294–97.

Smith, G. P. (1984). The critical issue of excellence and equity in competency testing. *Journal of Teacher Education, 35*, 6–9.

Snyder, N., J. Messer, & J. S. Cangelosi. (1977). *BOCAS manual*. Jacksonville, FL: Duval County School System.

Soar, R. S., D. M. Medley, & H. Coker. (1983). Teacher evaluation: A critique of currently used methods. *Phi Delta Kappan, 65*, 239–46.

Spearritt, D. (1988). Factor analysis. In J. P. Keeves (Ed.), *Educational research, methodology, and measurement: An international handbook* (pp. 644–54). Oxford, England: Pergamon Press.

Stallion, B. K. (1988, April). *Classroom management intervention: The effects of mentoring relationships on the inductee teacher's behavior*. Paper presented at the annual meeting of the American Educational Research Association, New Orleans.

Stanley, S. J., & W. J. Popham. (1988a). Introduction: A dismal day in court. In S. J. Stanley & W. J. Popham (Eds.), *Teacher evaluation: Six prescriptions for success* (pp. xi–xii). Alexandria, VA: Association for Curriculum and Supervision.

Stanley, S. J., & W. J. Popham, (Eds.). (1988b). *Teacher evaluation: Six prescriptions for success*. Alexandria, VA: Association for Curriculum and Supervision.

Steere, B. F. (1988). *Becoming an effective classroom manager: A resource for teachers*. Albany, NY: State University of New York Press.

Stenhouse, L. (1988). Case study methods. In J. P. Keeves (Ed.), *Educational research, methodology, and measurement: An international handbook* (pp. 49–53). Oxford, England: Pergamon Press.

Stiggins, R. J. (1988). Revitalizing classroom assessment: The highest instructional priority. *Phi Delta Kappan, 69*, 363–68.

Stiggins, R. J., N. F. Conklin, & N. J. Bridgeford. (1986). Classroom assessment: A key to effective instructions. *Educational Measurement: Issues and Practices, 5*, 5–17.

Stiggins, R. J., & D. Duke. (1988). *The case for commitment to teacher growth: Research on teacher evaluation*. Albany: State University of New York Press.

Stones, E. (1987). Student (practice) teaching. In M. J. Dunkin (Ed.), *The International encyclopedia of teaching and teacher education* (pp. 681–85). Oxford, England: Pergamon Press.

Struyk, L. R. (1990). *A self-evaluation model for examining transition time in the classroom*. Unpublished doctoral dissertation, Utah State University, Logan.

Sudman, S., & N. M. Bradburn. (1982). *Asking questions: A practical guide to questionnaire design*. San Francisco: Jossey-Bass.

Taft, R. (1988). Ethnographic research methods. In J. P. Keeves (Ed.), *Educational research, methodology, and measurement: An international handbook* (pp. 59–63). Oxford, England: Pergamon Press.

Tenbrink, T. D. (1986). Writing instructional objectives. In J. M. Cooper (Ed.), *Classroom teaching skills* (3rd ed.) (pp. 67–110). Lexington, MA: D. C. Heath.

Tennessee Department of Education. (1985). *Tennessee Career Ladder Better Schools Program: State model for local evaluation*. Nashville: the Department.

Testing for teacher certification: State-level examples. (1982). *Educational Measurement: Issues and Practices, 1*, 21–24.

Thomas, M. D. (1979). *Evaluation of educational personnel.* Bloomington, IN: Phi Delta Kappa Educational Foundation.

Thorndike, R. L. (1988). Reliability. In J. P. Keeves (Ed.), *Educational research, methodology, and measurement: An international handbook* (pp. 330–43). Oxford, England: Pergamon Press.

Tucker, M., & D. Mandel. (1986). The Carnegie Report—A call for redesigning the schools. *Phi Delta Kappan, 68,* 24–32.

Tuckman, B. W. (1988). *Testing for teachers* (2nd ed.). San Diego, CA: Harcourt Brace Jovanovich.

Utah State Board of Education. (1985). *Career ladders in Utah: A content analysis of Utah's career ladder plans for 1985–86.* Salt Lake City: the Board.

van den Bergh, H., & M. H. Eiting. (1989). A method of estimating rater reliability. *Journal of Educational Measurement, 26,* 29–40.

Veldman, D. J., & J. E. Brophy., (1974). Measuring teacher effects on pupil achievement. *Journal of Educational Psychology, 66,* 319–24.

Vold, D. J. (1985). The roots of teacher testing in America. *Educational Measurement: Issues and Practices, 4,* 5–7.

Weber, W. A. (1986). Classroom management. In J. M. Cooper (Ed.), *Classroom teaching skills* (3rd ed.) (pp. 271–357). Lexington, MA: D. C. Heath.

Weimer, M., J. L. Parrett, M. Kerns. (1988). *How am I teaching?* Madison, WI: Magna Publications.

Weinstein, C. E., E. T. Goetz, & P. A. Alexander. (Eds.). (1988). *Learning and study strategies: Issues in assessment, instruction, and evaluation,* San Diego, CA: Academic Press.

Williams, D., L. Howard, D. McDonald, & M. Renee. (1984). Why teachers fail. *Newsweek, 13,* 64–70.

Wise, A. E., L. Darling-Hammond, M. W. McLaughlin, & H. T. Bernstein. (1984). Teacher evaluation: A study of effective practices. (A report prepared for the National Institute of Education.) Santa Monica, CA: The Rand Corporation.

Wittrock, M. C. (Ed.). (1986). *Handbook of research on teaching* (3rd ed.). New York: Macmillan.

Wolfgang, C. H., & C. D. Glickman. (1986). *Solving discipline problems: Strategies for classroom teachers* (2nd ed.). Boston: Allyn and Bacon.

Wolman, B. B. (Ed.). (1989). *Dictionary of behavioral science* (2nd ed.). San Diego, CA: Academic Press.

Worthen, B. R., & J. R. Sanders. (1987). *Educational evaluation: Alternative approaches and practical guidelines.* New York: Longman.

Wright, B. D. (1988). Rasch measurement models. In J. P. Keeves (Ed.), *Educational research, methodology, and measurement: An international handbook* (pp. 286–92). Oxford, England: Pergamon Press.

Zeller, R. A. (1988). Validity. In J. P. Keeves (Ed.), *Educational research, methodology, and measurement: An international handbook* (pp. 322–30). Oxford, England: Pergamon Press.

Zumwalt, K. (Ed.), (1986). *Improving teaching: 1986 ASCD yearbook.* Alexandria, VA: Association for Supervision and Curriculum Development.

Zumwalt, K. (1989). Beginning professional teachers: The need for a curricular vision of teaching. In M. C. Reynolds (Ed.), *Knowledge base for the beginning teacher* (pp. 173–84). Oxford, England: Pergamon Press.

Index

Accreditation of teacher education programs, 106

Achievement: and change in the state of the art of evaluations, 209; and classroom observations, 45, 55, 261–262; and curriculum development, 136; and formative evaluations, 129, 136, 141–142, 261–262; and learning variables, 101; and measurement, 105–106; and questionnaires, 110–111, 112; and student needs, 146; student opinions about, 110–111; teacher's assessment of, 156–157, 261–262; and the teaching-cycle analysis approach, 147, 148, 156–157; and teaching performance, 98, 110-111; tests for assessing, 101–106. *See also* Student outcomes; Tests

American Council on Education, 106

Anecdotal records, 116–117

Aptitude tests, 102

Basic Literacy and Arithmetic Skills Tests, 107

Beginning teachers, 163–173, 208, 246–249

Behavorial Observation for Citizenship Attitudes and Skills. *See* BOCAS

Biases, 45–46

BOCAS (Behavorial Observation for Citizenship Attitudes and Skills), 55, 57, 80, 219–222

California Achievement Tests, 107

California Basic Educational Skills Test, 107

Career ladder programs, 175

Certification of teachers, 10, 106, 109

Classroom management: and the teaching-cycle analysis approach, 146

Classroom observations: and achievement, 45, 55, 261–262; advantages/disadvantages of, 46–47; appropriate uses of, 47–56; and biases, 45–46; and cost effectiveness, 58–59; and cut-off scores, 59; definition of, 44; designing of, 50–53; and developing a measurement, 56, 59, 62; and field tests, 58, 59; and formal assessment, 44–46, 56, 71–74, 81; and formative evaluations, 56, 57, 260–263; frequency of, 48; and indicators, 48–50, 59, 62; and informal assessment, 46, 56, 70, 81–83; instrument for, 45, 47, 53, 56–58, 60–62, 63–64, 68, 77-80, 213-215, 231–233, 236–238; and internal consistency, 68–74, 80–83; interpreting results of, 53; and